To Clint McDonald —
I hope you enjoy this
book and a portrait of
a great man. And thanks
for raising the wonderful
Courtney. You did a great
job. With best wishes,

Peter Walker

Ronald Reagan

RONALD REAGAN

The Power of Conviction and the
Success of His Presidency

PETER J. WALLISON

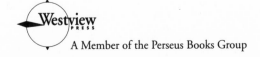

A Member of the Perseus Books Group

Copyright © 2003 by Peter J. Wallison

Westview Press books are available at special discounts for bulk purchases in the United States by corporations, institutions, and other organizations. For more information, please contact the Special Markets Department at the Perseus Books Group, 11 Cambridge Center, Cambridge MA 02142, or call (617) 252–5298, (800) 255-1514, or email j.mccrary@perseusbooks.com.

Published in 2003 in the United States of America by Westview Press, 5500 Central Avenue, Boulder, Colorado 80301–2877, and in the United Kingdom by Westview Press, 12 Hid's Copse Road, Cumnor Hill, Oxford OX2 9JJ.

Find us on the World Wide Web at www.westviewpress.com

Library of Congress Cataloging-in-Publication data

Wallison, Peter J.
　Ronald Reagan: the power of conviction and the success of his presidency/
Peter J Wallison.
　　p.　cm.
　Includes bibliographical references and index.
　ISBN 0-8133-4046-2 (alk. paper)
　1. Reagan, Ronald　2. United States—Politics and government—1981–1989.
　3. Political leadership—United States—Case studies.　I. Title
　E876 .W325　2003
　973.927'092—dc21
　　　　　　　　　　　　　　　　　　　　　　　　　　　　　20020155555

The paper used in this publication meets the requirements of the American National Standard for Permanence of Paper for Printed Library Materials Z39.48–1984.

10　9　8　7　6　5　4　3　2　1

For Frieda

CONTENTS

Preface   ix

1   Introduction: Understanding Reagan   1

2   Idea Man   21

3   Conviction Politician   45

4   The Person Who Was President   81

5   Meet the Press   111

6   Of Loyalty, Leaks, and the White House Staff   137

7   Iran-Contra: The Cover-Up   167

8   Iran-Contra: In the Dark   203

9   Iran-Contra: Recovery   237

Epilogue   281

Notes   283

Index   293

PREFACE

Throughout American history, how a particular president actually conducted his office has been a puzzle for historians and biographers, who have had to look for insights to his autobiography, if any, to the papers or tapes he left behind, and to the recollections of those who worked with him. But in Ronald Reagan's case, it was different. There, an independent scholar, Edmund Morris, a Pulitzer Prize–winning biographer of Theodore Roosevelt, was given an opportunity to enter the White House, stay for several years, and report on what he saw.

The decision to permit Morris this access was apparently made by Nancy Reagan and Michael Deaver, then Reagan's deputy chief of staff and longest-serving aide. Some might think it strange that a scholar and independent biographer was permitted this unprecedented access to a president who has been so lightly regarded by the press, by historians, and by the intelligentsia generally. One would imagine that if Ronald Reagan were as intellectually challenged and as disengaged as his detractors suggested, it would have been in the interests of those closest to him to conceal these deficiencies, not expose them to an unsympathetic observer.

But this paradox simply suggests one of the many mysteries about Ronald Reagan: what was it that Nancy Reagan and Mike Deaver saw that others, at some distance, could or would not see? A hint of this came with the publication in 2001 of *Reagan in His Own Hand,* a collection of over 670 radio addresses—on every conceivable major national issue—that Reagan had researched and written himself between 1974 and 1979. This body of work seemed inconsistent with the public image of Reagan as an affable fellow, a great communicator, but not of substantial intellectual weight or engaged on policy matters.

As it turned out, Edmund Morris—as accomplished a writer and biographer as he is—was the wrong man to do the definitive biography of Ronald Reagan as president. Morris, as shown by his work on the Roosevelt biographies, is a brilliant writer on personality, but by his own admission he has no interest in policy. Ronald Reagan, however, was precisely the opposite. His *only* interest was policy. He had no peculiarities of personality; there was nothing particularly colorful about him; he was a kind, old-fashioned, formal, and intelligent man, who also happened to be the president of the United States. And—worst of all from Morris's point of view—Ronald Reagan was a shy man who did not like to talk about himself. Morris's book, *Dutch: A Memoir of Ronald Reagan,* is full of his frustration in trying to discover Reagan's eccentricities from independent sources, or to pry out of Ronald Reagan himself the inner thoughts that make for an absorbing biographical work.

If the purpose of admitting Morris to the White House was to show the world what Ronald Reagan was really like, it was doomed from the start. Ronald Reagan was interested in ideas, not in Ronald Reagan. If Morris had been in the Lyndon Johnson White House, he would have come away with something significant, for Johnson was clearly interested in Johnson. Little prying would have been necessary. But no independent biographers were allowed to observe Johnson, or Kennedy, or Carter, or Clinton—all of whom no doubt, if they had had the confidence to open themselves to independent observation, would have provided wonderful raw material for a writer of Morris's skill.

In the end, then, what Nancy Reagan and Mike Deaver saw in Ronald Reagan was never discovered by Edmund Morris. *Dutch* failed to capture the essence and uniqueness of Ronald Reagan because these lay not in his personality but in how his unique capabilities, and his unique way of conducting his presidency, contributed to his success.

No amount of pounding could get the (literally) square Ronald Reagan into the round hole of an Edmund Morris biography.

Oddly, despite his enormous impact on American government and politics, there has been only one other attempt to write a full-scale biography of Ronald Reagan. That work is *President Reagan: The Role of a Lifetime,* by Lou Cannon, a journalist who covered Reagan both as governor of California and as president. As the title of Cannon's book implies, he saw Reagan through the prism of Reagan's initial profession as an actor. His book is a thorough record of Reagan's presidency, and a sympathetic one in many respects, but it does not see Reagan's governing style in an historical context, nor account for Reagan's undeniable success on any basis other than his acting skill.

Yet from my perspective, having served in his administration for a total of five years and in his White House for one, Ronald Reagan was unique among politicians and modern presidents. First, his interest in and commitment to his ideas in the broadest sense—in a philosophy of government that he had developed and honed over the years—transcended anything else one might say about him. Throughout his presidency, he had a sign on his desk that said: "There is no limit to what a man can do or where he can go if he doesn't mind who gets the credit." To Reagan, this was more than a motivational aphorism. He truly did not seem to care whether he received the credit for what he achieved, as long as his ideas were accepted and implemented. As he said in his autobiography, "I'd come to Washington to put into practice ideas I'd believed in for decades."[1] This attachment to ideas is highly unusual among politicians, let alone those who have the drive and ambition to reach the nation's highest office.

In addition, Reagan had convictions. By this I don't mean simply that he believed strongly in his ideas. His commitment went beyond that; unlike his predecessors—with the possible exception of Lincoln—he was willing to put his presidency on the line for his convictions, to take enormous political risks because he believed that the cause in which he was acting was the right one.

Finally, Reagan had a philosophy—a fully thought-out and consistent way of looking at government and its relationship to the American people that proceeded from premises to conclusions. No other modern president has allowed himself to be guided so completely by a philosophy. It was this philosophy, too, more than anything else, that he successfully communicated to his fellow citizens through his speeches, and was the source of a singular unity of purpose in his administration that other presidents have achieved only in national crises. As he said in his farewell address, "I won a nickname, 'the Great Communicator.' But I never thought it was my style or the words I used that made a difference: It was the content. I wasn't a great communicator, but I communicated great things."

To be sure, Reagan's style of governing and personal qualities gave rise to difficulties. He believed strongly in the management principle that a chief executive had to delegate responsibility, and thus he delegated enormous amounts of authority; and he had a sunny, almost naïve belief in the innate goodness of people, and thus made no concerted effort to find out whether things were being done as he would have wished. He staked his presidency on only a few core ideas, and left the rest to his staff and cabinet to work out within the philosophical guidelines he had laid out. The one great scandal and setback of his presidency—the Iran-Contra affair—flowed directly from his hands-off management style and was prolonged and deepened by his strong sense—his conviction—that he had not adopted the wrong policy and had not made a mistake in delegating the authority to pursue it. Yet if, as it appears, the Iran-Contra scandal—a foreign policy blunder—was the only significant adverse result of his management style in an eight-year presidency, it is difficult to criticize him for obsessive delegation overall.

These elements seemed to me to set Ronald Reagan apart from other presidents, before or since. Yet no one had written about him in this way. Most books about Reagan, both those that praise him and those that do not, have been and will be about his policies. But what was truly unique about Reagan was not his policies—it was how and why he succeeded in getting his policies accepted and implemented.

For that reason, and because I couldn't foresee that anyone else who observed him functioning in the White House would do so, I decided to
write this book.

While serving as the president's counsel, I kept a complete diary—
initially only for my children and grandchildren. As it turned out, however, the year in which I served, mid-1986 to mid-1987, was a pivotal
year in Reagan's presidency. When it began, he had reached his highest
level of popularity and approval, and this position was sustained until
the advent of the Iran-Contra crisis in November 1986. Up to that time,
he had surmounted the Bitburg controversy, bombed Libya, walked
away from Mikhail Gorbachev at Reykjavik in order to preserve his
Strategic Defense Initiative, and seen the enactment of his tax reform,
the most thoroughgoing in 30 years. Then, almost simultaneously, his
party lost control of the Senate, and the Iran-Contra crisis descended on
the White House. In my diary I recorded these momentous events, and
my observations of how, in his unique way, Ronald Reagan was responsible for and reacted to them.

This book is based on that diary, and thus reflects only my own perspective and analysis. However, I hope the views I express will stimulate
others to take a more careful and thoughtful look at a president who
shaped not only his own era but—through his ideas and philosophy—
the era in which we live today.

INTRODUCTION: UNDERSTANDING REAGAN

*There is no limit to what a man can do or where he
can go if he doesn't mind who gets the credit.*
—SIGN ON RONALD REAGAN'S OVAL OFFICE DESK

Ronald Reagan stood among the Justices of the Supreme Court, his head thrown back as he laughed at another story by Thurgood Marshall. It was November 25, 1986, and the President of the United States was entertaining the Justices of the Supreme Court at lunch in the White House. Ranged around him in a convivial group, wine glasses in hand, were Justice Marshall, Chief Justice William Rehnquist, and Justices William Brennan, Byron White, Sandra Day O'Connor, Harry Blackmun, Lewis Powell, and Antonin Scalia. The humor continued through the lunch that followed in the small East Wing family dining room, as Reagan and Marshall—both world-class raconteurs—competed to top one another with funny stories on everything from their boyhoods to baseball. Their supply seemed endless, the room rocked with laughter, and no one at the table wanted it to end.*

---

* I marveled at Thurgood Marshall's store of anecdotes. Here was another public man, like Reagan, who did not reveal in his public role the full scope of his gifts. I was sitting next to Justice White, and as the funny stories rolled on I turned to him and asked whether he'd not heard most of these before. "No," said White, who'd served many years with Marshall on the Court and was laughing along with the rest of us, "they're always wonderful and they're always new."

To look at Ronald Reagan that afternoon, you could not have imagined that he had a care in the world. His charm seemed as genuine that day as on any other—and the warmth he displayed during that lunch broke down whatever ideological barriers might otherwise have separated him from Justices Marshall and Brennan, the two leading liberals on the Court.

Presidents have to speak at every event they attend, even an informal lunch with the Supreme Court, and as the dessert was cleared Reagan got up to make a short speech. His prepared text was a somewhat stilted paean to the Supreme Court and the rule of law, but he set it aside and, as he often did, drew from his side jacket pocket a few notes he had jotted down on the short notepaper he used for occasions like this. As the Justices sat quietly looking on, Ronald Reagan gave them a sense of what it meant to him to be President of the United States. He referred to himself as a steward of his office, holding it in trust for the American people and hoping to pass it along to his successor intact. It must have been a particularly meaningful message for the members of the Supreme Court, who were themselves also links in the great chain of government established by the Constitution. And it was another graceful moment for Reagan, in which his listeners were moved both by his humility and the palpable sense of awe and respect he still felt for the office he held.

In the six months I had been counsel to the president, I had never been more proud of Ronald Reagan—or, on this day, more intrigued by his behavior. For November 25, 1986, was a memorable day for another reason. That morning, Reagan had met with the leaders of Congress and told them that there had been a plan to use the proceeds from the sale of arms to Iran for support of the anti-government rebels in Nicaragua—known as the Contras. As a result of this discovery, the President's national security adviser, Vice Admiral John Poindexter, had resigned, and Lt. Colonel Oliver North, a National Security Council staffer responsible for the Iran arms sales project and the plan to divert funds to the Contras, had been dismissed.

With this disclosure, the Iran arms sales—which had previously seemed nothing more than a bizarre policy blunder—became the Iran-Contra affair—a full-scale scandal, the largest and most potentially consequential of the Reagan presidency. As this pleasant lunch proceeded, the press briefing room—not 100 yards away—was in utter chaos. Attorney General Edwin Meese was attempting, with few facts—and many of them inaccurate—to answer a hurricane of questions. If it had been authorized by the President, the diversion of funds was reminiscent of the extra-constitutional action that was the essence of Watergate, and for the first time since the Iran arms transactions became public in early November, the dread word "impeachment" was heard in responsible quarters.

How was it possible that Reagan could carry on through this lunch with such seeming poise and genuine enjoyment, when only a few hours earlier he had announced an event that would shake his administration to its foundations?

Years later, when President Clinton was in the midst of the Monica Lewinsky scandal, the press indulged itself in a kind of pop psychology that attempted to explain Clinton's ability to "compartmentalize" his troubles—to segregate them from his day-to-day activities so that he could carry on as President despite the scandal breaking around him. This capacity was linked to Clinton's past—to his alcoholic stepfather and the traumas of his youth—as a way of explaining his strange ability to remain functional in the face of gross humiliation and public disgust with his behavior.

Whether or not this speculation was true of Clinton, it is not my view of Reagan. Ronald Reagan was unique among modern presidents. Other presidents might be said to have had general views about what they wanted to achieve in office, but they were pragmatic politicians first: their primary objective was to attain and hold power. Reagan was different; he was a conviction politician—an idealist—for whom the implementation of certain major ideas and principles meant more than personal power or aggrandizement.

It follows that his ability to remain poised and convivial at lunch with the Supreme Court, only hours after the plan to divert funds was disclosed, was a reflection of this unique aspect of his nature. The Iran-Contra affair, as important as it was to the press, threatened none of the achievements of the six years he had been in office. It was an embarrassment, to be sure, and he never really understood why the American people did not accept his explanation of what he had done, but political embarrassment does not appear to have been of great concern to him. Later, I found that he had not been reading press reports about the arms sales, or even consulting what he might have written in his diary about his own actions and decisions.

Indeed, although I did not recognize it at the time, the speech he gave at lunch that day said it all: Ronald Reagan, although he was the President of the United States, saw himself as merely an instrument of some larger purpose; his definition of success was not his personal place in history, but the adoption and success of his ideas. He appears to have had no desire for power alone, merely what he could do with it to achieve his purposes, and if he worried about his place in history it was not apparent.

This analysis is consistent with Reagan's frequent remark—especially after the March 1981 attempt on his life—that he thought God had saved him for a purpose. While many tend to discount these expressions from politicians, it may well be that Ronald Reagan—as in so many other things then and now regarded as unsophisticated or hokey—was quite serious about this. If this is one's outlook, the mere holding of personal power is not the point; power must be used for a purpose. In this light, the enormous setback of the Iran-Contra scandal—which might have been devastating to someone as self-absorbed as, say, Bill Clinton—was not debilitating to Reagan. It did not rob him of his sense of achievement as president, or detract from the significance of the changes he had already brought about. By the sixth year of his presidency, in fact, Reagan had achieved much of what he had set out for himself and his administration—at least in domestic matters—and the Iran-Contra affair, while painful because of the American people's refusal to believe his explanation, did not threaten the gains he thought he had already made.[1]

And there may have been a third element. Ronald Reagan may simply not have believed that he did anything wrong, and one day would be proved right. As he wrote to a friend, Lorraine Wagner, with whom he had corresponded for 51 years, "Thank you for your kind words about our present troubles [Iran-Contra]. I think there is a kind of political lynching going on, but my conscience is completely clear, so I'm not losing any sleep." Still, the Iran-Contra scandal had a major impact on Reagan's effectiveness as president. For the four months that it continued, the administration was brought to a standstill. Reagan's support among the American public fell significantly, and he was never again able to attain the level of credibility as President that had made him an awesome political force through his first six years. Nevertheless, at least one of his greatest achievements—the first arms-reduction agreement with the Soviet Union—was yet to come. Only a person who had a serene confidence in his own judgment and convictions could—after the trauma of Iran-Contra and as his term in office was drawing to a close—have discounted the anxieties and doubts of his advisers and negotiated this historic agreement with the Soviet Union.

Certainly there can be differing interpretations of the lunch with the Supreme Court, and those who have always disparaged Ronald Reagan and been baffled by his success will no doubt see in his behavior the same "disengagement" that they considered a characteristic of his presidency. Reagan's refusal to become involved in the details of his administration—indeed his apparent disinterest in these details—is not a matter of dispute. I saw many instances of this myself, and the fact of Reagan's disengagement has been cited again and again as an example of his "cognitive limitations,"[2] his disinterest in policy generally,[3] his excessive delegation of policy-making responsibility to his advisers,[4] or the cause of the Iran-Contra scandal.[5]

But this picture of Reagan has left political scientists, presidential historians, and commentators with a major unanswered question—if Reagan was so limited intellectually and so disengaged from his own administration, why was he so successful as a president? That success, surely, is undeniable. During Reagan's presidency, the United States shook off more than a decade of economic stagnation and began a 20-year period of almost uninterrupted growth; U.S. companies became highly efficient and competitive globally, leaving other nations and regions far behind; the free-market system Reagan had championed became the model for economic reform, replacing government-directed or socialist economics around the world; the Soviet empire—the "evil empire" so famously identified by Ronald Reagan—the chief superpower rival of the United States, came apart shortly after Reagan left office (with the Soviet Union itself following three years later—an outcome many independent observers credited to Reagan's eight years of relentless pressure); and the American people returned from a period of self-doubt and timidity to their accustomed self-confidence and sense of optimism.[6] At the same time, the huge government deficits—cited by many as a result of Reagan's purportedly misguided policies—left no discernible scar on the American economy. Unless we are to say that a president has no responsibility for what happens while he is in office, these facts stand as a challenge to the conventional image of Ronald Reagan largely created and propagated by the media and his political opponents.

And if political science is in any sense a science, it must be able to deal with another apparent contradiction. Reagan's success as president challenges the conventional notions about what it takes for a president to succeed. When Reagan took office, learned political scientists and pundits were saying that the presidency was too big a job for one man, that we should be thinking about a co-presidency, or an office of the presidency as adopted by many large corporations. But Reagan achieved all his major and ambitious goals, and he made it look easy. He seemed to coast, and so effortlessly that he acquired a reputation for laziness.

Indeed, the most prominent and acclaimed modern student of the presidency, Professor Richard E. Neustadt, devotes several chapters to Ronald Reagan in his 1990 book, *Presidential Power and the Modern Presidents*,[7] noting that the Reagan presidency poses a challenge to his thesis that successful presidents acquire influence not just through their formal powers, but through the skill with which they maneuver in the Washington community and the impression they establish in the country about how successfully they are functioning in office.[8] Above all, a successful president, in Neustadt's view, must make a sophisticated appraisal of his position, bringing to bear all his resources—information, advice, and a knowledge of details—in order to maximize his chances of success in any given case.

To Neustadt, Reagan lacked many of the skills and capacities that a successful president needs: "He seems to have combined less intellectual curiosity, less interest in detail, than any President at least since Calvin Coolidge—about whom I remain unsure—with more initial and sustained commitments, more convictions independent of events or evidence, than any President since Woodrow Wilson championed the League."[9] Yet Reagan had to be accounted successful: "[H]is presidency restored the public image of the office to a fair (if perhaps rickety) approximation of its Rooseveltian mold: a place of popularity, influence, and initiative, a source of programmatic and symbolic leadership, both pacesetter and tonesetter, the nation's voice to both the world and us."[10] Moreover, "the very combination—the incuriosity and delegation on the one hand, the commitments and convictions on the other—at once framed Reagan's operating style and seemingly accounted for his impacts on the course of public policy. In anybody's reckoning, these were substantial. . . ."[11] So Neustadt recognizes Reagan's presidency as a kind of paradox: "[I]t qualifies all prior generalizations about presidential power and about work in the White House. Thus it calls for acknowledgment here."[12]

Ultimately, Neustadt reconciles his view of Reagan with his thesis about successful presidents by pointing to the Iran-Contra scandal. This he sees as a demonstration that a president who is not interested in detail and not deeply knowledgeable about a subject with which he is dealing will eventually encounter serious trouble. As we will see, however, the Iran-Contra scandal—despite the enormous press coverage it received—was, at most, a foreign policy blunder, and (apart from failing to protect the marines in Beirut) probably the only serious mistake in Reagan's

eight years in office. It cannot be compared, for example, to Kennedy's
Bay of Pigs disaster, or Johnson's deepening of the U.S. commitment in
Vietnam—errors of two presidents who came far closer to Neustadt's
ideal than Reagan. And ultimately, Reagan could have reduced the impact of the Iran-Contra affair if—like Kennedy in the much more serious case of the Bay of Pigs invasion—he had simply been able to admit
that he made a mistake.

Although Professor Neustadt acknowledges Reagan's success—while
pointing out the dangers of Reagan's incuriosity and disinterest in detail—he makes no concerted effort to explain how Reagan achieved as
much as he did. Others, however, have generally attributed his success to
the mesmerizing effect of his celebrity and his speeches, to the political
agility and PR brilliance of his staff and media managers, or simply to
extraordinary luck. To his critics, Reagan's ideas, to the extent that they
had validity, were simplistic and hackneyed, but were attractively presented according to a well-written script; he was, in the end, what he was
in the beginning—an actor, playing the role of president. A good example of this assessment is Frances Fitzgerald's book, *Way Out There in the
Blue*.[13] The Reagan that appears in this work is uninterested in policy,
confused, and ignorant, plunging ahead with ill-considered nostrums
and protected only by his retainers, his skills as an actor, and simple
good luck. To Fitzgerald, Reagan avoided catastrophe only because his
many errors and misconceptions had either not yet come home to roost
when he left office, or had misfired.[14]

Reagan's two serious independent biographers—Lou Cannon, a
journalist who covered Reagan both as a governor and as President, and
Edmund Morris—did not identify a credible key to his success, relying
in slightly different ways on the conventional explanation that his success was related to his background as an actor. The title of Cannon's
book, *President Reagan: The Role of a Lifetime*,[15] was obviously chosen to
emphasize the link between Reagan's presidency and his past career.
Chapter headings such as "The Acting Politician," "The Acting President," "Offstage Influences," and "An Actor Abroad" say it all. Morris,
in *Dutch: A Memoir of Ronald Reagan*, traces Reagan's acting career in

detail, from school plays through Hollywood and beyond. Describing Reagan's triumphant address to a joint session of Congress after his second inauguration, Morris notes that "as roar built on roar," Reagan "was at last what he had never been on stage or screen, a great actor."[16]

Yet these somewhat facile explanations of Reagan's success are ultimately unsatisfactory. Reagan, for example, insisted upon and achieved enormous changes in the nation's fiscal structure, changing the U.S. tax system in significant ways—one might say revolutionary ways—twice during his presidency. After a sharp and painful recession shortly after he took office, the U.S. economy roared back, economic growth continued into the next decade, and the stock markets reached unprecedented levels. By the end of his term, Reagan had negotiated the first strategic arms reduction agreement with the Soviet Union. Perhaps most important, the American people, after the defeat in Vietnam, the oil embargo, the taking of U.S. diplomats as hostages in Iran, and the malaise of the Carter period, experienced a new sense of confidence. Changes of this dimension don't happen because of mere luck. Similarly, the precipitous decline in Reagan's popularity during the recession of 1981–82, and again during the Iran-Contra affair, demonstrates that his extraordinary communication skills had their limitations, while his refusal to change course despite these setbacks and the pleas of his much-vaunted advisers shows that there was far more to him than clever managers.

Efforts like those of Cannon and Morris to account for Reagan's success have failed because they assumed he must be assessed within a conventional frame of reference. This template, largely developed by Professor Neustadt and other political scientists after Franklin Delano Roosevelt's presidency, evaluates a president as a master politician who achieves his goals by skillfully wielding the manifold formal and informal powers of his office. Such a president, like FDR himself, seldom has a clear philosophy on entering office, but he succeeds by responding flexibly and effectively to challenges he confronts day by day. Above all, he is expected to intervene decisively in the process of policy development, to negotiate his legislative program through the shoals of Congress, and to maintain firm control, indirectly through his staff or directly through contact with his cabinet, of all the major decisions and initiatives of his administration.

In the media's simplified formulation of this idea, the president "runs the country." During the Reagan administration, the comedy program *Saturday Night Live* created a famous skit in which Reagan was portrayed as friendly and grandfatherly in public, but when his visitors leave and the door closes, he barks orders at his cowering staff and sends them scurrying to do his bidding. In a sense, this satire was a way of overcoming the cognitive dissonance between the successful Reagan the comedy writers could observe and the manipulative personality they had been taught to expect in a successful president. Scholars, too, puzzled by this contradiction, have reached for some highly unlikely explanations. Historian Barton Bernstein, for example, has speculated that perhaps Reagan learned as a young man to hide his intelligence because it was not valued in the Midwest world in which he grew up. (That is— shocking as it may sound—Reagan might actually have been intelligent!) However, Bernstein warned, those who accept this radical notion will also have to accept the fact that an intelligent Reagan could not escape blame for the Iran-Contra affair.[17]

As we will see, there is no mystery here; Reagan made no effort to control his administration in the conventional sense beloved of presidential scholars and accepted by the media. He was successful because he developed and pursued an entirely different model for carrying on his presidency. Unlike any modern president, he led with ideas—with a consistent philosophy expressed through his speeches—and despite the enormous pressures brought upon him during his two terms in office, he refused to be shaken from the core concepts with which he had sought election. In other words, the convictions and commitments, the apparent disinterest in detail, the delegation of authority—the very characteristics that Richard Neustadt found so antithetical to achievement of a president's objectives—were ultimately the sources of Reagan's success.

Despite reaching the highest office in the land, Ronald Reagan was not a driven man. If anything, his dominant mode—to his staff as well as to outsiders—was passivity. He could not and did not manipulate people as Franklin Roosevelt did, control events behind the scenes like Eisenhower, twist arms or browbeat like Lyndon Johnson, promote a personal image or style like Jack Kennedy, seek to build a coalition of the disgruntled like Richard Nixon, master details like Jimmy Carter, or happily debate policy options like Bill Clinton. He was polite, cordial, and unassuming to all around him—sometimes to a fault—and although he could speak firmly or sharply on matters he cared about, never in my hearing did he raise his voice in anger to a staff member or a political opponent.

In addition, Reagan had a startlingly benevolent view of human nature and motivations, bordering on naïveté. Revealingly, he wrote in his autobiography that, unlike his beloved wife, Nancy, he believed the best of people until they proved otherwise[18]—a credulousness that would be unimaginable in presidents before or since. For this reason, although he had an extraordinarily acute sense of how to appeal to the American people, probably because he thought of himself as one of them, he was not a particularly good political analyst. His idealism caused him to believe that other politicians and his opponents would react more positively, more public-spiritedly, and with more rationality than most experienced observers of politics and politicians would assume. As noted by Don Regan, who saw him almost every day in every conceivable context for more than two years, "there was simply no guile in the man."

In his book *Ronald Reagan: How an Ordinary Man Became an Extraordinary Leader,* Dinesh D'Souza attempted to explain Reagan's success when he wrote: "Reagan's greatness derives in large part from the fact that he was a visionary—a conceptualizer who was able to see the world differently from the way it was. While others were obsessed and bewildered by the problems of the present, Reagan was focused on the future. This orientation gave Reagan an otherworldly quality that is often characteristic of great men."[19] Although this observation captures some of the ways in which Reagan was different from other presidents, it does not explain how his visionary qualities led to his success.

Indeed, if Reagan is viewed as a visionary—with his eyes set on the future—we immediately encounter a contradiction. The radio addresses collected by Kiron Skinner and Annelise and Martin Anderson in *Reagan in His Own Hand*[20]—only a selection from among more than 1,000 such addresses that Reagan researched and wrote himself between 1974 and 1979—reveal a man deeply interested in and conversant with a wide range of the political issues of the day. As Edmund Morris pointed out in his biography of Reagan, his intense interest in politics and political issues long preceded any apparent interest in public office, and may have been responsible for the failure of his first marriage. And as Michael Deaver noted in *A Different Drummer*,[21] during their extensive travels together Reagan spent virtually all his time reading and writing on policy matters.

The subjects Reagan researched and wrote about in developing his radio addresses covered virtually all the issues that would confront a president who was deeply engaged in the policies and programs of his administration. It would not be an exaggeration, therefore, to say that—at least with respect to his personal efforts to inform himself and develop his views about the matters he would have to address as president—Reagan was as prepared to assume the presidency as any of his predecessors or successors, and probably more than most.

Yet it is undeniable that, after he became president, Reagan showed little interest in many of the same issues he had talked about in his radio addresses or that might have absorbed the attention of someone who was truly interested in politics or policy. Thus, either Reagan spent a great deal of time feigning an interest in political issues and policy before he became president, or he consciously decided to limit his intervention in the decisions of his administration in order to achieve some other objectives. I believe the latter is closer to the truth, and can be seen, in hindsight, as one of the sources of his success as well as the appearance that he was "disengaged."

It is a further demonstration of the uniqueness of his presidency that Ronald Reagan has become a powerful myth in present-day politics—using the term not in its sense as a fantastical story but as the Greeks did (and political scientists still do), as a collectively accepted idea that provides a foundation for a belief system. In American politics today there is a distinct ideology—a belief system—known as "Reaganism," which refers to a set of ideas that are thought to embody the underlying principles that Ronald Reagan pursued during his administration. Reagan's admirers believe that the precepts of Reaganism are identifiable and that they led the country out of the wilderness and into its current position as the unchallenged leader of the world.

It doesn't matter whether this is true—although I believe in general it is—but the fact is that no Republican candidate for the presidency can hope to be nominated by his party today unless he can show that he is an ideological descendant of Ronald Reagan. As recently as the 2000 election, John McCain—while presenting himself as the maverick candidate for the Republican presidential nomination—was required to prove to Republican voters that despite his reputation as a reformer he was at heart a follower of Ronald Reagan. His inability to do so—despite the vast and favorable attention he received from the media—is as likely to have been the cause of his defeat as the quality of the Bush campaign.

There is no similar following for any other modern president. Despite his enormous popularity and success, no set of principles for governing survived Franklin Roosevelt, and it would be absurd to speak of Trumanism, Nixonism, Carterism, or Clintonism. The Kennedy legend—despite its hold on the imaginations of Americans—is one of style rather than substance. While Reagan is still alive, National Airport in Washington, major public buildings, and an aircraft carrier have been named or renamed for him, and so many more proposals for renaming other landmarks have been advanced in the Republican Congress that even so stalwart a Reagan supporter as columnist George Will has declared them unseemly.

There are two reasons for this attachment to Reagan. First, he represented a set of ideas and values. The Republican Party was founded on opposition to slavery—an idea ultimately based on moral values. Abraham Lincoln began his rise from obscure prairie lawyer to Republican nominee for president when he began to call Americans back to the basic ideals of the Founders articulated in the Declaration of Independence—particularly that all men are created equal.[22] As historian William Lee Miller wrote of Lincoln: "His speeches, or rather the moral-political argument presented in his speeches and the clarity and force with which it was presented, was the essential ingredient in Lincoln's rise."[23] There remains a strong moral core in Republicanism to which both Lincoln and Reagan appealed. Moreover, although many educated Americans today tend to think about politics in terms of interest groups and power relationships, and the media largely cover politics in these terms, ideas and principles are still what ultimately move people. As John Maynard Keynes wrote, "the world is ruled by little else."[24]

Second, Reagan's ideas, like Lincoln's, reformulated Republicanism so that it tapped into traditional American values—support for private sector-based economic growth and individual opportunity, and opposition to the growth of government and the bureaucratic state. This reoriented and reinvigorated the GOP as a party of change, persuaded Americans that there was another way to think about government, and created an historic turning point in the direction of the United States. After Reagan, and the Republican takeover of the House of Representatives in 1994—which occurred largely on the strength of Reagan's ideas—those who would expand the size and scope of the federal government's role in the economy had to sustain a heavy burden of proof. It may be too early to call the last quarter of the twentieth century the Reagan Era, but it would not at this point seem extravagant to do so.

Nevertheless, although Reagan's ideas were important as an intellectual framework for his party and many other Americans, it was how Reagan chose to implement his ideas—how he conducted his presidency—that ultimately accounts not only for his popularity but also for his success.

Reagan's approach to the presidency flowed naturally from his view of government. First articulated in "The Speech" in support of Barry Goldwater that brought him to public attention as a political force in 1964,[25] and further explicated both in his radio addresses and his speeches during the 1980 campaign, Reagan's concept of government's role was radically at variance with the conventional politics of the day. Of course, it is well known that Reagan believed in limited government, but it has not been as clear that his reason for this view was an extraordinary faith in the American people. Ultimately, Reagan was an opponent of big government because he thought its bureaucracy, its paternalism, and its taxation would reduce the ability and incentives of the American people to innovate, compete, and produce better lives for themselves.

In his 1981 Inaugural Address, Reagan said, "In this present crisis, government is not the solution to our problem. Government is the problem." This extraordinary and provocative statement was not a political slogan; it fully reflected his view that the best thing the U.S. Government could do for the American people was to get out of their way. Indeed, it seems that Reagan's optimism about America sprang from his belief that the American people could do anything they set out to do, if given the opportunity and the tools. Accordingly, when Jimmy Carter, in his now infamous "malaise" speech, seemed to blame the profligacy of his countrymen for the nation's troubling condition, Reagan said, "People who talk about an age of limits are really talking about their own limitations, not America's."[26]

Thus, it becomes understandable why Reagan might have had limited interest in the issues and programs that did not form the core of his agenda. If we take him at his word—and with Ronald Reagan there is always good reason to do so—we should not expect him to think that (apart from defense and law enforcement) most of what government does is necessary or important. He was committed to reducing the role of government in the nation's life. Once he had removed what he regarded as obstacles to the American people's productivity—punitive tax rates, excessive regulation, trade restrictions—and raised national morale through his unique blend of faith, optimism, and stubborn insistence on distinguishing between right and wrong, Reagan could reasonably believe he had done on the domestic front all that his presidency required. The efforts of the American people—whose potential, to him, was limitless—would take care of the rest.

Lou Cannon caught the significance of this economy of interest in describing the first meeting between Reagan—recently elected—and President Carter. Carter was astonished, reports Cannon, by Reagan's apparent lack of interest in the briefing Carter had provided. Cannon writes: "Reagan's problem was not an inability to grasp what Carter was telling him but a lack of curiosity about anything he deemed irrelevant to his immediate agenda. Carter's interests were so broad that he often seemed to lack focus, even in private conversation. Reagan's range was narrow, but his agenda was compelling. He wanted to get on with the business of cutting government spending, reducing income taxes, and building up the military. All other policies seemed to him beside the point."[27]

Thus, several threads, woven together, begin to define the outward appearance of Reagan's presidency. Because he thought he had achieved most of what he set out to do, he was relatively unruffled by setbacks that did not undo his accomplishments—even including the Iran-Contra affair; because he was more concerned about establishing his core ideas than in maintaining decision-making control over his administration—and believed strongly in the value of delegation— he gladly delegated authority to those he trusted to follow his principles while he focused relentlessly on a few key concepts central to his philosophy; and because he saw a few objectives—such as reducing the role of the government in the economy—as foundational, and thus vastly more important than others, he could relegate to low priority many of the policies and programs that routinely come to the president's desk, thus accounting for his appearance of disengagement.

But although this interpretation of Reagan accounts in substantial part for his unconventional behavior as president, it still doesn't fully explain his success. This, I believe, was the result of a combination of factors—only a few of which have been identified by commentators or biographers since the end of his administration.

First, unlike any president in the twentieth century, Reagan had a fully developed philosophy of government when he assumed office. Because he made his philosophy so clear both before and after he became president—principally through his speeches—it was fully assimilated and could be implemented by the members of his administration. For example, since there was no question that Reagan wanted to reduce the role of government in the economy, it was not necessary for him to press his administration for specific deregulatory programs; these welled up from the cabinet departments as they sought to respond to Reagan's well-known overall objectives. For those who served in the Reagan administration, the slogan "Don't just stand there—undo something" contained as much truth as humor. When I was General Counsel of the Treasury, Don Regan returned one day from a cabinet meeting and told the top Treasury staff that the President had acknowledged the difficulty of cutting the growth of government but said, "If not us, who? And if not now, when?" We all knew what he meant, and what was expected of us. This in itself reduced the extent to which the President had to intervene in the policy-making process.

This interest in ideas and principles sets Reagan apart from other presidents. It suggests why it is wrong to judge him by whether he read his briefing papers, stayed on top of the details of programs, or cared if his chief of staff was James Baker or Donald Regan. He was simply operating on a different plane. Because of the firmness with which he held his ideas, and the single-mindedness with which he communicated and pursued them, it was not necessary for him to take personal command of everything his administration did. Instead, he focused on the principles he thought important and counted on his subordinates to implement them. Indeed, he seemed relatively indifferent to the specifics of less important policies and uninterested in how programs were structured—even if he would have structured them another way—as long as these policies and programs reflected a rough consensus of his advisers and remained generally within the boundaries his principles implied.

Reaganism—as it came to be understood by friend and foe alike—was very much the intellectual product of Ronald Reagan. The central ideas, the philosophy of government, that he initially outlined in The Speech, were further explicated and developed in the radio addresses of the 1970s and were largely implemented in his presidency. As discussed in Chapter 2, Reagan's administration, as no other administration in modern American history, was guided and given purpose by a president's philosophy and ideas.

There are ideas, and there are convictions. While many commentators have noted that Reagan focused on only a few major objectives, and largely achieved them, few have recognized that these were more

than simply priorities. Indeed, Reagan saw the major ideas and principles he wanted to establish as fundamental or essential to the purposes
of his presidency. For Reagan, these ideas rose to the level of convictions—fundamental beliefs on which compromise was not easy. In support or furtherance of these convictions, Reagan was willing to take extraordinary political risks. Most famously, he stayed the course against
changes in his economic plan through one of the most serious reces-
sions since the Great Depression, and in the process changed the way
the government would henceforth respond to economic downturns.
These and other stands—some of them even more politically risky—
established his credibility for an unearthly steadfastness of purpose, increasing the respect he was accorded by the public and his bargaining
power with Congress. The significance of Reagan's convictions to the
success of his administration is the subject of Chapter 3.

Finally, it is important to recognize that all political success cannot
be rationally explained. The ease with which Reagan conquered and reoriented Washington during his eight years in office was also in part the
product of a strange magnetism, of something within him that drew
others to follow and believe in his mission. We don't know why or how
this aura exerts its power, but we have a name for it: charisma.

As described in the work of the sociologist Max Weber, who sought
to characterize and define different kinds of authority, the elements of
charismatic authority are identifiable, although their source is mysterious:
"There is the authority of the extraordinary personal gift of grace
(charisma), the absolutely personal devotion and personal confidence in
revelation, heroism, or other qualities of individual leadership. This is
'charismatic' domination, as exercised by the prophet—or in the field of
politics—by the elected war lord, the plebiscitarian ruler, the great dema-
gogue, or the party leader. . . . [T]he leader is personally recognized as the
innerly 'called' leader of men. Men do not obey him by virtue of tradition
or statute, but because they believe in him. If he is more than a narrow
and vain upstart of the moment, the leader lives for his cause. . . ."[28] Reagan certainly lived for his cause, and his extraordinary persona—one of
the reasons people believed in him— is the subject of Chapter 4.

However well Weber's description applies to Reagan—and it does seem particularly apt to those of us who were privileged to work with him—it is important to keep in mind how Reagan saw himself. Indeed, Reagan's view of himself was one of the sources of his personal charisma. On this, we have Reagan's own words, written in reply to a question from Peggy Noonan:

> I never thought of myself as a great man, just a man committed to great ideas. I've always believed that individuals should take priority over the state. History has taught me that this is what sets America apart—not to remake the world in our image, but to inspire people everywhere with a sense of their own boundless possibilities. There's no question I am an idealist, which is another way of saying I am an American.[29]

CHAPTER

2

IDEA MAN

*I won a nickname, "the Great Communicator."
But I never thought it was my style or the words
I used that made a difference: It was the content. I
wasn't a great communicator, but I communicated
great things.*
—RONALD REAGAN IN HIS FAREWELL ADDRESS,
JANUARY 11, 1989

Shortly before the Iran-Contra scandal erupted, *Fortune* magazine fea-
tured an admiring article on Reagan's management style, praising him
for creating an orderly administration by choosing good people and
delegating to them the authority to act. The article became something
of an embarrassment for *Fortune* after the scandal broke, since at the
very least it raised questions about Reagan's management style. Indeed,
the Tower Board—the three-member board that Reagan appointed to
review the Iran-Contra matter—attributed the crisis to Reagan's poor
management of the National Security Council staff.

Reagan himself was never embarrassed by the critical light the Iran-
Contra affair had thrown on his management style. In his autobiography, he wrote:

I don't believe a chief executive should supervise every detail of what goes on in his organization. The chief executive should set broad policy and general ground rules, tell people what he or she wants them to do, then let them do it. . . . I think that's the cornerstone of good management: Set clear goals and appoint good people to help you achieve them. As long as they are doing what you have in mind, don't interfere, but if somebody drops the ball, interfere and make a change.[1]

The critics of Reagan's management style seem unaware that when an executive delegates a great deal of authority, lapses of this kind will inevitably happen; the trick is to minimize the errors while maximizing the efficiency and leverage with which the CEO's policies are carried out. What is perhaps most remarkable about the Reagan administration is that major mistakes happened so seldom. Delegating responsibility can be good or bad, depending on who ultimately ends up with the authority. If the Iran-Contra matter had been managed by someone other than Oliver North—lightly overseen by Robert McFarlane and John Poindexter—Reagan might have reached the end of his second term without a serious scandal in his administration. But the possibility that authority will fall into the hands of an Oliver North is one of the ever-present dangers of delegation. There are few management techniques that are free of any countervailing deficiencies, and delegation of authority is not one of them.

In any event, as Reagan's autobiography makes clear, delegation of authority alone was never the key to Reagan's success as president. The *Fortune* article missed the real story even if the Iran arms sales had not occurred. Any executive can delegate responsibility to subordinates, and the best executives are frequently the ones who are able to hand over the most responsibility. Delegation in itself is not the key issue; the problem is assuring that subordinates do what the boss would do in the same circumstances. In saying, "As long as they are doing what you have in mind, don't interfere," Reagan put his finger on the key difficulty—making sure that subordinates understand both what the chief executive wants done, and how they are to go about doing it. The key to Reagan's success as a delegator—and indeed as president—was his ability to make clear to the members of his administration what he wanted them to do, the Iran-Contra affair notwithstanding. He provided this clarity and direction through his speeches.

Ironically, although Reagan was not the kind of executive envisioned by Richard Neustadt in his groundbreaking study of the presidency, Reagan—through the clear philosophy he articulated—appears to have found a means to the same end that Neustadt envisioned as one of the key attributes of a successful presidency: the president's personal capacity to influence the conduct of the people who make up his own government. Neustadt writes:

> Like our government structure as a whole, the executive establishment consists of separated institutions sharing powers. The President heads one of these; cabinet officers, agency administrators, and military commanders head others. . . . Everything somehow involves the President. But operating agencies owe their existence least of all to one another—and only in some part to him. Each has a separate statutory base; each has its statutes to administer; each deals with a different set of subcommittees at the Capitol. . . . All agency administrators are responsible to [the president]. But they are responsible to Congress, to their clients, to their staffs, and to themselves. In short, they have five masters.[2]

In other words, one of the first requirements for a successful presidency—in Neustadt's terms—is to knit together an administration into a cohesive whole, with cabinet members, agency administrators, and White House and other staffs working together to carry out the president's priorities. Neustadt presents this as a foundational presidential objective, difficult to achieve for all the reasons outlined above. But Reagan did this with ease by tying his administration together with ideas. As John Podhoretz noted in his book on the first Bush White House:

> In a White House motivated at least in part by ideas—as the Reagan administration was, and as the Johnson administration was—every

staffer could feel he was part of the policy process because he understood the philosophical and theoretical outlines of the administration policy. In the Reagan White House, the outlines were quite simple: Reagan was philosophically opposed to the growth of government, the growth of taxation, and the spread of Communism. He was pro-life, anti-gun control, opposed to judicial activism. With this ideological outline in mind, White House staffers from assistants to the president to secretaries in the New Executive Office Building could go about their business with little confusion. But in the Bush White House, it was very difficult to feel a part of things in the same way, because staffers had no idea from one day to the next where the administration stood on *anything*. Policy was an ever evolving thing, always under negotiation.[3]

As a candidate and as president, Reagan outlined in radio commentary and speeches a set of principles and goals that were recognized as a distinct philosophy of government and were absorbed and assimilated by those who ultimately became the political appointees and senior members of his administration. As a result, decisions that in other administrations would routinely have gone to the White House were made at the cabinet level or lower, by officials confident that they were doing what the President had in mind. This gave the administration a far more cohesive and orderly look—at least on matters of policy direction—than prior and subsequent administrations, where cabinet officers were not sufficiently clear about the President's priorities to step out on their own. This accounts for the consistent and businesslike tone noted by the *Fortune* magazine article and other observers prior to the advent of the Iran-Contra scandal. To be sure, there were disputes among cabinet members and White House staff, but these were over how the President's principles would be implemented, not over the philosophy of government from which they sprang.

This strong sense of the President's philosophy and goals also enabled the cabinet departments to play a much more important role in policy development than had been the case in prior administrations. Since the Kennedy administration, virtually all administration policy initiatives had originated at the White House and were staffed out by the cabinet agencies, which drafted the legislation and supporting documentation and worked with Congress to get it passed. In the early 1970s, the President's Advisory Commission on Executive Organization—known as the Ash Council for its chair, Roy Ash—recommended the creation of an institutional body within the White House staff to be known as the Domestic Council. This organization, headed by an executive director who would report to the president, was intended to be the domestic policy analog of the National Security Council, and to establish within the White House a powerful institutionalized domestic policy staff that would continue from administration to administration. The Ford and Carter administrations continued this structure, and domestic policy in both administrations was initiated and directed by the White House staff.

The Domestic Council, as a powerful centralized staff unit within the White House, was never revived in the Reagan administration. Instead, a decentralized structure of separate cabinet councils was organized, each with assigned responsibilities over sectors of domestic policy and headed by a cabinet officer. The Cabinet Council on Economics, for example, was headed by the Secretary of the Treasury. The White House staff intersected with these cabinet groups through a member of the White House domestic policy staff, who served as the staff director of one or more councils.

Whether or not deliberately so designed, the cabinet council structure was a reasonably effective means for encouraging the cabinet departments themselves to initiate many of the policies and programs of the Reagan administration. This was possible because the Reagan appointees at the departmental level understood Reagan's philosophy of government and attempted to carry it out within their areas of authority, seeking approval of their initiatives through the consultative cabinet council process. Initiatives that were developed through this process eventually went to the President, who gave final approval. In most cases, there were a series of options for decision by the President, but these ordinarily concerned how a policy or program was to be implemented, rather than whether to proceed with it at all.

There were deficiencies in the system, discussed in Chapter 6, but clearly, a decentralized system in which initiatives were developed at the cabinet level could not have worked at all if Reagan's ideas and principles had not provided the necessary philosophical framework. In most administrations, cabinet members—and indeed the White House staff itself—have no idea what the president intends to do. There might have been vague promises during the campaign—Bill Clinton's promise to "end welfare as we know it" is an example—but what this means, if anything, when the candidate becomes the president, awaits direction by the new chief executive. Until this direction comes, it is fruitless— indeed it can be a sign of disloyalty—for a cabinet department or officer to begin a policy initiative that might signal a direction the president has not approved.

For this reason, all policy development in the Executive Branch must begin with what the president wants to do. In most administrations, this is something of a mystery. Most presidents, apart from campaign speeches and perhaps a record as a governor or a senator, have not articulated a plan or fixed set of programs for their administrations in advance of taking office. Thus, in his book, *Intellectuals and the American Presidency*,[4] Tevi Troy points out that many presidents recruited a resident intellectual for the White House staff as a source of policy and program ideas, or at least as a link to the intellectual community where such ideas were thought to reside.

Such a function would have been superfluous to the Reagan White House; the President had very clearly formulated policy ideas, many of them already expressed in the speeches and radio addresses of the 1960s and 1970s and in his speeches during the 1980 campaign. In addition, the cabinet departments were headed and staffed by political appointees who understood and agreed with Reagan's philosophy and thus had some sense of what the President would do if he were making the decisions that confronted them day to day. Neustadt quotes a presidential aide from Eisenhower's administration: "If some of these cabinet members would just take time out to stop and ask themselves, 'What would I want if I were President?' they wouldn't give him all the trouble he's been having."[5] Just so. Reagan's clearly articulated philosophy and ideas enabled the members of his administration to make decisions at subordinate levels that were, more likely than not, consistent with what Reagan himself would have done in the same circumstances.

Thus, the extraordinary degree to which Reagan delegated authority does not seem quite as risky as some students of the presidency, including Neustadt, have suggested. Indeed, Reagan seemed well aware of this, noting in his autobiography that delegation of authority was appropriate as long as subordinates are "doing what you have in mind." To a great extent, Reagan achieved this degree of control over his subordinates through their acceptance of his philosophy and ideas. But as shown by the Iran-Contra affair, making sure that subordinates are doing what the president has in mind requires subordinates with the good judgment to understand not only what the president really intends but how he would carry out his intentions. Yet, despite the failure of management represented by the Iran-Contra episode, it would not be fair to use that one instance, as Neustadt has suggested, to indict Reagan's management style as a whole. During his eight years in office, Reagan achieved an extraordinary amount by combining a coherent philosophy of government with a great deal of delegated authority. That style should now be recognized as another way for a president to achieve success.

My experience at the Treasury Department illustrates both how the Reagan management style worked in practice and why it was successful. During the 1980 campaign—and in meetings with his cabinet after election—Reagan made clear that he wanted to reduce the federal government's regulatory role in the economy. Although Treasury has few regulatory responsibilities, one of them is in banking and financial services. The Office of the Comptroller of the Currency—the chartering authority and regulator of national banks—is a bureau within the Treasury Department, and Treasury has always been the department that has followed developments in the banking and financial services field for the administration in office.

In the early 1980s, there was considerable congressional and academic policy interest in some form of deregulation in the banking field—

particularly through modification or repeal of the Glass-Steagall Act—so that banks could compete in the securities business. The proposals on the Hill were quite modest, and followed closely the ideas laid down in prior years. Banks, which were already permitted under Glass-Steagall to underwrite and deal in the general obligation bonds of states and municipalities, would be given additional authority to underwrite and deal in municipal revenue bonds—securities backed by specific revenue streams and not by a general obligation of the state or municipality. This was not much in the way of deregulation, and certainly not what Ronald Reagan meant by reducing the role of the government in the economy. Of course, Ronald Reagan had never addressed specifically—before or after the campaign—either the Glass-Steagall Act or the general question of reforming the regulation of banks. But in his strong statements about the importance of deregulation, Reagan in effect authorized the Treasury Department to develop a robust program of deregulation in this area.

Accordingly, in Treasury Secretary Donald Regan's first testimony on a pending banking bill, he advanced a proposal that changed the nature of the debate. Rather than simply offering banks one more relatively minor securities activity, Regan suggested that bank holding companies—ordinary corporations that control banks—be permitted to engage in a full range of financial activities, including underwriting and dealing in corporate securities and offering all types of insurance. This would amount to a substantial modification in the scope of Glass-Steagall and free banking organizations to enter other financial services activities. It would also permit securities firms and insurance companies to enter the banking business by acquiring banks, thus contributing to the desire for enhanced competition that ultimately underlay Reagan's deregulatory philosophy. It was a radical approach at the time, but this very structure was finally adopted in 1999, with the enactment of the Gramm-Leach-Bliley Act.

The important point, however, is that this idea originated with the Treasury Department, and was approved through the cabinet council process established for policy development in the Reagan administration. Eventually, the proposal went to the President for approval, but this was close to a formality by the time it occurred. We all knew that a significant change in the government's role in the economy was what Ronald Reagan wanted, and the deregulation plan advanced for the banking industry was part of Treasury's contribution to the implementation of the President's philosophy. Other agencies, too, came forward with their own policy proposals, and it is likely that all of them conformed to the philosophy that Ronald Reagan had articulated in the campaign and in his speeches as president. This was delegation in the Reagan administration, and was successful only because the President led through the communication of his ideas and principles—not by making decisions on a case-by-case basis.

Others have also seen Reagan's speeches and the ideas they contained as the central element through which Ronald Reagan led his administration and the country. As one of Reagan's principal speechwriters, Tony Dolan, noted:

> Ronald Reagan knows how important his speeches are. Not only do they provide a statement of purpose for the government, it is through his speeches that managers understand where they're going. And especially is that important in our form of government, where we do not have a parliamentary majority. Here you have to mobilize public opinion to make the government work in the direction the president wants, and Ronald Reagan—or any president for that matter—does that through his speeches.[6]

Reagan's speeches in turn influenced what his cabinet members said, also lending a coherence to his administration. In his book on Reagan's use of speeches as an instrument of governance, *The Bully Pulpit*, William Ker Muir Jr. notes, "The President's words were frequently read by the cabinet speechwriters. 'I look at the Reagan speeches. I try to let them influence me,' said one. Another recalled, 'Reagan's State of the Union speech [in 1985] really did move me very strongly, and at a number of levels. . . .'"[7] In other words, Reagan's speeches as president infused his entire administration with a sense of direction, and that was ultimately reflected in the actions and statements of his cabinet members.

To a very substantial degree, Reagan's speechwriters simply revised the words he had written himself many years before he became President. Tony Dolan captured this process perfectly:

> "People say that the president is the great communicator. He's not. He's the great rhetorician. He uses words. He uses logic. There is substance in every paragraph. His arguments flow from one point to the next. And he uses anecdotes and statistics to back them up. He has a philosophy. He develops it. And he adheres to it. . . . [T]he Reagan speechwriters' major function is to plagiarize the president's old speeches and give them back to him to say."[8]

In other words, the speeches Reagan made in the 1980s echo the radio addresses he researched and wrote after leaving the California governorship in 1974, which in turn elucidate and expand upon the ideas that Reagan first articulated in The Speech. "You know," said a speechwriter in the Department of Agriculture quoted by Muir, "Reagan came to Joliet, [Illinois], years ago, maybe it was 1976, and I still have a copy of his speech, and it is not much different from the things he said in 1980 and even today. . . ."[9] Thus, far from being a mouthpiece for his speechwriters and staff—as Reagan was so often presented in the press—Reagan was frequently the fountainhead of the ideas the writers incorporated into his speeches. In this sense, Ronald Reagan was not simply a spokesman for a philosophy of government he came to represent; he was the source of that philosophy.

Indeed, the ideas that Ronald Reagan framed in his radio addresses became the ideas that shaped his presidency. Sometimes almost word for word. Thus, in his first major speech as president, on February 5, 1981, he dealt with the weak state of the economy and what to do about it:

> Some say shift the burden to business and industry, but business doesn't pay taxes. Oh, don't get the wrong idea. Business is being taxed. . . . But business must pass its costs of operations—and that

includes taxes—on to the consumer in the price of the product. Only people pay taxes, all the taxes. Government just uses business in a kind of sneaky way to help collect the taxes.[10]

Compare this statement to his radio address on July 31, 1978, where he used an example of the corner grocer who must include his tax bill in the cost of his groceries:

> What all this adds up to is that gov't. can't tax things like businesses or corporations, it can only tax people. When it says it's going to "make business pay," it is really saying it is going to make business help it to collect taxes.[11]

To many observers, obsessed with the notion that Reagan was an actor in the presidency, Reagan's speeches were less about policy than about performance. Lou Cannon writes, for example: "Reagan was largely removed from the unending debate that raged within his administration on the distinction between speeches and policy. He never confused a speech with a fact-finding expedition. Instead, Reagan recognized the salesman's truth that salesmen sell themselves before they sell their products, and he used his speeches to reaffirm his personal relationship with the American audience. This point was lost on the bickering disciples who battled among themselves about the purposes and meaning of 'the Reagan Revolution.'"[12] This comment itself misses the point. The words in Reagan's speeches outlined and refined his policies and principles the way regulations apply the more general principles embodied in statutes. The speeches were fought over not because the policy direction was unclear, but because the details of implementation were important.

Naturally, his critics would see Reagan's focus on speeches as evidence of his shallowness, or his role as a performer. Thus, in *Way Out There in the Blue*, Frances Fitzgerald recounts the following from an interview with Henry Kissinger: "Kissinger discovered that the best way to get Reagan's attention was to talk about what he ought to say publicly on an issue. If there was talk of a speech or a public statement, Reagan would sit up and his eyes would come back into focus."[13] This should hardly be surprising. Reagan understood the importance of his speeches in setting a direction for his administration and the country.

Fitzgerald also quotes John Sears, a former Reagan campaign manager, who thought that Reagan's management style came from his days as an actor: "He gave the speeches and made the appearances—and the rest was the work of his staff."[14] But even the highly critical Sears—who was fired by Reagan during the 1980 campaign—admitted that there were limits to how far staff could stray in making policy decisions: "You could do almost anything you wanted, and you didn't have to check with anybody. You could do all these amazing things. . . . Reagan wasn't involved. . . . He let everybody—as long as they stayed within a bit of a framework—do anything they wanted. . . . What he was doing in his speeches was setting limits in the form of principles."[15] Making allowances for Sears's animosity toward Reagan, we can see in this statement the outlines of the same management style that Reagan brought to the presidency: he set the boundaries with statements of principle, and left the rest to his subordinates.

Even some of Reagan's closest advisers were never able to see the bigger picture on which Reagan alone seems to have been focused. Thus, Lou Cannon notes, in describing Reagan's views concerning nuclear disarmament:

> By 1980, Reagan was a familiar figure on the national political stage. There seemed nothing enigmatic about him. He was stereotyped as a likable and decent man who was lacking in intellectual candlepower. Most reporters focused on the maneuvers of Reagan's strategists rather than on Reagan's inner goals. Often, the strategists were also focused on themselves. They respected Reagan's performance skills and paid little attention to his larger purposes. This attitude was compounded when Reagan reached the White House; many of his advisers viewed his dreamy imaginings and original ideas as irrelevant to his presidency. "We were always dazzled by the success of his approach and never quite willing to trust it," said one of Reagan's foreign policy advisers.[16]

But one man's "dreamy imaginings" are another man's inspirations, and to Reagan and most members of his administration the ideas he advanced in his speeches were the essence of his presidency and his governing style.

Reagan believed in the power of ideas—not simply programmatic ideas, but ideas broadly construed to include political and economic theory, a philosophy of government—a systematic and coherent statement of the role of government in a democratic society that could be called an ideology. Things were as they were, Reagan believed, because of ideas in this broad sense—about economics, government, and themselves—that the American people had come to accept over the years since the Great Depression. To Reagan, change could come only with a change in these prevailing ideas.

Thus, Reagan's "revolution" was indisputably a revolution of ideas—an effort to change the American people's conception of the proper role of government. If he was successful in this effort—if his ideas took hold—a change in the direction of the country, a change toward the smaller less intrusive government he wanted, would follow.

Indeed, to an extent virtually unknown among presidents, Reagan was an active participant in the ongoing war of ideas over the proper role of government. In their influential 1981 book *Free to Choose*, Milton and Rose Friedman wrote of the effect of the Depression on the American people's view of the role of government: "In the realm of ideas, the Depression persuaded the public that capitalism was an unstable system destined to suffer ever more serious crises. The public was converted to views that had already gained increasing acceptance among intellectuals . . . the change in the public's perception of the proper role of private enterprise on the one hand and of the government on the other proved a major catalyst for the rapid growth of government, and particularly central government, from that day to this."[17] The change in public attitudes, according to the Friedmans, extended beyond the public sphere. Noting that the Depression was seen by the public as a failure of capitalism, even though later scholarship has shown that government policy itself was the principal cause of the Depression's severity, the Friedmans point out that the myth of market failure "led the public to join the intellectuals in a changed view of the relative responsibilities of individuals and government. Emphasis on the responsibility of the individual for his own fate was replaced by emphasis on the individual as a pawn buffeted by forces beyond his control. The view that government's role is to serve as an umpire to prevent individuals from coercing one another was replaced by the view that government's role is to serve as a parent charged with the duty of coercing some to aid others."[18]

Reagan intended, with his speeches as president, to reverse the changes in public perception the Friedmans had identified. To do this, he sought to call forth the individualism and sense of personal responsibility of the American people . . . to make them believe again that they could cure the nation's problems themselves rather than depending on government. As he said in his first Inaugural Address:

> In this present crisis, government is not the solution to our problem; government is the problem. From time to time we've been tempted to believe that society has become too complex to be managed by self-rule, that government by an elite group is superior to government for, by, and of the people. Well, if no one among us is capable of governing himself, then who among us has the capacity to govern someone else? All of us together, in and out of government, must bear the burden. . . . It is my intention to curb the size and influence of the federal government and to demand recognition of the distinction between the powers granted to the federal government and those reserved to the states and the people.[19]

Reagan's weapon in this effort was not the political power he held as president. It was the ideas he would put before the American people. As he said in a 1981 speech to the Conservative Political Action Conference:

> It's been said that anyone who seeks success or greatness should first forget about both and seek only the truth, and the rest will follow. . . . And history must also say that our victory, when it was achieved, was not so much a victory of politics as it was a victory of ideas, not so much a

victory for any one man or party as it was a victory for a set of principles—principles that were protected and nourished by a few unselfish
Americans through many grim and heartbreaking defeats. . . . Our
goals complement each other. We're not cutting the budget simply for
the sake of sounder financial management. This is only a first step toward returning power to the states and communities, only a first step
toward reordering the relationship between citizen and government.[20]

Reagan's faith in ideas may be unique among modern American
presidents. He does not appear to have sought the presidency for its
own sake, or for its trappings, or even as the culmination of a life-long
goal. Instead, he sought the presidency to implement a set of firmly
held ideas about government's proper role that he—virtually alone
among major public figures at the time he ran—believed. Reviewing
the presidents in the twentieth century, one would be hard pressed to
identify any—except possibly Woodrow Wilson—who was interested
more in ideas than in gaining and holding power. Ironically, in the
sense that he believed that ideas were more important than individuals
or power relationships, Ronald Reagan—no matter how it may gall
those who have scorned the quality of his intelligence and called him an
actor or a lightweight—was an intellectual.

The sheer number of radio addresses in *Reagan in His Own Hand* is
testimony to this view. What other modern president—before or after
becoming president—ever researched and wrote, himself, over a thousand commentaries on public issues of his day? This suggests an inten-
sity of commitment that belies claims that he was lazy or disinterested
in policy. Both Michael Deaver, who traveled with Reagan for many
years before he became President, and Nancy Reagan have remarked on
the fact that he was always reading and writing. Deaver writes: "In all
my years with Reagan—on the campaign plane or in the White
House—I watched him devour countless books, white papers, position
papers, memos and biographies."[21] And Nancy Reagan recalls: "Nobody thought that he ever read anything, either—but he was a vora-
cious reader. I don't remember Ronnie sitting and watching television. I

really don't. I just don't. When I picture those days, it's him sitting behind that desk in the bedroom, working."[22]

According to the editors of *Reagan in His Own Hand,* about 670 of these essays, written in his own hand between 1975 and 1979, were saved and are now in the Reagan Presidential Library in Simi Valley, California. Of these, 27 percent were on foreign and defense policy, 25 percent on economics, 15 percent on government and individual liberty, 10 percent on energy and the environment, and the balance were distributed more or less evenly among a myriad other issues that were of importance at the time.[23] This effort reflects not only immense intellectual discipline but a powerful motivation—a motivation that could only have been the result of a belief that it is ideas that ultimately shape the world.

And these were not small ideas. On November 16, 1976, Reagan's essay for his radio address included a parable he had written about a little red hen. I include it here in full because it illustrates a great deal about Reagan's intellectual gifts, his skill as a rhetorician, and the ideas with which he was challenging his audience.

Once upon a time there was a little red hen who scratched about the barnyard until she uncovered some grains of wheat. She called her neighbors and said, "if we plant this wheat, we shall have bread to eat. Who will help me plant it?"

"Not I," said the cow.

"Not I," said the duck.

"Not I," said the pig.

"Not I," said the goose.

"Then I will," said the little red hen. And she did. The wheat grew tall and ripened into golden grain. "Who will help me reap my wheat?" asked the little red hen.

"Not I," said the duck.

"Out of my classification," said the pig.

"I'd lose my seniority," said the cow.

"I'd lose my unemployment compensation," said the goose.

"Then I will," said the little red hen, and she did.

At last it came time to bake the bread. "Who will help me bake the bread?" asked the little red hen.

"That would be overtime for me," said the cow.

"I'd lose my welfare benefits," said the duck.

"I'm a dropout and never learned how," said the pig.

"If I'm to be the only helper, that's discrimination," said the goose.

"Then I will," said the little red hen.

She baked five loaves and held them up for her neighbors to see.

They all wanted some and, in fact, demanded a share. But the little red hen said, "No, I can eat the five loaves myself."

"Excess profits," cried the cow.

"Capitalist leech," screamed the duck.

"I demand equal rights," yelled the goose.

And the pig just grunted.

And they painted "unfair" picket signs and marched round and round the little red hen, shouting obscenities.

When the government agent came, he said to the little red hen, "You must not be greedy."

"But I earned the bread," said the little red hen.

"Exactly," said the agent. "That is the wonderful free enterprise system. Anyone in the barnyard can earn as much as he wants. But under our modern government regulations, the productive workers must divide their product with the idle."

And they lived happily ever after, including the little red hen, who smiled and clucked, "I am grateful, I am grateful."

But her neighbors wondered why she never again baked any more bread.[24]

This is a very clever piece of political writing, making several points simultaneously. In the nursery story on which it is based, the point is the simple one that people who don't do the work don't have a right to share in the product. But Reagan makes this simple idea operate on this and several other levels, and changes the conclusion so that it drives home an even more subtle point. First, of course, there is the refusal to help. This Reagan turns into a lampoon of the excuses commonly heard at the time from the uncooperative and the nonproductive ("That would be overtime for me!"). Then, when the bread is baked, he ridicules the whining and name-calling of the non-productive ("Capitalist leech!"). Finally, he satirizes a government policy that takes from the productive and gives to the non-productive ("our modern government regulations"). But then he adds a further telling point. The little red hen is seemingly content, but she doesn't bake any more bread. In other words, people may comply with this policy—may even agree that it has an ethical basis—but in the end nothing can make them produce the wealth that others rely on.

It is also a commentary on Reagan's impact on American political discourse that many of the excuses and complaints he cites in this parable are no longer heard. The ideas concerning personal responsibility and the relationship between work and success that Reagan preached took hold during his time in office and have grown stronger in public opinion polls as the generation that formed their views during the 1980s became the adults of the 1990s. In one series of polls, asking Americans whether they preferred smaller government with fewer services or larger government with many services, the 40 percent of Americans who preferred smaller government in 1976 had grown to 63 percent in 1996.[25] Similarly, those who were willing to agree with the proposition that the best government is one that governs least increased from 32 percent in 1973 to 61 percent in 1996.[26] And between 1983 and 1997, the percentage of Americans who believed that government was responsible for the well-being of its citizens declined from 43 percent to 16 percent, while those who believed individuals were responsible for their own well-being increased from 46 percent to 66 percent.[27] Reagan had achieved what he set out to do—reverse the trend toward greater government power cited by Milton and Rose Friedman in 1981.

Other Reagan essays were more pointed than the metaphorical red hen story. On July 31, 1978, Reagan talked about ancient Rome and its lessons for contemporary policies:

We can envy a little the Roman postal system that extended north into Europe & south to Egypt and guaranteed safe delivery. Roman justice made possible such things as commercial contracts, property laws, marriage & divorce, wills, trusts, etc. . . .

But it was in the growth of govt. intervention that we should find a warning. They set interest rates, devalued the currency, created a wheat subsidy & then dumped wheat on the mkt. There were extensive public works like our New Deal-W.P.A.; a welfare system & food stamps. Believe it or not they had a depression & created a Home Loan Corp., an Agricultural Adjustment Admin. Which plowed under half the grapes to stop overproduction of wine and their basic coin the Denarius sank lower & lower in purchasing power. They of course didn't have printing press money but they increased the money supply by adding copper to the silver in the Denarius. It went from 94% silver to only 2/100's of 1% in Rome's final days.[28]

This is a key point in any understanding of Ronald Reagan and his presidency. Unlike other presidents before and after him, he was not focused on checking off items on an agenda of specific programs so that he might be accounted in history as effective; and, as many have noted, he didn't really seem to care who was on his staff or how their duties were distributed. What mattered to Ronald Reagan were issues of the broadest kind: What is the proper place of the government in the lives of the American people? How can government create an environment in which people will be productive? How can we create incentives for greater productivity? These were the issues he preferred to address in his speeches, and, as we have seen, these ideas had an effect.

This way of governing is quite different from what we have come to expect from presidents. Since Franklin Roosevelt, the model president has been the master manipulator—of the press, Congress, his staff and administration, or the public itself, and sometimes all at once. Fred I. Greenstein, a scholar of the presidency, catches the flavor of this approach in his assessment of political skill as an element of presidential success. Citing Professor Neustadt's work on the presidency, Greenstein writes:

> The classic statement of the centrality of political skill to presidential performance is Richard E. Neustadt's *Presidential Power,* which has been described as the closest approximation to Machiavelli's writings in the literature of American politics. The question Neustadt addresses is how the chief executive can put his stamp on public policy in the readily stalemated American political system. Neustadt's prescription is for the president to use the powers of his office assertively, build and maintain public support, and establish a reputation among fellow policymakers as a skilled, determined political operator.[29]

The presidents who have been deemed successful by historians and political scientists have by and large been able to achieve their goals through building and managing political coalitions that would not otherwise easily work together. The Roosevelt New Deal coalition, made up of the white and black South, northern blue-collar workers, and intellectuals, was a classic of this kind. Kennedy, Johnson, and Nixon also put together coalitions to gain office and to govern.

But these coalitions were not coalitions brought together by ideas. Roosevelt had no fixed philosophy of government when he assumed the presidency, and soon reversed the course he had promised during the campaign. Kennedy promised to "get the country moving again"—but did not suggest during the campaign that he would achieve this by cutting taxes. Johnson's War on Poverty was not a philosophy; it was a pragmatic application of the idea that government spending could effect major change in society.

Reagan's coalition, on the other hand, was a coalition based on ideas, on a way of viewing government's role in the economy and in daily life. In this sense, it was unlike any coalition in modern times—perhaps any coalition since Lincoln's. Indeed, David Donald's biography of Lincoln shows clearly that Lincoln, an obscure former Congressman from the frontier, gained national attention only when he began to make speeches about values and ideas; and it was his appeal to the nation's better angels—its values as expressed in the Declaration of Independence—that held the Union together through its most trying period.[30]

To be sure, Reagan was helped in seeking the presidency by the dreadful state of the economy in 1980, but in light of his controversial tenure as governor of California, his radio addresses between 1975 and 1979, and his speeches during the campaign, there could have been little doubt among those who voted for him where he stood on the issues and what he intended to do with his presidency. He was elected by people who had come to accept, albeit tentatively, the proposition that perhaps the government had grown too large, too intrusive, and too expensive. Now they wanted to see whether Reagan's prescription worked.

Thus, in his first Inaugural Address, which he largely drafted himself, Reagan made clear that his would be a different administration, wielding power in a different way: "We are a nation that has a government—not the other way around. And this makes us special among the nations of the earth. Our government has no power except that granted to it by the people. It is time to check and reverse the growth of government, which shows signs of having grown beyond the consent of the governed."[31]

It is noteworthy—and typical of Reagan—that this address articulated a philosophy of government, not a litany of programs. Reagan *was* interested in policy, but in its broadest sense: the policies that flowed from the acceptance and implementation of first principles about how the government should operate, and how it should relate to the citizenry and the private sector generally. Perhaps for this reason, Reagan was not particularly interested in programs or details, and certainly not in those programs or details that did not reflect his priorities—tax policy, deregulation, free trade, restoring American military power, and restoring the confidence of the American people.

Since so spare a set of interests was not what was expected of a president, Reagan paid a high price in the scorn of the media, members of Congress, and even some members of his staff, who saw his disinterest in programs and details as emblematic of laziness, disengagement, and intellectual limitation. Yet in reality, Reagan might have had his priorities correctly aligned. The important thing, he believed, was to change people's views of government, and this required concentrated attention to a few key ideas. This was Reagan's goal, and he sought to accomplish it through his speeches rather than through attending to the myriad day-to-day issues that routinely appear on the agendas of our presidents.

That Reagan largely accomplished his objectives should go a long way toward validating the unconventional methods that he used. Reagan's ideas, advanced in his speeches, left a policy legacy that can be seen clearly in the presidencies of at least two of his successors—Bill Clinton and the second George Bush. After Clinton's disastrous effort to saddle the economy with a national health plan redolent of the New Deal and the Great Society—in other words, to reverse the ideology of a smaller, less intrusive government established by Reagan—he declared that "The era of big government is over" and spent the rest of his presidency proposing small costless initiatives as a way of meeting the media's standards for being an activist president. Meanwhile, the powerful economic engine created by Reagan's policies of lower taxation and less regulation, more competition and freer trade, sustained Clinton's popularity to the end of his two troubled terms. Although the duration of his administration—and the philosophy on which it is based—is not yet clear, the first major initiative of George W. Bush was to cut taxes, relying on what could be called a new Reaganomics approach.

As Peter Rodman, a foreign policy official in several Republican administrations observed, referring to Reagan: "The striking thing about this president. . . is that he has placed his stamp on this government by virtue of a coherent philosophy everyone understands. . . . I doubt if any president has so permanently and so widely left his mark on government as Reagan."[32]

Thus, Reagan accomplished considerably more through his ideas and his speeches than those of his predecessors who have been praised and admired by historians for their relentless and occasionally successful efforts to enact an agenda of specific programs. Roosevelt's New

Deal ran out of steam after the beginning of World War II, even though the inability of Congress to terminate agencies or programs has kept many of its artifacts alive in Washington. Truman, Eisenhower, Kennedy, Johnson, Nixon, Ford, and Carter left nothing behind except larger and more diverse bureaucracies, because their administrations were not based on ideas or principles. It would be absurd to try to identify the influence of Harry Truman on John F. Kennedy or Jimmy Carter, but the influence of Ronald Reagan on Bill Clinton's ability to reconstitute a big-government program, and on the campaign and early initiatives of the second George Bush is plain to see.

There are, accordingly, no modern templates or precedents against which to measure or assess Ronald Reagan in his own terms. If he had been a failure, an effort to identify the ways in which he was unique would be a waste of time; in that case he could be judged by the usual standards. But Reagan was undeniably a success—more successful in changing his country than any president since Franklin D. Roosevelt— and for that reason it is important to understand how he achieved his objectives. Many commentators, judging him according to conventional standards, professed to be mystified by his success, but that is because they believed there was only one way for a president to succeed. Reagan proved that there was another way—perhaps even a better way—by basing his administration on the power of ideas.

Since his ideas were large in conception and limited in number, Reagan might be said to have reigned rather than ruled; that is, he did not seek as president to inject himself or his views into every program or controversy of his administration, but reserved his interventions for those issues that were central to his philosophy. Ultimately, he succeeded because he showed the American people that his vision worked—that they could accomplish much more for themselves without government than they could by asking government to do things for them. This is exactly what Reagan intended, and in changing the way the American people thought about their government and themselves, Reagan changed the United States. And since ideas do not respect borders, in changing the United States he changed the world. It's all there in his first Inaugural Address:

If we look to the answer as to why for so many years we achieved so much, prospered as no other people on earth, it was because here in this land we unleashed the energy and individual genius of man to a greater extent than has ever been done before. . . .

It is no coincidence that our present troubles parallel and are proportionate to the intervention and intrusion in our lives that result from unnecessary and excessive growth of government. . . .

In the days ahead I will propose removing the roadblocks that have slowed our economy and reduced productivity. Steps will be taken aimed at restoring the balance between the various levels of government. Progress may be slow, measured in inches and feet, not miles, but we will progress. It is time to reawaken this industrial giant, to get government back within its means, and to lighten our punitive tax burden. And these will be our first priorities, and on these principles there will be no compromise.[33]

As many presidents have found, it is easy to make pledges and reject compromise in speeches, especially in an inaugural address. The difficult part comes when they must govern in the real world. Then we discover whether those who claim to have convictions can in fact stay the course.

3

CONVICTION POLITICIAN

There are simple ideas—just not easy ones.
—RONALD REAGAN, IN MANY CAMPAIGN SPEECHES

If it weren't for David Stockman, we would never have known how tough and committed Ronald Reagan really was. Stockman, Reagan's first budget director, was not a believer in the supply-side economic theory that came to be known as Reaganomics—not while he was in the government and not after he left—but it is from Stockman's book, *The Triumph of Politics,* that we get a sense of Ronald Reagan's unshakeable belief in the tax and economic policies on which he staked his presidency.

Shortly after Congress passed Reagan's initial tax package in July 1981, the first indications of what would become a serious recession began to appear. By many measures, the recession of 1981–82 was one of the worst economic downturns since the Great Depression of the 1930s. In February 1982, the prime rate stood at 16.5 percent, unemployment was 8.4 percent—over 10 million people—and the economy was steadily declining. The nightly news relentlessly recorded and reported the hardships of the unemployed and the underemployed. Reagan's popularity, measured by the Gallup Poll's approval/disapproval ratio, declined from a 60/29 ratio in July 1981 to 41/47 in July 1982.

Moreover, with congressional elections approaching in November 1982, panicky Republicans in Congress were imploring the President to take some concrete steps that would show he was responding to the economic distress their constituents were feeling. The president's party normally loses seats in an off-year election, and with a serious recession grinding the country's economy, the looming election of November 1982 looked like an oncoming train.

It seems almost absurd in retrospect—so much has Ronald Reagan reshaped Republican and even some Democratic thinking—but at the time Reagan was being urged by virtually all his advisers, as well as by Republicans in the House and Senate, to *raise* taxes. In his book, Stockman describes his shock on realizing in the fall of 1981 that OMB's forecast for 1982 and beyond was for triple-digit deficits "as far as the eye could see," and he recounts the efforts of key senators as well as the entire top White House staff to convince the President to roll back at least a portion of the tax cuts that Reagan had won just three months before.[1]

The argument for tax increases was that deficits caused high interest rates, which in turn were contributing to the seriousness of the recession and preventing economic recovery.* This position was hard to counter, since both the projected deficit and interest rates were at near historic highs. Reagan, however, seemed to understand that all this pressure to roll back the tax cuts was really a surrender to the false economic policies that had brought the country to the current crisis. He had promised the American people a new economic policy—one in which tax cuts would stimulate productivity and growth—and he was going to deliver it whatever the short-term political cost.

In a speech to the nation from the Oval Office on February 5, 1981, only three weeks after taking office, Reagan made clear that his economic program was going to be nothing like that of his predecessors:

---

* When Regan told the President that raising taxes in the midst of a recession was a bad idea, Stockman wrote that Regan's position "was a non sequitur, and it was ignorant twaddle." David Stockman, *The Triumph of Politics* (New York: Harper and Row, 1986) p. 347. In light of later developments in the economy, and economists' more sophisticated understanding of the relationship among deficits, interest rates and inflation, Stockman's absolute certainty about the correctness of his position now looks misplaced.

I've put a freeze on pending regulations and set up a task force under Vice President Bush to review regulations with an eye toward getting rid of as many as possible. I have decontrolled oil, which should result in more domestic production and less dependence on foreign oil. And I'm eliminating that ineffective Council on Wage and Price Stability.

But it will take much more. And we must realize there is no quick fix. At the same time, however, we cannot delay in implementing an economic program aimed at both reducing tax rates to stimulate productivity and reducing the growth in government spending to reduce unemployment and inflation.[2]

Despite this ardent determination, few people—even some among Republican officeholders—believed Reagan could not be talked out of his position. In one particularly revealing moment recounted in Stockman's book, Reagan was confronted by Senate Budget Chairman Pete Domenici, a Republican, who tells him that there is no way to cut the deficit without raising revenue—to which Reagan responds "Dammit, Pete, I'm just not going to accept this. This is just more of the same kind of talk we've heard for forty years."[3] Stockman had set up the meeting with Domenici in the hope that it would sway Reagan, and the episode is presented in his book as an indication of how hard it was to deal with this stubborn and seemingly ignorant man.

Reagan himself was fully aware of the pressure he was receiving. Late in 1981, he wrote in his diary: "The recession has worsened, throwing our earlier figures off. Now my team is pushing for a tax increase to help hold down the deficits. I'm being stubborn. I think our tax cuts will produce more revenue by stimulating the economy. I intend to wait and see some results."[4]

All through 1982, Reagan's diary entries reflect pressure on him from Republicans and Democrats alike to raise taxes—pressure that he steadfastly resisted. In the face of this, dutifully recorded by Stockman as a demonstration of Reagan's irrational stubbornness, Reagan wouldn't budge. This former movie actor, whose "cognitive limitations" (in Fred Greenstein's delicate phrase) supposedly made him prey to the blandishments of his advisers, was apparently able to stand almost alone—not only in the face of his advisers' disapproval but also in defiance of pleas from his party's establishment. Only Don Regan, then Reagan's treasury secretary, backed the President's position. Reagan's response to all—"Stay the course"—has since become shorthand for the political courage to carry through with an idea or principle despite fierce opposition.

Reagan understood that the recession was caused in large part by the efforts of the Federal Reserve to wring inflation out of the economy, and believed that increasing taxes would only make the recession worse. This seems obvious to most economists now, but at the time it was an untried theory much at variance with conservative Republican orthodoxy, and Reagan stood by it for the completely unconventional reason that he actually believed it. Of course, he did not want deficits—he had always argued against deficit spending—but if the choice was between deficits as far as the eye could see and instituting a new economic policy in which he believed, then deficits there would be.[5] On January 22, 1982, for example, Reagan wrote in his diary: "I told our guys I couldn't go for tax increases. If I had to be criticized, I'd rather be criticized for a deficit than for backing away from our economic program."[6]

Reagan clearly understood that his economic policy would result in deficits but thought that getting inflation under control through monetary policy while stimulating the economy through tax cuts would eventually result in the economic growth that would eliminate the deficits. Reporting on a discussion among Regan, the President, and himself, Stockman writes disapprovingly of Regan's statement that the budget should not be balanced "on the back of the taxpayers." To which the President, referring to the balanced budget that Stockman wanted, responded, "No, Don is right. I never said anything but that it was a goal. A balanced budget, yes. That's where we have to be aiming to come out. Whether it comes then or is delayed or not—well, you're still heading to the point where the lines cross."[7]

As it turned out, when Reagan's tax cuts took effect productivity in the economy increased, and inflation and interest rates came down. As

Don Regan and the Treasury economists had been arguing all along, there is no relationship between deficits and interest rates. Many economic studies have since shown this, but it was Reagan's extraordinary conviction on this point—his belief that the economy would recover without tax increases—that made a real-life demonstration possible. Although deficits continued at the level David Stockman regarded as horrific, lower inflation and interest rates—as well as Reagan's productivity-enhancing tax cuts—produced an historic economic expansion that continued into the next decade.

Reagan believed that among the first steps required to turn the economy around was to stop inflation, and the way to do that was to allow the Federal Reserve's medicine to work as quickly as possible. It is clear now—after the publication of Reagan's radio addresses from the mid-1970s—that this was Ronald Reagan's policy all along, reflecting his view that inflation must be arrested, even if it meant the country must suffer through a recession. It should come as no surprise, then, that Reagan did not interfere with or desire to jawbone the Fed as it tightened money through 1981 and into 1982. In a radio address on February 27, 1975, for example, Reagan prefigured his intention to stay the course on economic policy as president:

> I've talked at some length in these broadcasts about the need to zero in on inflation and not push the panic button because of recession. Now the leaders in Cong. are making it very evident that pol. considerations will determine what they do—not what is good for the country. . . . Recession must not be allowed to deepen into depression but if inflation is to be stopped we have to sweat out a certain period of recession. Unfortunately some politicians overreact to any increase in unemp. and start looking at the next election instead of the next generation.[8]

Anyone who has spent time in the White House or politics generally knows how difficult it is to follow the prescription that Reagan—as a private citizen—outlined in 1975. The complaints are loud and

never-ending; they come from supporters, friends, and advisers, from
Congress, and from members of the cabinet, all of whom are responding to complaints and calls for action they have received from their
own friends, constituents, and family members. The press coverage is
invariably negative—because the news business thrives on crisis. In the
midst of a recession, there are no news reports about companies that
are weathering the storm, or laid-off employees who have found jobs
or started their own businesses, even though these things always happen. It was easy for Reagan to talk about "sweating out" a recession
when he was a radio commentator; however, actually taking the heat as
president required a toughness and conviction that few in politics have
ever exhibited.

Yet this stance was absolutely essential to the success of Reagan's program. One of the central purposes of the tax cuts enacted in 1981—in
addition to creating the incentives necessary for accelerated economic
growth—was to limit over time the federal government's access to the
nation's wealth. Reagan was well aware that reversing the tax cuts would
not end the deficits—it would only provide more temporary revenue
that Congress would spend. The only way to stop government spending
was to place a limit on the government's taxing power, to reduce the percentage of the economy that the government could take in taxes. It was
essential to make a stand against this—no matter what the cost—if the
presidency he had envisioned was to have any meaning. Again, Stockman, although disapproving and critical of what he saw as Reagan's economic ignorance, quotes Reagan making exactly this point to Domenici
in the same meeting described above. 'I don't question your concern
with the deficit and all," says Reagan. "But there was once an economist,
maybe you haven't heard of him. He said when government starts taking
more than 25 percent of the economy, that's when the trouble starts.
Well, we zoomed above that a long time ago. That's how we got this economic mess. We can't solve it with more tax and spend."9

Ironically, Stockman follows this quote with: "The room fell silent.
The President never mentioned who the anonymous economist was.
Now the nation would begin an experiment to find out if he was right."
As it turned out, he was.

The conviction that helped Reagan withstand this enormous pressure, even from people within his own party and within his administration, was a long-held belief that his tax cuts would eventually result in much greater economic growth. When in fact the economy began to grow strongly in 1982, he recognized the moment by gently noting in a radio address, "They don't call it Reaganomics anymore."

Reagan recalled this difficult period in his autobiography: "Nancy sometimes calls me stubborn. Well, in this case, I *was* stubborn. I thought I was right. It was going to take time for the tax cuts to generate the kind of economic resurgence we needed to bring down interest rates, inflation, and unemployment. I believed we just had to wait it out."[10] Reagan's stubbornness and faith in his own convictions eventually paid off. Eight years after Reagan stayed the course, Lawrence Lindsey summarized the results of Reaganomics in *The Growth Experiment:*

> Two years [after the enactment of the Reagan tax cuts] the nation had embarked on the longest and strongest peacetime economic expansion in history, an expansion that would eventually bring more than twenty million new jobs to a once-discouraged American work force and revitalize states and regions of the country that shortly before seemed doomed to years of frustration and decline. The prime force behind this recovery was a revolution in economic policy that was scorned by many orthodox economists. This new direction in economics, though not without its flaws, revitalized the economy while simultaneously subduing inflation and reducing the burden of government on American business and families. This new wave of economic thought is still controversial. But its effects have made the U.S. once again the leader of the world economy and inspired nations throughout the industrialized and developing world to dramatically revise their own economic strategies.[11]

Reagan's willingness to stay the course on his economic policy was a revelation in Washington. The media missed it, but the political class did not. A president who would stand his ground in the face of the enormous pressure Reagan endured might be crazy, but he was a force to be reckoned with. This impression was strongly reinforced by another episode in which Reagan again demonstrated the extraordinary lengths to which he would go to turn the country in a new direction.

In August 1981, Reagan dismissed virtually all the nation's air traffic controllers—the employees of the Federal Aviation Administration who guide airplanes in and out of airports—after their union struck for higher wages. Here again, Reagan seemed heedless of the enormous political risks he was assuming, since he must have realized that an airplane crash while the air traffic control system was understaffed would have been a political disaster for which he alone would take the blame. But Reagan was elected as a law-and-order president, at a time when governments at all levels seemed unable to take decisive action against powerful interests. A failure of the federal government itself to stand up to pressure—a failure simply to enforce the law against a striking union—would have undermined Reagan's effort to show that his administration would be different.

Although in retrospect many have seen Reagan's action in this case as a central element of his successful economic policy, at the time it was highly controversial. The unions, of course, saw it as a Republican effort to break union power, and indeed many economic historians date the moderated wage demands of the Reagan period to this event. Many in the press and public saw it as a threat to the collective bargaining system itself. But again Reagan had addressed this issue before, and had decided what his policy would be. In a radio address on May 25, 1977, he took up the question of whether public employees such as teachers have the right to strike against the government.

Reagan began by quoting Franklin D. Roosevelt: "A strike of pub. emps. manifests nothing less than an intent on their part to prevent or obstruct the operations of govt. until their demands are satisfied. Such action looking toward the paralysis of govt. by those who have sworn to support it is unthinkable & intolerable." Then Reagan continued with his own views:

> F.D.R. summed it up pretty well. His words mean that those who
> choose govt. employment become a part of the govt. establishment

and are sworn to uphold it. Their employers are not their immediate superiors, or even the elected representatives of the people. Their true employers *are* the people. No amount of rhetoric or reciting clichés such as "2nd class citizens" can change the fact that there is a fundamental difference between private & pub. employment.[12]

Most politicians, confronted with this crisis and mindful of the potential consequences of an air disaster, would have sought a face-saving solution—a commission, a White House meeting followed by a compromise, or submitting conciliatory legislation to Congress. In particular, one wonders what the ideal president of Richard Neustadt's conception would have done. How much advice would he have sought? How much detail? Would any of this have helped him reach the right decision, or would it simply have enabled him to extricate himself from a difficult situation without assuming the implicit risks? Would that have been a solution or only a temporary fix? One is left with the sense that Neustadt's president would have adopted a policy that somehow allowed the air traffic controllers to retain their jobs, but required them to moderate their wage demands. Not Reagan. He had long before articulated the views that would shape his response, and he stood by them.

Given what Reagan wanted to achieve with his presidency, however, in a sense he had no choice. Here his prior convictions dovetailed with another element of his program—restoring the confidence of the American people in themselves and in their government. Reagan assumed office after Vietnam, after the failure of the Carter presidency, after the humiliation of the Iran hostage crisis, and the failure of even the much-admired U.S. military to accomplish a rescue. He could see that Americans had lost confidence in the steadfastness of their leaders and were unsure of themselves. Having been pushed around by Iranian mullahs, the Organization of Petroleum Exporting Countries (OPEC), runaway inflation, and a stagnating economy, the country could be forgiven for believing that things were out of control. Now, the air traffic controllers were threatening further havoc, attempting to extort a significantly higher wage package because of their stranglehold on the transportation economy. If Reagan was to restore the confidence of the American people, he had to show the country that someone could control events.

In addition, inflation psychology had taken hold in the United States, and to a large extent was a cause of inflation itself. Wage demands and wage increases caused price increases, which in turn produced demand for higher wages. Most employees and consumers assumed that higher wages and prices were inevitable. By calling a halt to this cycle, Reagan changed the nation's outlook. Labor unions became more cautious about striking to demand higher wages, and businesses to giving in to strike threats. With this enormously risky political step, in other words, Reagan began the process of cooling inflation psychology just as the Fed's policies were cooling down the economy.

In his statement on the controllers' strike, delivered in the White House Rose Garden on August 3, 1981, Reagan made clear that his action was linked, not just to the general principle that public employees have no right to strike, but to two other principles that were central both to his philosophy and to his effort to change the views of the American people about their ability to control their own lives—individual obedience to the law and individual acceptance of personal responsibility. He quoted a controller who had resigned from the union and reported to work—"How can I ask my kids to obey the law if I don't?"—and read aloud the oath that all government employees take when they enter upon their jobs: "I am not participating in any strike against the Government of the United States or any agency thereof, and I will not so participate while an employee of the Government of the United States or any agency thereof." Later, Reagan added another element of the event's significance: "I think it convinced people who might have thought otherwise that I meant what I said."[13]

It did. These two decisions relatively early in his presidency—staying the course on the recession of 1981–82 and firing the striking air traffic controllers—established Reagan's credibility for many of the controversies that lay ahead, substantially increasing his bargaining power with a Congress that had not recently seen a president who could not be forced into compromise. He would need this credibility; on the issues he considered important—and which formed the core of his reasons for seeking the presidency—Reagan's goals were not modest. We may take for granted the realities we see around us today—a U.S. economy that is the unchallenged world leader, a military establishment that makes the United States the world's only superpower, and a nation generally confident and optimistic about the future despite the tragedy of 9/11—but it is necessary to recall that when Ronald Reagan entered office none of these things seemed within reach. The American economy was in the grip of stagflation, our diplomats were captives in Iran, the Soviet Union was expanding, having recently established control of Afghanistan, and these were the days of "malaise" for the American people.

To change this pattern, Reagan intended to stimulate economic growth and investment by cutting taxes, improve the efficiency of the economy through enhanced competition and reduced government regulation, improve America's security by reaching an accommodation with the Soviet Union for a reduction in nuclear arms, and restore the American people's optimism and confidence about their future. These were goals he had talked about for 20 years before he became president, and the fact that they were unique to him—and not the work of advisers or speechwriters—has now been conclusively demonstrated with the publication of his radio addresses.

The policies and programs that were related to or furthered these goals—his economic program and the dismissal of the air traffic controllers are only two examples—received Reagan's persistent attention throughout his presidency. Significantly, however, other policies and programs—including many that he had written and spoken about over the years—were left largely to others. Here, Reagan seemed simply to follow the recommendations of his cabinet or other advisers, often waiting for a consensus to develop. This created the impression that he had no interest in policy or was "disengaged" from his own administration. It is curious that this idea should have acquired so much currency. As Edmund Morris points out in his biography of Theodore Roosevelt, *Theodore Rex*, TR selected certain issues as priorities for his presidency, and left the rest to the ministrations of his party—and no one ever accused him of being disengaged.

But Reagan began his presidency with the handicap of his past as an actor, despite his successful tenure as the governor of California, and as with most images adopted by the media, this initial introduction to the political world was difficult to shake. The notion that Reagan was uninterested in or ignorant on matters of policy, that he was merely a spokesman for his advisers—a view that, not coincidentally, enhanced the prestige and importance of his advisers—became deeply ingrained in the press. For example, Lou Cannon, a reporter who had covered Reagan for many years, both before and after he became president, and devoted significant attention to Reagan's policies in his biography, simply assumed that Reagan's apparent disinterest in some policies came from their unfamiliarity, causing Reagan difficulty in understanding their complexity. Writing about Reagan's early months in office, Cannon noted: "What Reagan was actually trying to do was focus on issues that had never crossed his mental horizon before he entered the White House."[14] With the publication of Reagan's radio addresses, however, we now know that between 1974 and 1979, Reagan had written tidy and powerful essays on virtually every issue he confronted as president. That an observer as close to Reagan as Cannon could have missed this fact reflects the power of the pervasive notion in Washington that Reagan was disengaged, lazy, intellectually limited, and the tool of his advisers on matters of policy.

In light of what we now know about Reagan's familiarity with a broad range of national policy issues before he assumed the presidency, it is difficult to escape the conclusion that his focus on certain policies and objectives—to the exclusion of others—was deliberate. He had apparently decided, before he took office, that he would limit his objectives to the very few outlined above, and leave the rest to his cabinet and advisers—whose work he would support and direct through his speeches. This rigorous setting of priorities is borne out in Reagan's autobiography, *Ronald Reagan: An American Life,* where he devotes over 50 pages to tax policy, 60 pages to economic policy, and almost 30 pages to trade policy—all core elements of his agenda—but makes only passing references to anticrime legislation, education, welfare, and Social Security, and does not mention at all many of the issues that were important to his conservative constituency or were major issues during his administration—abortion, drugs, gun control, and foreign aid.

The price Reagan paid for this economy of goals—the perception of laziness and disengagement, as well as ignorance and shallowness— seemed to trouble him from time to time, but did not alter his course. This was not true of his outer-directed successors, who—despite the success of the Reagan strategy—elected to scatter seeds widely rather than appear uninvolved in the work of their respective administrations.

It is important to recognize that Reagan's core issues were few and carefully chosen because the foundation of his political philosophy was an intense and unshakeable faith in the American people. Over and over in his speeches the same theme occurs: if we can get the government out of the way, the American people can solve the country's problems. Government action, accordingly, was just not that important in Reagan's world. He made this clear in his autobiography, referring to the difficult period of recession early in his administration:

> As I look back on those times now, I realize that the turnaround took a little longer than I expected. But I always expected it to come. I believed the economic recovery program would work because I had faith—faith in those tax cuts and faith in the American people. I felt we were going to solve our problems because we had a secret weapon in the battle: our factory workers, our farmers, our entrepreneurs, and others among us who I believed would prove once again that the American people were gifted with and propelled by a spirit unique in the world, a spirit tenaciously devoted to solving our problems and bettering our lives, the lives of our children, and our country—and if these forces could be liberated from the restraints imposed on them by government, they'd pull the country out of its tailspin.[15]

Given this view of the resourcefulness and ambition of individual Americans, Reagan was unlikely to see the importance of most of the things the government might be doing. These might be well-intentioned, and might make marginal or temporary improvements here and there, but they were as likely to impede the progress of individuals as to advance it. Accordingly, most of the initiatives that bubble up through the bureaucracy or in Congress were of little interest to Reagan; they were not central to his belief system or worth the expenditure of substantial amounts of political capital. This philosophical approach enabled Reagan to focus on only a few initiatives, while believing at the same time—because of his faith in the American people, acting without the government's intervention—that he was realistically addressing the many ills that are regularly called to the president's attention. If this analysis is correct, one would expect to see Reagan strongly and stubbornly attached to some ideas, but only weakly interested in others.

Indeed, it is possible to divide Reagan's strength of commitment or engagement into two groups—those issues that he regarded as central to his presidency and those that were important to conservatives and Republicans but not among his core issues. In many ways, this breakdown explains Reagan's tenacious interest in some ideas, and his apparent disengagement and passivity with respect to many of the initiatives pressed by his staff and cabinet. In my time in the administration and at the White House, I saw Reagan in both modes.

On the core issues he considered important to his presidency, Reagan—far from disengaged—was an active participant in his administration's policy development, legislative strategy, and dealings with Congress. On the domestic side, these included cutting taxes, promoting freer trade, encouraging domestic and foreign competition, and reducing the government's role in the economy through deregulation and elimination of price controls. All were large subjects that Reagan had spoken about in radio addresses and speeches prior to becoming President. In *Reagan in His Own Hand,* there are 30 radio addresses on economics and tax policy alone, and these issues were centerpieces of his 1980 campaign. As Margaret Thatcher is reputed to have said: "He only had five or six ideas, but all of them were big and all of them were good."

Between 1974 and 1979, Reagan made at least ten radio broadcasts on taxation and its relationship to the economy and economic growth.

These showed him reading extensively in economic history and theory and becoming increasingly committed to the supply-side view that tax reductions would produce the incentives necessary to reverse the nation's economic stagnation. For example, in a broadcast on November 28, 1978, he quoted the following statement by Andrew Mellon, the secretary of the treasury under Presidents Harding, Coolidge, and Hoover:

> The high tax rates inevitably put pressure upon the taxpayer to withdraw his capital from productive business & invest it in tax-exempt securities or find other lawful methods of avoiding the realization of taxable income. The result is that the sources of taxation are drying up; wealth is failing to carry its share of the tax burden; and capital is being diverted into channels which yield neither revenues to the govt. nor profits to the people. . . . What rates will bring in the largest revenue to the govt., experience has not yet developed, but it is estimated that by cutting taxes in half, then govt., when the full effect of the reduction is felt, will receive more revenue at the lower rates of tax than it would have received at the higher rates.[16]

At other points in his radio broadcasts he cited Milton Friedman, Arthur Laffer, and Allan Meltzer, all contemporary supply-side economists. Supply-side economics held a natural attraction for Reagan, because it is based on the assumption that people respond to incentives, resulting in economic growth when taxes are lowered. Although some biographers, searching for an underlying rationale for Reagan's adoption of supply-side economics, have pointed to the high taxes he must have paid as a successful actor, it is more likely to have sprung from other sources. Supply-side economics fits particularly well with Reagan's fundamental view that the American people could solve the country's problems if government simply got out of the way.

Reagan's autobiography and diary entries provide ample evidence of his involvement in both the adoption of his initial tax plan by Congress, and in resisting modifications of that plan as huge deficits developed in subsequent years. Describing the effort to pass the plan in July 1981, he wrote: "I knew that, if we were going to get it passed, it wouldn't be enough to make Congress see the light; I had to make 'em feel the heat. That Monday [July 27] I spent virtually every minute from early in the morning to until seven thirty at night on the phone or in meetings with congressmen lobbying for tax cuts. . . ."[17]

Reagan did the same thing the following day, and up until the final vote on July 29, when he wrote in his diary: "The whole day was given over to phone calls to Congressmen. . . . I went from fearing the worst to hope we'd squeak through. . . . Then late in the afternoon came word that the Senate had passed its tax bill (ours) 89 to 11. Then from the House where all the chips were down, we won 238–195. We got 40 Democrat votes. On final passage almost 100 joined the parade making it 330 odd to 107 or thereabouts."[18] Diary entries over the two-month period leading up to the vote are dense with Reagan's descriptions of his involvement in the tax and deficit debate. [19]

To be sure, Reagan eventually agreed to a modest rollback of the tax reductions he had won in 1981. But this seems to have been the result of accepting a promise from the Democrats in Congress that they would agree to cuts in spending that were twice the tax increases Reagan had allowed. Donald Regan, the treasury secretary at the time, also believed an agreement along these lines had been reached.[20] Looked at from the perspective of Reagan's priorities, an exchange of this kind makes sense. Reagan was interested in stimulating the economic growth he believed would follow from tax cuts, but he also wanted to cut the growth of government. Trading some tax increases for even larger cuts in government spending fit well with what he saw as an effort to back the government out of the economy.

But the spending cuts never materialized. In his autobiography, referring to virtually the whole of his first term, he explained his compromise on taxes this way: "During the next three years, I was under almost constant pressure to abandon the economic program. Along the way, I made some compromises: To win congressional approval of additional spending cuts and show the financial community we were serious about reducing the deficit, I made a deal with the congressional Democrats in

1982, agreeing to support a limited loophole-closing tax increase to raise more than $98.3 billion over three years in return for their agreement to cut spending by $280 billion during the same period; later the Democrats reneged on their pledge and we never got those cuts."[21]

After this experience, Reagan showed himself to be virtually impervious to pleas for further tax increases—in spite of the fact that the country was running record deficits. When Congress threatened to increase taxes, Reagan adamantly refused to go along, famously remarking, Clint Eastwood-like: "Go ahead; make my day." He had clearly decided, consistent with his philosophy, that as between deficits and low rates of taxation, he preferred the latter. Not only would low tax rates stimulate economic growth, but as long as the Democrats denounced deficits in order to gain increased taxes, the deficits themselves would cause them to accept reduced government spending.

Reagan was again deeply involved in policy-making and legislative strategy in his second term—with the structuring, campaign for, and ultimate enactment of the Tax Reform Act of 1986. From the time he discussed and approved significant tax reform in 1984, through the passage of the 1986 legislation, Reagan's role was pivotal. Most political observers had thought tax reform was impossible, and submitting a significant reform proposal to Congress would either be a waste of time or produce a feeding frenzy by special interests, but Reagan—again exhibiting a willingness to commit his political capital for major policy initiatives—determined to try, and after the plan was developed at Treasury, he participated in revising it and selling it to Congress and the American people.

Free trade was another area to which Reagan devoted considerable personal effort, addressing the subject directly at all eight of the economic summits he attended and recording in his autobiography the difficulties he had in persuading his counterparts to break down protectionist barriers. Here is his account of why he was committed to free trade:

> The principles underlying my support of free and fair trade are pretty simple: The operation of the free market is based on the concept that people make a product or produce a service which they hope other

people will want to buy. Then, in millions of separate decisions, consumers choose which products and services they want to buy. . . . Free
competition and the law of supply and demand determine the prices
and the winners and the losers in the competition. . . . *For the free
market to work, everyone has to compete on an equal footing* [emphasis
in original]... Free competition produces better products and lower
prices. However, when governments fix or control the price, impose
quotas, subsidize manufacturers or farmers, or otherwise intervene in
the free market with artificial restrictions, it isn't free and it won't
work as it is supposed to work.[22]

It's easy to see how this view fits in with Reagan's general philosophy of encouraging competition rather than regulation to control
prices, and why he was strongly committed to free trade. Trade protec-
tionism was one more example of government interference in the economy, and freer trade and market competition improve both the quality
of products and prices to consumers. To Reagan, the competition that
comes with free trade would only enhance the quality of life for Americans. "It's true," he said, "that we now have tougher competitors over-
seas than we used to have, but America is tougher, too. We've proved
that we can respond to competition, as we always have. As a nation we
have always thrived on competition, and we always will."[23] Reagan's
first major speech as a candidate for president was devoted to freeing
trade with Mexico, and during his administration the United States entered the U.S.-Canada Free Trade Agreement and began the negotiation
of a similar agreement with Mexico that was ultimately completed as
the North American Free Trade Agreement (NAFTA) during the succeeding Bush administration.

This pro-competition approach infused the policies of the Reagan
administration in many ways, some of them quite subtle. Many commentators, for example, have considered the Reagan administration to
be just another Republican government, favoring the interests of American big business. But this is a mistake. If the Reagan administration
had a favorite economic player, it was the entrepreneur, the self-made

risk-taker. And if it had a favorite *bête noire* it was the bureaucrat, both public and private. When, in late 1986, Richard Darman—then deputy secretary of the treasury—made a speech in Japan at which he referred to big business in the United States as a "corpocracy,"[24] he evoked surprise among those in the media who thought he was out of step with Republican orthodoxy. But Darman was reflecting a theme that fit well with Ronald Reagan's own outlook. The people whom Ronald Reagan admired, and who admired him and supported his political rise, were generally not the successful bureaucrats who had reached the top of major U.S. corporations. They were successful entrepreneurs who built businesses themselves and outran their competitors.

Thus, just as one of Reagan's priorities was to increase competition through free trade, he also wanted the market to take productive assets out of the hands of bureaucracies that were not using them effectively. It has been little noted, for example, that the Reagan administration gave no comfort at all to the corporate managements that were threatened by the raiders and takeover artists of the 1980s. In general, Ronald Reagan agreed that where the managers of large U.S. corporations were slothful and inefficient in the use of the resources they controlled, or that corporate directors were not holding managers responsible for a better and more profitable use of the company's assets, they should be replaced. And, to Reagan, the market was the place where this issue should be decided.

That Reagan understood the importance of who controlled the assets of a society cannot be doubted. In one of his radio broadcasts, on April 16, 1979, he discussed the difference between other economic systems and our own by focusing on the term "capitalist":

> Actually all systems are capitalist. It's just a matter of who owns & controls the capital—ancient king, dictator or private individual. We should properly be looking at the contrast between a free mkt. system where individuals have the right to live like kings if they have the ability to earn that right and govt. control of the mkt. system such as we find today in socialist nations.[25]

With this view, Reagan could not see any point in preventing raiders from taking over corporations, breaking them up, and selling off the pieces for more than the company as a whole was valued by the market. These breakup valuations simply meant that a company's managers were not using its assets efficiently. Thus, despite the pleas of corporate executives for the federal government to do something about the takeover frenzy—which, it was said, was destroying fine companies and causing unnecessary unemployment—Reagan and his administration refused to act. Eventually, corporate directors got the idea, and began to look carefully at whether their companies were being operated as profitably as they could be, whether managers were adding value for shareholders or merely seeing to their own comfort. The result, in part, is the internationally competitive U.S. corporation of today, and the extraordinary growth in productivity of the 1990s.

Defense and foreign policy was another area where Reagan had strong convictions, and where he took an active part in developing and implementing policy. His autobiography devotes more than 30 pages to defense spending, over 75 pages to arms control, and over 30 pages to foreign policy generally. Reagan came into office having promised both to increase defense spending and reduce nuclear arms. Shortly after his inauguration, he proposed a "zero-zero" option for Europe—in which both NATO and the Soviets would reduce their intermediate-range nuclear missile stocks to zero in Europe—and attempted to start talks on reducing strategic nuclear arms. As usual with Reagan, there was a theory or vision behind these seemingly contradictory moves. He believed it would be impossible to bring the Soviets to the bargaining table on weapons reduction until they were convinced that they could not gain any military advantage over the United States. He noted in his autobiography, "[I]t was obvious that if we were ever going to get anywhere with the Russians in persuading them to reduce armaments, we had to bargain with them from *strength,* not weakness."[26] As Lou Cannon observed in an essay on Reagan's relationship with Mikhail Gorbachev: "Reagan, although not strong on technological detail, knew what he wanted to accomplish. He viewed the military buildup he had advocated to confront Soviet expansionism as a means, not an end. The President was convinced that the Soviet Union could not compete with the United States and that the buildup would lead the Soviets to the bargaining table."[27]

This was not a new idea for Ronald Reagan. During the 1980 campaign he said, "I think there is every indication and every reason to believe that the Soviet Union cannot increase its production of arms. . . . I think the Soviet Union is probably near the very limit of its military output. They've diverted so much to the military that they can't provide for the consumer needs. . . ."[28] As usual, this position was linked to a concept of how to accomplish a result. As Reagan told the *National Journal* in March 1980, "[The Soviets] know that if we turned our full industrial might into an arms race, they cannot keep pace with us. Why haven't we played that card? Why haven't we said to them when we're sitting at the SALT table, 'Gentlemen, the only alternative to you being willing to meet us half way on these things is an arms race'? And maybe we wouldn't have to have the arms race because that's the last thing they want us to do."[29] These statements are a demonstration—despite the efforts of his critics to attribute subsequent events to Reagan's luck—that when he entered office Reagan had a clearly formulated concept that his defense buildup was a means to an end: that once the Soviets understood the United States would not waver in its determination to increase its defense capacity, they would either come to the bargaining table or lose faith in their future. In the end, as we now know, it was both.

Reagan's 1980 campaign positions, too, were fully consistent with what he had said in his many radio addresses during the 1970s. In this five-year period, according to *Reagan in His Own Hand,* he researched and wrote at least 40 radio addresses on defense and intelligence policy, including ten on SALT II alone. On November 28, 1978, he addressed a question that was quite similar to the question he faced on the Strategic Defense Initiative (SDI) eight years later—whether the United States should give up a technological lead over the Soviets in the interests of reaching an arms-control agreement. In this case, the lead was in depressed trajectory missiles, and Reagan said: "The question that should be asked is, what will the Soviets give up if we agree to sacrifice our technological lead? If the object of the Salt II talks is to reduce the possibility of war, what better way is there than to stay so far ahead in weaponry that Russia's imperialistic desires will be inhibited?"[30]

This background sets the stage for what happened at Reagan's meeting with Mikhail Gorbachev at Reykjavik, Iceland, in 1986, when Reagan refused to trade his Strategic Defense Initiative for a broad agreement on strategic arms limitation with the Soviet Union. SDI, proposed initially in 1983, provided another opportunity for Reagan to demonstrate his unshakeable commitment to certain goals, this time in foreign and defense policy. Since the idea was opposed by many of Reagan's advisers, it also demonstrates his deep involvement and formative role in this aspect of his administration's activities.

Even though SDI had not been conceived when Reagan was preparing his radio addresses in the mid-1970s, he made clear that he was not satisfied with a world in which the safety of populations depended on Mutually Assured Destruction (known by its acronym, MAD)—the policy of deterring attack by maintaining the capacity to destroy the attacker. In a radio address on June 27, 1978, Reagan expressed doubt that the Soviets accepted the underlying premises of this policy, and hence whether the United States was truly safe in relying on this mechanism to assure its strategic security:

> Do the Russians subscribe to our belief in "mutual assured destruction" as a deterrent to war? Apparently we think so but just as apparently the Russians do not. We say "thermonuclear war is unthinkable by either side." The Russians have told their own people that while it would be a calamity it is not unthinkable; that it very well might happen & if it does the Soviet U. will survive & be victorious."[31]

Reagan here was pointing at a conceptual flaw at the heart of the MAD policy. For the system to work, both sides had to believe that use of nuclear weapons was unthinkable and had to believe that the other side thought so too. This is a considerable weakness. If either side comes to believe that the other no longer believes that a thermonuclear exchange is unthinkable, it will be tempted to launch a first strike, and the first-mover advantage is so significant in this game that it makes sense for a country that thinks a thermonuclear war is unthinkable to launch the first strike if it comes to believe that the other country no longer thinks so. The problems get even more complex if either side believes the other is no longer convinced that it will be destroyed in a nuclear war; in that case a pre-emptive strike may be the most sensible policy, and knowing this, its adversary might be tempted to launch first. To Reagan, there had to be a better way.

SDI offered such an alternative, but perhaps only a president with Reagan's strength of conviction could have brought it to the fore in defense policy and sustained it against attack. As David Gergen notes: "I doubt SDI would have gotten off the drawing boards under any chief executive other than Reagan. Another president would have vetted the idea within government. The Pentagon and State Department would have strenuously opposed it, especially in the expansive form Reagan proposed. The proposal would surely have leaked as well, and outside experts would have shot it full of holes."[32]

If SDI could be made to work, ballistic missiles could be destroyed by space- or ground-based systems that would form a defensive umbrella over the United States. Such a system would make nuclear weapons obsolete, but it would also have upset the strategic balance between the United States and the (now defunct) Soviet Union by eliminating any confidence the Soviet Union might have had that the United States would not launch a first strike. Thus, to be truly effective and consistent as a policy, the United States had to offer SDI technology to the Soviets—which is exactly what Reagan did when he met with Soviet General Secretary Mikhail Gorbachev at Reykjavik in 1986.

There are a number of differing accounts of what happened at Reykjavik. Particularly mooted is the question of whether Reagan agreed with Gorbachev to ban all nuclear weapons—which would have placed the United States and other Western nations at what was then thought to be a disadvantage in conventional weapons vis-à-vis the Soviets[33]—but there is no disagreement that Reagan left the meeting and abandoned the talks with Gorbachev when the General Secretary insisted that the Soviets would not agree to any set of nuclear arms reductions until it was first agreed that SDI would be confined to laboratory testing.

Returning to the United States, Reagan was greeted with a barrage of complaints for allowing SDI—which was, after all, only an unproven concept—to stand in the way of a significant disarmament agreement. From the left were declarations that Reagan had proved himself the fool they had always known him to be; from the right were accusations that Reagan apparently did not understand the basis of U.S. defense policy. After his initial disappointment at Reykjavik, however, Reagan recovered his balance and noted in a speech to the nation that although the proposal on the table at Reykjavik was the complete elimination of ballistic missiles by 1996, "there was no way I could tell our people that their government would not protect them against nuclear destruction."[34] Reagan realized that even if an agreement in principle had been reached on the elimination of strategic nuclear weapons, negotiations on details would drag on for years, leaving the world exposed to the danger of nuclear war. By that time, too, Reagan had probably realized that Gorbachev's seemingly desperate effort at Reykjavik to stop the development of SDI was a validation of Reagan's own views—that the Soviets had great respect for the technological and productive capacities of the United States and would go to great lengths to shackle or limit the development of U.S. technology that had military implications.

Nevertheless, it is difficult to imagine what strength of conviction it required for Reagan to walk away from what would have been a world-historic arms agreement in order to preserve a concept or vision to which he had become committed. Subsequent reports have cast doubt on whether the deal, if it had been made, would have been favorable to the United States and its NATO allies. However, even if one does not agree with the choice Reagan made, it was a remarkable display of fortitude and commitment to an idea. Few U.S. presidents could have resisted the chance to return to the United States with an agreement from the Soviets that could have been portrayed as the beginning of the end of the Cold War and the threat of nuclear destruction.

Once again, Reagan demonstrated his unwillingness to compromise on ideas he believed were essential to what he wanted to achieve with his presidency. And once again, the conviction—and the idea— outweighed the prospect of a personal triumph. From the time he entered office, Reagan was searching for a way to place the defense of the United States on a firmer footing. An enormous increase in defense spending was certainly one of these ways, but the uncertainties associated with basing our policy on MAD still appeared to haunt him. With only two years left in his presidency, Reagan could not abandon an idea that, in his view, promised Americans a future safety they could never otherwise have hoped for in a world of nuclear weapons. As Lou Cannon noted in a 2000 essay:

> [B]oth Reagan and Gorbachev acknowledged that the doctrine of mutual assured destruction (or MAD) had preserved the peace but that it was impossible that this could continue in perpetuity with thousands of nuclear missiles on hair-trigger alert. . . . Because they feared the status quo, Reagan and Gorbachev were willing to take risks to change it, as they did most notably at the 1986 Reykjavik summit, where the two leaders galloped ahead of subordinates in discussions about banning all nuclear weapons. They didn't quite succeed, but a summit that was seen as a failure led to the INF treaty and subsequent nuclear arms reductions.[35]

The Intermediate Nuclear Force (INF) treaty was the first agreement between the United States and the Soviet Union that actually reduced arms. In a sense, by proving that the Soviets were willing to deal despite Reagan's refusal to abandon SDI, it validated Reagan's decision at Reykjavik to walk away from any agreement that would prevent the development of the SDI technology. We now know, too, that the SDI idea was no harebrained scheme unique to Reagan. The George W. Bush administration resolved to pursue it even though this would require the United States to withdraw from the ABM treaty with Russia. And despite outcries in Congress and the press that this would never be accepted by the Russians, it was.

Nor is there any doubt that Reagan's support of SDI was part of a fully thought-out negotiating strategy of which Reagan himself was the architect. In early November, a few weeks after he returned from Reykjavik, I attended a conference with Reagan to prepare him for a meeting with some selected members of the press. Also present were John Poindexter, national security adviser; Alton Keel, Poindexter's deputy; Don Regan, White House chief of staff; Larry Speakes, deputy press secretary; and Dennis Thomas, an assistant to the president.

The meeting had been called to discuss the President's position on the then-unfolding Iran-Contra matter, but having completed that discussion, Thomas suggested that the President should be prepared for a question on whether he had agreed to eliminate all nuclear weapons at Reykjavik or only strategic weapons such as ballistic missiles. This had become a major issue, discussed at length in the press.[36]

Reagan briefly outlined his discussion with Gorbachev. He noted that Gorbachev had referred repeatedly to the elimination of "nuclear weapons" rather than "strategic weapons," so that finally Reagan asked him what he had in mind. According to Reagan, Gorbachev said he wanted to eliminate all nuclear weapons in ten years, and Reagan responded by saying that that was something to be discussed when Gorbachev came to Washington.

At this point, Poindexter suggested that Reagan tell the press that he favored only the elimination of all strategic *missiles*—a policy that would be advantageous to the United States because of our superiority in stealth technology and cruise missiles. But Reagan declined to do this. Speaking uncharacteristically sharply to Poindexter, he said that he did in fact want to eliminate *all* nuclear weapons "eventually," but could not see how the Soviets would find it in their interests to eliminate strategic ballistic missiles alone. So while Reagan denied that he had actually agreed with Gorbachev to eliminate all nuclear weapons, he made it unambiguously clear that this was ultimately his policy.

The tone Reagan took with Poindexter was initially surprising, because he seldom raised his voice or contradicted his advisers—preferring in most cases to hold his peace and simply not do what had been recommended—but in this case Poindexter had intruded into an area that Reagan thought he knew well, that involved one of his core objectives, and in which he had developed a policy and a strategy of his own. When these factors were present, Ronald Reagan was clearly in command.

Another example of Reagan's stubbornness—this time in support of his commitments—was the Bitburg episode, a painful period for Reagan and the White House that arose out of Reagan's desire to effect a symbolic reconciliation with Germany 40 years after the end of World War II. During a visit to the White House in late 1984, German Chancellor Helmut Kohl suggested to Reagan that he visit a cemetery for the German war dead, and the President agreed to visit a cemetery at Bitburg, in a district near the Rhineland-Palatinate that Kohl represented in the Bundestag, the German federal parliament. The visit would take place in May 1985, in connection with an economic summit to be held in Bonn.

Not unlike the decision to fire the air traffic controllers, Reagan's decision to visit Bitburg offered little tangible political gain but was fraught with political risk, and when the schedule for the visit was announced in April 1985 it produced some controversy, especially among Jewish groups. But that was minor compared to the firestorm that erupted when it was revealed that among the dead in the Bitburg cemetery were 47 members of the Waffen SS, part of Hitler's elite guard. Mike Deaver, who had visited the cemetery on an advance trip in February, 1985, said that he could not determine who was actually buried there because it was covered with snow. Now the President was in a box. He had promised his friend Helmut Kohl that he would visit Bitburg, and had either to go back on his word or plunge ahead. Typically, Reagan kept his word. Although he might have blamed Kohl and the Germans for suggesting Bitburg, and used this as an excuse to change his plans, he did not. Don Regan, who was White House chief of staff at the time, explains why:

> [T]he President would not be moved from his determination to keep his promise to Kohl. It was Kohl himself who had chosen Bitburg. . . . The Chancellor telephoned Reagan, and in another

emotional conversation lasting some twenty minutes, pleaded with
him not to abandon his plans. To do so, Kohl told him, would cost
him his Chancellorship. . . . This strengthened the President's determination to carry out the visit as intended. . . . [He] saw a larger
issue: his credibility as a leader who kept his word and stood by his
friends and allies despite high political costs.[37]

Regan comments: "This was the first tough Presidential decision to
which I had been an eyewitness as Chief of Staff. In my view Reagan
had come through with flying colors. He had reasoned and reacted as a
President—choosing the future over the past and the long-term interests of the nation over the passions of the moment."[38]

There were, however, a number of areas where Reagan declined to
exert his will. These cases typically involved policies or programs that
were not part of his core agenda—the reasons he ran for president. In
these cases, he would seldom express preferences but would await the
development of a compromise or consensus among his advisers and
cabinet officers. Even where he clearly had views, he would not insist
that they be adopted if it appeared to him that his advisers or cabinet
officers felt strongly otherwise.

This often gave the impression that he was manipulated—that he
was not in control of his presidency—and accounts for the many descriptions by insiders and former White House staffers of a policy-making process in which the President himself did not seem to be engaged.
Indeed, my diary is full of references to Reagan seeming passive and uninterested in policies or programs that were being hotly debated in front
of him. I have come to believe, however, that as important as these issues
were to the people who debated them, Reagan had decided that they
were relatively minor matters; in these cases, always recalling that these
discussions were occurring within a philosophical framework Reagan
himself had established, he was simply presiding over a process of implementing his policies rather than participating in their development.

One vivid example of this occurred in the debate over drug testing
for government employees, an issue that arose late in 1986. The Reagan

administration was firm in its opposition to illegal drugs. The Justice Department was eager to enforce existing drug laws and to toughen the laws where they were considered inadequate. Nancy Reagan had taken on this issue as one of her personal causes, and her slogan, "Just say no," was credited with raising awareness of the drug issue among teens and with the reduction in teenage drug use that occurred during the Reagan administration. However, Reagan himself had not spent much time on the drug issue prior to becoming president. Of the hundreds of radio addresses in *Reagan in His Own Hand*—on issues ranging from the snail darter to SALT II—few touched on the issue of drugs.[39]

It was in this context that the Justice Department, as the lead agency of the Domestic Policy Council (DPC), one of the cabinet councils, proposed that the administration adopt a program of testing all proposed new government employees for drug use. Ed Meese, the attorney general, introduced the subject at a meeting in July 1986. The initial proposal was to require urinalysis testing of all new applicants for federal employment and all current federal employees in national security, safety, or law enforcement positions. I opposed this idea as too broad and likely to be unconstitutional. I could see reasons to test employees in sensitive positions such as law enforcement, safety, and national security, but to test applicants for all positions—on a regular or random basis—seemed to me to go too far. I argued that the courts generally sought a balance in this area between the privacy interests of the individual and the interests of the government; although the government was permitted to test for drugs where it could be shown that it had a compelling interest in the performance of its employees, it would in my view be difficult to justify testing all employees or even all prospective employees.

Meese strongly disagreed with my views, and debate on this issue, among others, proceeded through several meetings of the DPC until the group finally met with the President on July 25, 1986. In accordance with established procedures, the President had received a memo in advance of the meeting; in this case, the memo recommended a program of extensive testing that, it promised, would eliminate 50 percent of federal government employee drug use within three years. Carlton Turner, the administration's drug czar, told the President about the great success that had been achieved with the military drug-testing program, and what was necessary to have an effective program on the civilian side. I had not had the time or opportunity to brief the President on this issue. Although I had sent a memo that morning to Regan, with which I'd hoped he would brief the President, I doubted that Regan had done so, and I turned out to be right.

Nevertheless—much to everyone's surprise—Reagan weighed in with some very definite views. To my delight, he thought all testing should be voluntary, and that before any program of testing was begun the government and the federal employee unions should work out the procedures. If someone is found to be taking drugs, said the President, the remedy should be treatment and not dismissal. Moreover, to set an example and encourage others to volunteer, the President said he would take the first drug test. Since none of these ideas—except voluntary testing—were in the memo I had sent to Regan that morning, and which I doubted had been communicated to the President in any event, what we heard in that meeting was the authentic voice of Ronald Reagan. That he favored persuasion over mandated compliance was also consistent with his view on much larger issues—that to change course it was necessary to change minds.

The authentic voice of Ronald Reagan was also a gentle one. The President advanced these views in the quiet and tentative way in which he often reflected his initial thoughts on a subject. Reagan, despite—or perhaps because of—the great authority he wielded as President, had a powerful respect for the opinions of those he considered more expert than himself. In matters that he had not worked out fully in his own mind, he accepted the views of experts without objection. It may be that Meese, after long experience with Reagan, understood this tentativeness as a signal that the President—despite the lack of ambiguity in his statements on drug policy—was not firmly committed to the views he expressed, because the program for involuntary drug testing of federal employees marched on.

By late July, the Justice Department had prepared draft legislation that would have authorized mandatory drug testing for all employees of the federal government, testing by private employers, and testing by schools. It included federal preemption of all state laws to the contrary—surprising for an administration that was supposed to value federalism. At virtually the same time, the head of the small domestic policy staff in the White House, Jack Svahn, sent a check-the-box memo to the President requesting decisions on a number of questions—including whether there should be mandatory testing of all federal employees—without any reference to the serious constitutional and privacy issues involved. It seemed to me the President had already given his views on this question—quietly but firmly—and I was distressed to see the issue still coming back in a number of different forms.

It was becoming clear that the political operatives in the White House and cabinet wanted a strong statement by the President on the drug issue and didn't much care to address the constitutional niceties. Yes, there would be criticism from the Democrats and the civil liberties constituencies about mandatory testing, but the President—who was scheduled to give a speech on the subject the following week—would be making a strong statement and that's what would linger in the minds of the public. The polls, indeed, were showing the public seriously concerned about the prevalence of drugs in society. Thus, in this case, Ed Meese and the Justice Department had allies within the White House. Meese wanted a substantive policy that included mandatory testing because he thought it was good policy; the politicos wanted a red-meat statement because they thought it was good politics. The President's speech would be coming shortly after a statement he had made on South Africa that had been widely criticized in the press for saying nothing new; the White House political staff didn't want that to happen again.

However, Reagan kept his balance. On the day the issue was supposed to be decided by the President, I met in Regan's office before the regular 8:00 A.M. staff meeting with Regan, Dennis Thomas, an assistant to the President, Al Kingon, cabinet secretary, and David Chew,

White House staff secretary. One last time, I made my pitch about constitutional and privacy questions, and Regan, somewhat piqued by
what he had regarded as technical objections, asked me what constitutional questions I was talking about. I explained that the kind of urine
test that was necessary for drug testing was not what we were accustomed to in the doctor's office. In order to prevent cheating, someone
had to be in the room with the tested person. I pointed out that this
was highly intrusive. For the first time, Regan seemed to understand the
dimensions of the problem, and later told me that he brought this
vividly to the attention of the President. "Would you want people
watching you while you take a leak?" Regan told me he asked the President. Of such things is policy made.

Possibly as a result, when the President met with the DPC later that
day, he had seemingly decided that only applicants for sensitive positions would be tested, not those already holding these positions. In the
course of the discussion, Reagan made clear that he did not want to
fight about such questions as the scope of testing because that would
detract from the program he had in mind. The point, he said, was to
convince the American people to be drug-intolerant—again, the power
of ideas—and that goal would not be advanced by allowing fights to develop over drug testing. That, it seemed, was that.

But of course it wasn't. The President's drug policy had to be embodied in an executive order, and in early September that gave the proponents of mandatory testing another bite at the apple. I argued against
mandatory testing in the DPC meeting, but a clear majority of the
membership—with the exception of Bill Brock, then secretary of labor,
and Connie Horner, head of the Office of Personnel Management—
favored it. The proposed executive order required mandatory testing for
all applicants and incumbents in sensitive positions and authorized
agency heads to require mandatory testing of employees in non-sensitive
positions under certain circumstances. The executive order went to the
President with a covering memo that noted the sentiments of the DPC
in favor of mandatory testing for all applicants and testing of all incumbents in sensitive positions. The President approved the executive order,

which in many respects reversed his earlier decision that all testing should be voluntary or be limited to applicants for sensitive positions.

Thus, while Ronald Reagan had unshakeable views in some areas, he was far less committed to other positions that he seemed to regard as of lesser importance. In these cases, he allowed his subordinates to have their way, even if his own instincts on an issue might be different. It was understandable, then, that many people who participated in the White House policy development process came away with the view that Reagan was disengaged and manipulated by his advisers.

At other meetings, Reagan seemed deliberately to refuse to signal any interest—pro or con—on issues that did not involve his core commitments. These included such things as substantial congressional cuts in foreign aid even though the cuts had been denounced by Secretary of State George Shultz, or on social issues that were important to significant elements of his constituency. In some cases, this was simply an expression of Reagan's custom to avoid committing himself in a meeting at which outsiders were present—preferring to wait for a private discussion with key advisers. But at issues lunches with the top White House staff—where the staff met every Monday with the President to discuss policy and political questions—there were many examples of Reagan's refusal to be drawn into statements of support for conservative hot-button issues.

At these lunches, after each of us had reported to the President about what we were working on and where the next grenade might be expected to originate, the floor was open for staff to bring up any subject they wanted. Pat Buchanan, the White House communications director and a strong conservative, would often try an opening like "Many of your Christian supporters think . . ." or "Some people in the Justice Department hope that you'll. . . ." He was obviously hoping to get a supporting remark from Reagan that could be taken back to conservative groups or given to the press, but Reagan almost uniformly simply nodded and refused comment. Sometimes, however, he would muse about something tangentially related to the subject, such as—in response to a sally about abortion—how sexual mores had changed since he was young. This was only barely relevant to the issue, and to an

uninitiated observer might have seemed just another example of Reagan's disengagement, but should better be viewed as part of a strategy to
avoid personal involvement in issues that might interfere with his main
objectives.

Why did Ronald Reagan resist involvement in these controversial
issues—even though many of them were policies he campaigned on
and spoke about in his radio addresses? One explanation might be that
he was husbanding his political capital. By avoiding participation in or
association with issues that were highly controversial and divisive, he
could avoid polarizing the country—and jeopardizing his support in
Congress—about issues that were, in the scheme of things, of only minor significance. It is not hard to imagine this as a possible rationale,
since Reagan clearly had a hierarchy of objectives for what he wanted to
achieve. The items that he ignored or avoided were not the major issues
on which his presidency was founded.

This could explain why he avoided identification with some of the
more divisive social issues that were part of the political debate in the
United States, but what accounts for his diffidence in pressing his views
on how the drug-testing initiative should come out? Here, we might see
at work some of the craftiness that Richard Neustadt thought was a requirement for successful presidents. Given that all Reagan's advisers and
cabinet officers were functioning within a philosophical framework he
himself had laid out, whether the federal employee drug-testing program came out one way rather than another was perhaps of less importance than keeping the loyalty and support of his cabinet and staff, and
promoting the idea of cabinet government. In order to do both, he
might have thought, it was necessary to go lightly in overturning the
decisions that came out of cabinet councils. Neustadt argues that presidents must bargain to get their way, even with their own cabinet members, who have strong and occasionally opposing institutional interests.
It is not inconceivable that Reagan saw an implicit bargain here—an
agreement on his part to interpose his views only in cases where his core
purposes were involved, but in other cases to stay his hand in deference
to the institutional and other interests of his cabinet and staff.

Indeed, Ronald Reagan did not seek the presidency to preside over the government or to do the many (relatively) minor things that flow to the president's desk. He had large ideas and large changes in mind; most of all, he wanted to change the American people's view of the proper role of government, not decide how particular programs should be structured. He could stay the course—exhibit political courage worthy of a profile—where he thought the issue was related to his principal goals, but if he was satisfied that his administration was working within the ideological framework he had set out, he was content to let his subordinates work out their differences and come to him with a compromise plan. In this—once again—Ronald Reagan was not a conventional president.

4

THE PERSON
WHO WAS PRESIDENT

*I often wonder how far I might have gone if I'd
studied.*

—Ronald Reagan, in a commencement
speech at Eureka College

On February 21, 1986, a bright and sunny late winter day in Washington, I walked into the Oval Office with Don Regan, the White House chief of staff, to meet my new client. As we entered, the President got up from his desk and came over to meet us. We shook hands, and I said something fairly ordinary and banal about being honored to meet him and to have this opportunity to serve as White House counsel.

At this remark, Reagan looked genuinely uncomfortable. His head bobbed in the way that is so familiar to people who have seen him on television, and he seemed at a loss for words. The impression I got was that Ronald Reagan—although he had been president for five years— was embarrassed by praise or expressions of admiration or gratitude. I also had the sense that he was somewhat shy. These impressions grew stronger as I saw more and more of him in the months to come.

That Ronald Reagan was shy will seem incomprehensible to some—after all, he was constantly required to meet people, and seemed to do it with extraordinary grace—but Mike Deaver, who knew Reagan best, drew the same conclusion, and I think this is the simplest and best explanation for the fact that he was thought by some of his staff to be "remote." This, and one other thing: Reagan was not interested in Reagan as a subject; he did not enjoy talking about himself, and when others praised him in his presence he found it embarrassing. As Reagan saw himself, he was an ordinary man, with an extraordinary mission; making him the central focus of attention diminished the significance of that mission.

After describing my background briefly, Regan handed the President my résumé, which he studied carefully. As it happened, I had been a partner of the law firm that for many years had done Reagan's tax and other legal work, and he remarked on this. As his eyes worked down the page, Regan interjected that the President shouldn't be concerned that I'd gone to Harvard—I was, Regan averred, in all other respects an estimable fellow. The President looked up, feigning disappointment, and quipped that he'd grown up on Frank Merriwell stories, implying that he would have been happier if I'd gone to Yale. The official photo shows all of us laughing at this point, with the President looking down at my résumé and smiling broadly.

As always in the Oval Office, the President was impeccably dressed in a business suit. It is now well known that, out of respect for the office, Reagan never took off his suit jacket while there. This simple fact speaks volumes about the man. It was not just that he had respect for the history or symbolism of the physical place, but that he saw the presidency as something much larger than himself—another example of his unwillingness to treat himself, or to be treated, as a special person.

This became clear to me at a large lunch given at the White House in July 1986 for those who were working on fundraising for Reagan's presidential library. After lunch, the President got up to make some remarks. His prepared statement was not memorable, but at one point he stopped and seemed to ad lib a few thoughts that would not have been written by a speechwriter. As I remember his words, Reagan said: "I hope you will all keep in mind, while you are raising funds for this worthy project, that it is not for me that this library is being constructed. I will hold the office of the presidency only for a few years, and after me there will be many more presidents. This library is important because it will contain materials that reflect a period in history that people in the future will want to study. That is what gives your efforts real significance."

This modesty about himself extended to many of the things Ronald Reagan did as president. One example was his almost obsessive desire to be punctual. He did this, I believe, because of his reluctance to keep waiting the people who had appointments to see him at particular times—even though there is hardly a person in the world who would not sit and wait all day, if necessary, to get a chance to meet with the President of the United States. Reagan, even as president, never seemed to see himself as exalted above others. Keeping other people waiting offended their dignity even if it might have served his convenience.

Another example was his correspondence with ordinary Americans. One morning in late July 1986 David Chew, the White House staff secretary, brought me a few sheets of yellow legal-size paper on which the President had written several responses to letters received at the White House. Chew's purpose was to have me review what the President had said in response to criticism of the Supreme Court on the abortion issue. We both wanted to be sure that Reagan's letter conformed to what he had said in the past; these informal letters, after all, were not the place to break new policy ground.

What amazed me, however, was that the President was writing his own responses to these letters—that at least in these cases the correspondents were getting the real thing and not the perfunctory response of a programmed assistant in the White House Correspondence Unit. I wondered how many of them realized this. In any event, as I looked at what the President had written, I noticed two things in particular—the striking lucidity of his prose and the fact that he had written out the inside addresses of those he was writing to. It seemed as though Reagan did not want to bother his secretaries to find this information, and so took the time himself to provide it.

I learned later that Reagan carried on an active correspondence with a number of people to whom he had been writing before he became president, and in some cases before he became governor of California. Recently, I came across a calendar with photographs of Reagan and excerpts of personal letters he had written for over 51 years to a friend named Lorraine Wagner. Letters from old friends like Lorraine Wagner were flagged by the White House Correspondence Unit and sent directly to him. In these cases, he wrote out his responses on yellow paper, and they were typed and sent out. In the few cases where the President got into policy issues in these letters, his secretaries had them reviewed by appropriate members of the White House staff. How many presidents, I wondered, kept up with friends—ordinary people all—after assuming their exalted office?

A more well-known example of Reagan's writing was his open letter to the American people after he learned that he had Alzheimer's disease. This letter can hardly be read without emotion. Dated November 5, 1994, and written on his personal stationery in his own hand, it ends with this:

> . . . In closing let me thank you, the American people for giving me the great honor of allowing me to serve as your President. When the Lord calls me home, whenever that may be, I will leave with the greatest love for this country of ours and eternal optimism for its future.
>
> I now begin the journey that will lead me into the sunset of my life. I know that for America there will always be a bright dream ahead.
>
> Thank you my friends. May God always bless you.
>
> Sincerely,
>
> Ronald Reagan

The fluidity, grace, and emotive power of Reagan's writing raises a question that many supporters avoid, perhaps because they do not want to dignify it with a defense: was Ronald Reagan an intelligent man? The common opinion among the elites is that he was not; even members of his staff have expressed uncertainty about this, or delicately left the subject alone. Fred I. Greenstein's phrase, that Reagan had "cognitive limitations," summarizes the conclusion of the intelligentsia concerning Reagan's mental capacities. The virtually universal acceptance of this idea has led biographers and others to attribute Reagan's success to something else—in most instances to his skills as an actor and a speaker.

But George Shultz has written: "I could tell dozens of stories about specific times when Ronald Reagan displayed detailed knowledge about policy issues, and when he took decisive action based on that knowledge—without the benefit of someone whispering in his ear or sliding a note into his hand. But so ingrained is the belief that he was an amiable man—not too bright, the willing captive of his aides—that it would probably not make much difference."[1]

The first serious question about this ingrained consensus was raised by the publication of *Reagan in His Own Hand.* Since these statements are in Reagan's own handwriting, there can be no question that he wrote them, and so the consensus about the quality of his intellect must now consider this question: Is it still possible to say of a man who researched and wrote these statements, who was a successful governor of California and a successful president of the United States that he had "cognitive limitations"?

What is intelligence? Anyone who has kept his eyes open to the world around him knows that there are many kinds of skills that we consider intelligence—the good test taker's ability to memorize and repeat facts and figures; the architect's ability to conceptualize space; the philosopher or mathematician's ability to reason symbolically; the lawyer's ability to recognize fact patterns in applying principles to facts; a doctor's ability to make a diagnosis.

The radio addresses show that Reagan possessed a rare and powerful intelligence—the ability to understand and summarize complex material in clear and understandable form. Many who read this material will probably be surprised by what they find—given the widely held opinion of the man's intellectual limitations—but I was not. There were at least two instances, before I joined the White House staff, when

I had seen first hand Reagan's extraordinary ability to summarize complex ideas in a way that reflected both his grasp of the concepts involved and his extraordinarily logical and lucid writing style.

My first experience with this occurred when I was counsel to Vice President Nelson Rockefeller in 1975. That year, shortly after the Watergate scandal, Seymour Hersh of the *New York Times* reported in successive stories that the Central Intelligence Agency had been spying on the American people. Coming so soon after Watergate and the Pentagon Papers case, this revelation sparked an outpouring of concern among the public and, of course, congressional hearings.

In order to forestall precipitate action by Congress, and to reassure the public, President Ford appointed a blue-ribbon commission—with Vice President Rockefeller as chairman—to look into the allegations that the CIA had overstepped its authority, or that its authority was overbroad to begin with. The other members included John T. Connor, CEO of Allied Chemical Corporation; Lane Kirkland, then the secretary-treasurer (and later president) of the AFL-CIO; C. Douglas Dillon, a former treasury secretary; Erwin N. Griswold, a former solicitor general of the United States and dean of Harvard Law School; Lyman Lemnitzer, a retired U.S. Army general; Edgar F. Shannon, president of the University of Virginia; and Ronald Reagan, then former governor of California. As the Vice President's counsel, I served as his principal staff assistant for the work of the commission and liaison with the commission's staff, all of whom were lawyers.

Reagan attended about half of the 20 or so meetings of the commission, and was said to have kept up with its work by going to a military base in California to read the highly classified materials with which the commission was dealing. Reagan's poor attendance record irritated Rockefeller, who was devoting a great deal of time to the commission's work and regarded Reagan as a lightweight who was not taking his responsibilities seriously.

When Reagan did attend meetings, he didn't say much, but seemed to listen attentively. At that point, there was not much about his contribution to the commission's work that particularly impressed me, and to be truthful I didn't expect much. I had been an active member of the Ripon Society—what was called at the time a liberal Republican group—and thought of myself as a Rockefeller Republican. I hoped and expected that Rockefeller would be able to maneuver himself from the vice presidency into the presidency, and if he were to do this it was clear that he would have to overcome the opposition—and possibly the candidacy—of Ronald Reagan. I considered Reagan a California phenomenon—a product of an eccentric state that was dominated by Hollywood values and extremist politics.

However, as the commission began to draft its report, a different Reagan—or rather a contributing Reagan—emerged. The work of the commission was heavily focused on legal issues. The key questions for resolution had to do with the scope of the CIA's charter—much of which was unwritten lore or vague authorities that had accreted over the years—and a good deal of the commission's time after the hearing of witnesses and the review of written background material was taken up with discussions by and with the staff lawyers about what was or was not a permissible CIA activity within the United States. The issues were bewilderingly complex and ambiguous even for lawyers, and must have been extremely difficult for those of the commission's members who were not trained in legal analysis. In my discussions with Rockefeller, it was reasonably clear that he saw the commission in political terms, primarily as a way of forestalling strong congressional sentiment for dismemberment or abolition of the CIA. He had relatively little grasp of the legal issues that were at the heart of the commission's work.

Rockefeller was a great natural politician who had a powerful personality and a serious interest in policy. He was dyslectic, which played hob with his spelling, but he had an excellent memory for facts and figures. He had great respect for intellectuals, kept in touch with them, and remembered what they told him. Because of these attributes, it never occurred to anyone to question his intellect. But Rockefeller was not an analytical or critical thinker. That is, he was not easily able to see that ideas he held in one area were inconsistent with or required the adjustment of views he held elsewhere. This made it very difficult for him to bring together varying technical views into a compromise, since his mind didn't probe into the underlying ideas that would form the foundation for compromise. As a consequence, Rockefeller was not able to offer much leadership in the actual drafting of the report. The staff drafts were unsatisfactory on certain of the key points, and for a while the commission seemed unable to develop a generally acceptable formulation of its views.

As the discussions went on inconclusively, Reagan started to write on a yellow legal pad that he brought with him. At first I thought he was simply taking notes. Then, on several occasions, when the discussion flagged, he would say something like "How does this sound, fellas?" and would read aloud what he had written. His draft language was usually a succinct summary of the principal issues in the discussion and a sensible way to address them. Often, the commission found that they could agree with his proposal, which went directly into the report. Douglas Dillon has also written about his surprise at the ease with which Reagan was able to do this.

Rockefeller was somewhat astonished by Reagan's success at this process, especially since Reagan appeared to do it so effortlessly. I don't know that it improved his opinion of Reagan, but it certainly changed mine. From that time on, I held a more respectful view of Reagan's intellect, and eventually concluded that, as between Reagan and Rockefeller, Reagan would make the better president.

The skill Reagan showed at summarizing complex issues is a key to the quality of his intellect. Understanding a complex issue in an intuitive sense is one thing, but—as any writer knows—adopting actual words to describe the concepts you have grasped can be quite difficult. The problem is that words have specific meanings, and once particular words are attached to an idea, they have confined it. That's fine if the idea is understood sufficiently well to be sure of its contours and boundaries, but if one's understanding is limited, it is difficult to choose the right words. Having a sufficient mastery of the subject matter to prescribe a solution is harder still. Reagan more than met these standards. Remarking on his letter to the American people about his

Alzheimer's, Edmund Morris, an extraordinary writer himself, described it as having "the simplicity of genius." Among a group of gifted and famous men, in the setting of the Commission on CIA Activities in the United States, Reagan was a standout.

Then, when I was at the Treasury Department in the first Reagan administration, I saw Reagan use this skill again, and it impressed me and the rest of the Treasury staff who were involved. The subject was the replenishment of the capital of the International Monetary Fund. The United States is the principal investor in the IMF, which was established to assist countries in overcoming the consequences of changes in relative currency values. As the size of the world economy grows, or if substantial portions of its resources are called upon to assist countries in need, the IMF requires larger amounts of capital to carry on its work. In the early 1980s, several Latin American countries—Mexico, Brazil, and Argentina particularly—suffered financial crises that required substantial IMF assistance. In order to enable the IMF to continue its assistance to these and other countries, the United States agreed with other IMF members to replenish the institution's capital, which required congressional authorization.

The Treasury Department was the lead agency for the administration's efforts to achieve IMF replenishment, and in early 1984 the Treasury staff was working hard on this problem. Congressional support for the idea was weak, even among Republicans, in part because the IMF's efforts in Latin America were seen in Congress and the country generally as an effort to bail out the big New York banks, which had lent heavily to the Latin American countries that were in trouble.

For weeks, Don Regan (then Treasury Secretary) had tried, without success, to get the President and the White House staff to take up the case for IMF replenishment by including a reference to the President's support for this initiative in one of his Saturday radio addresses. Even a few words from the President would go a long way with Republicans in Congress, who repeatedly told Treasury representatives that the President's silence on the matter indicated that he did not really support replenishment. There were many other issues of importance to the White

House at this point, and the President's words and support were the most precious commodity in Washington. Moreover, the complexity and unpopularity of the issue argued strongly to the White House political experts for keeping the President above the battle.

Finally, after persistent efforts, Regan got word that the President would say something about IMF replenishment in his Saturday radio address, and we were notified that we should expect to see the text of what the President would say some time around noon on the preceding Friday. Shortly thereafter, the White House advised that the President was writing the IMF portion of the address himself, and we should understand that—since this was the way the President wanted to state his case—we should not expect to do much editing other than to correct factual errors.

At the Treasury, we braced for what was coming. Not only did we have to act relatively quickly to get our comments back to the White House, but we expected to have the diplomatic problem of gently telling the White House that the President's formulation—if these were indeed the President's own words—did not make the best case or reflect the most sophisticated arguments in favor of the administration's position. It seemed hardly likely that whatever came over would be particularly useful, since the White House—and seemingly the President— had paid very little attention to the arcane debate over the IMF that had been going on for months.

However, when the draft came over from the White House, we had a couple of surprises. First, what the White House sent was a Xerox copy of what the President wrote, in longhand, on legal-size lined paper. Looking at his three paragraphs we were all amazed that they read as fluently as they did. Only a few words were crossed out or written over. The President had written several starkly coherent paragraphs on the IMF issue without having to make any substantial revisions in the flow of his argument. Few writers can draft on complex subjects so easily.

What's more, what the President had written was one of the best and simplest statements of the case for IMF replenishment that most of us had seen—and we had been writing this material for several weeks or months. The President focused his remarks on the relationship between

JANUARY 24TH, 1983 - The President in the Oval Office working on a speech. Note the yellow pad, on which he drafted formal speeches and letters to friends.

Courtesy of the Reagan Library.

AUGUST 3RD, 1981 - The President in the Rose Garden, with Attorney General William French Smith and Secretary of Transportation Drew Lewis, warning the Air Traffic Controllers that they will be fired if they strike.

Courtesy of the Reagan Library.

FEBRUARY 21ST, 1986 - First meeting with the President prior to becoming White House Counsel (from left: Don Regan, Peter Wallison, President Reagan).

Official White House photograph.

APRIL 14TH, 1986 - The President in the Oval Office, meeting with the press before his speech to the nation on the Libya bombing.

Courtesy of the Reagan Library.

JUNE 17TH, 1986 - The President meeting in the Oval Office with Warren Burger, William Rehnquist, and Antonin Scalia before the announcement of Burger's retirement as Chief Justice and the nominations of Rehnquist and Scalia, respectively, to be Chief Justice and Associate Justice of the Supreme Court (from left: Scalia, Rehnquist, Ed Meese, Burger, Peter Wallison, Don Regan, and the President.

Courtesy of the Reagan Library.

JUNE 20TH, 1986 - The President and First Lady Nancy Reagan in the Diplomatic Reception Room at the White House with Jeremy, Peter, and Rebecca Wallison. The President and Mrs. Reagan were on the way to Camp David for the weekend. *Official White House photograph.*

NOVEMBER 13TH, 1986 - The President speaking to the nation from the Oval Office. This was his first statement on the Iran-Contra affair.

Courtesy of the Reagan Library.

NOVEMBER 19TH, 1986 - The President in the White House East Room taking questions from the press on the Iran-Contra affair.

Courtesy of the Reagan Library.

NOVEMBER 25TH, 1986 - The President in the Family Dining Room at the White House enjoying another story from Justice Thurgood Marshall at a White House luncheon for members of the Supreme Court. With him from left to right: Chief Justice William Rehnquist, Justice Byron White and Peter Wallison.

Courtesy of the Reagan Library.

FEBRUARY 11, 1987 - The President's second meeting with the Tower Board (from left: John Tower, Edmund Muskie, Brent Scowcroft, Peter Wallison, Clark McFadden, Charles Brower, Rhett Dawson, David Abshire.)

Courtesy of the Reagan Library.

the IMF replenishment and the continued health of the U.S. economy. It was a persuasive statement, and the Treasury Department sent it back to the White House substantially unchanged.

These experiences, when added to the evidence of the radio addresses, suggest intellectual abilities in Ronald Reagan that have not been appropriately recognized. Other indications of his intelligence were his quick wit—off-the-cuff remarks that were celebrated when they came from Jack Kennedy but simply enjoyed when they came from Reagan—and his ability both to conceptualize a coherent philosophy of government and to implement it as president. It is important to remember that an ideology or philosophy is more than a belief system; it must be internally consistent, with the parts logically flowing from the same consistent premises. A person who can conceptualize and defend an ideology or a political philosophy, I would submit, has more than ordinary intellectual capacity.

In his foreword to *Reagan in His Own Hand,* George Shultz makes exactly this point. The reason the book is so important, he notes, is that

> [it] provides a key to unlocking the mystery of Reagan that has baffled so many for so long.
>
> How could a man of supposedly limited knowledge and limited intelligence accomplish so much? How did he get elected and reelected governor of our largest state? How did he get elected and reelected president of the United States? How did he preside over a time of unprecedented prosperity, the winning of the cold war, and the demise of communism worldwide? How?
>
> Well, maybe he was a lot smarter than most people thought.[2]

In the previous chapter I discussed Reagan's convictions—his willingness and ability to stay the course, to stick with an idea despite the opposition of just about everyone else. To David Stockman and the others who were pressing Reagan to change his economic plan and raise taxes, his refusal to do so was not conviction—it was just preternatural stubbornness. And Ronald Reagan was indeed a stubborn man—a trait that was both a strength and a weakness. When he stood by his embattled Labor Secretary, Ray Donovan, who was falsely accused of illegal activities in his contracting business before assuming office, Reagan earned the admiration of all those—in his administration and outside—who had watched presidents cut and run from their subordinates when the going got tough. And it was Reagan's stubbornness that caused him to continue with the Bitburg visit—although the protests in the United States were loud and powerful—because he had promised Chancellor Kohl he would do so.

The same Reagan stubbornness protected Don Regan for months after the Iran-Contra scandal broke, even though a massed chorus of Republicans and media commentators was calling for his head. There were even reports that the President and Nancy Reagan had fought over Regan's continuing role, with the President allegedly overheard telling his beloved Nancy: "Get off my back!"

Eventually, as discussed later, Regan went a bridge too far for Ronald Reagan, allowing himself to be quoted at a staff meeting as blaming Nancy Reagan for a controversial White House hire. With this, the President had had enough. But for several months during the Iran-Contra crisis, when politicians, pundits, Washington wise men, and his own wife told Reagan that the only way he could save his presidency was by getting rid of his chief of staff, the President stood his ground. He realized that Regan was being made a scapegoat for the errors of others, and it offended his sense of justice to yield to the demands for Regan's head.

On the other hand, Reagan's stubbornness was itself the reason that the Iran-Contra scandal grew to presidency-threatening proportions. It was readily apparent from almost the beginning that the issue could have been defused by Reagan saying that he had made a mistake in permitting the arms sales—initiated for another reason—to devolve into a trade of arms for the American hostages in Lebanon. The analog was President Kennedy's accepting blame for the Bay of Pigs fiasco, an event far worse in every substantive respect than the Iran-Contra affair. This, however, the President refused to do, going only as far as to say that "mistakes were made," and insisting that he had not intended to and did not deal with kidnappers. Finally, after meeting with the Tower Board—the presidentially appointed fact-finding group assigned to investigate the Iran-Contra matter—and being told that the board had found a one-to-one relationship between shipments of arms and expectations for the release of hostages, Reagan relented. In a statement to the nation, he admitted that by not properly overseeing how his policy was carried out he himself had made mistakes. From that moment on, it was all over but the shouting. But the damage to Reagan—to his reputation for straight shooting and good management of his office, to the orderliness of his policy-making process, and to his relationship with Regan—was already done. He would recover later, but the momentum of his second term was lost.

A lot has been written about Reagan's purported lack of interest in people, sometimes described as his "remoteness." His staff, in particular, complained that it was impossible to get close to him, to get beyond the affable man to the "real person" inside. Edmund Morris connects this to his acting vocation with the somewhat harsh statement that "Even as a teenager, he had taken no personal interest in people. They were, and remained, a faceless audience to his perpetual performance."[3] It's somewhat unclear how anyone can support such a generalization. Those who knew Reagan as a teenager would be quite elderly now, and their recollections of Reagan would not be trustworthy at this point.

In any event, this aspect of Reagan's character has attracted so much attention that Lou Cannon devotes a chapter to it. He writes: "Some thought that Reagan was oblivious to the needs of others. Others believed he knew their needs but opted to protect himself to compensate for some childhood hurt. Whatever they thought, the barrier made Reagan a magnet as well as a mystery."[4] I don't think one needs to search for reasons for Reagan's "remoteness" beyond a recognition that he was fundamentally shy, but Cannon's observation about the mystery and magnetism of Reagan may indirectly illuminate another reason why Reagan's interactions with his staff seemed—to some of his staff— to lack the intimacy they wanted.

Remoteness and mystery are qualities often associated with charismatic leaders, who are by definition magnetic. One of the reasons for this is that they frequently have a sense that they are an instrument for some greater purpose. Reagan's frequent comments, particularly after his narrow escape from assassination, that he had dedicated himself to God, are consistent with this analysis. David Gergen, a communications adviser in the first Reagan administration, noted "[Reagan] didn't make you feel needed. He made you feel like you were working there for a cause or for the success of the presidency, but not enough for him."[5] Gergen's insight is also consistent with a central thesis of this book—that Reagan consciously subordinated his persona to his cause. It would not be surprising in such a case for those around him to sense that Reagan did not need the stroking, the personal attention, or the reinforcement that many politicians crave. Reagan, unlike most politicians, was focused on his ideas, not on himself, and could well have assumed that others were similarly motivated. Rather than wondering about Reagan's supposed remoteness, presidential scholars who are interested in probing the minds of our chief executives might more profitably consider why Reagan was so deeply attached to ideas and policy, and had so little interest in directing attention to himself.

One of the episodes that is frequently summoned to illustrate Reagan's remoteness is his apparent unconcern about who was his chief of staff. Regan notes in his book that when he and James Baker decided to switch jobs—with Regan becoming White House chief of staff and Baker becoming treasury secretary at the beginning of Reagan's second term—Reagan seemed to have no comment or reaction. Regan describes him as "equable, relaxed—almost incurious."[6] This would indeed be unusual, considering the importance of the chief of staff in the Reagan White House, but it is misleading to take this reaction out of context. As Regan himself notes, when the idea was first presented to Mike Deaver—then the President's chief of staff—at a lunch with Baker and Deaver in December 1985, Deaver had the air of one who had already cleared the decision with the First Lady and knew what Reagan's reaction would be.[7] This is very likely to be true, so that the

President was probably fully aware of the plan before it was formally presented to him in an Oval Office meeting in January 1986. Under these circumstances, his reaction was perfectly understandable. Indeed, to have asked questions would have given the false impression that he had been taken by surprise.

Moreover, from Mike Deaver's accounts, we know that at the beginning of his administration the President was quite interested in who would be his chief of staff. He recruited James Baker and rejected the loyal Ed Meese because he realized that in order to get his ideas implemented he needed someone with Baker's skills. By the time Baker and Regan agreed to switch jobs, the President was embarking on his second term and his principal ideas on domestic matters had already been implemented. He had less need for Baker's skills and probably saw Regan as a contemporary and ideological soulmate who could help him defend the territory he had taken. It was Regan, after all, who alone had stood with the President in 1981 and 1982 when all his other advisers had wanted him to abandon his economic program in the face of rising deficits and recession.

In any event, to say Reagan was unaware of people around him, or uncaring of their feelings, was certainly not consistent with my observations or my own experience. One of my favorite examples of Reagan's attentiveness occurred at an issues lunch in late June 1986. At that lunch, Regan raised with the President the question of whether he should accept a possible invitation to address the House of Representatives on the issue of U.S. aid to the Nicaraguan rebels known as the Contras. The staff was divided, and Regan outlined the pros and cons as the President started on the soup course. The briefing took about ten minutes while the President ate and listened. When Regan had finished, the President asked where our friends on the Hill stood on the question—the only issue that had not been covered by Regan. Regan said that Dick Cheney, then a congressman from Wyoming and a leader of the Republicans in the House, favored the idea and had won over Bob Michel, the House minority leader. The President thought a moment, and then said, "You don't get anywhere if you don't try. I'll do it." Then, turning to Regan: "Now, Don, eat your soup." People who are focused on themselves, or uncaring about others, don't usually notice the inconvenience they are causing to others.

Reagan's caring nature was also shown by his extraordinary courtesy to everyone around him—his inability to be abrupt or peremptory, the soft-spoken way he advanced his own views, and the fact that he never in my presence raised his voice in anger to a subordinate. Indeed, Reagan's concern about others created problems for him. His continual worry about the welfare of the American hostages in Lebanon may have been responsible for the overzealousness of his aides in promoting the arms sales to Iran, which gave rise to the debilitating Iran-Contra affair. And Reagan's concern for a former aide created one of the first problems I faced after joining the White House staff: what to do about allegations that Mike Deaver, after leaving the White House staff, had violated the government ethics laws by contacting the White House about a matter in which he had allegedly been involved while working as a senior White House official.

This was a very painful exercise. I didn't know Deaver, but in looking at the issue for the first time, it seemed reasonably clear that he was a victim of a typical Washington press frenzy—coupled perhaps with some jealousy on the part of his rivals and the press about his meteoric rise to prominence in the private sector. Although I had my doubts about Deaver's culpability, my job was to keep the President from stepping into the issue on Deaver's side. For one thing, it might turn out that Deaver had in fact done something wrong, and I did not want the President to be accused of attempting to protect him when he had violated the law. In addition, since a decision to appoint an independent counsel to investigate Deaver was to be made by the Justice Department, a series of statements by Reagan to the effect that he thought Deaver was innocent would provoke charges of undue influence if Justice ultimately decided that a special counsel was not warranted.

But getting Reagan to keep quiet about his views on the Deaver matter was a tall order. My advice to him was that, if asked, he should say only that he could not comment because the matter was before the Justice Department. This seemed a relatively simple escape, and he seemed to agree with this formulation, but every time he got a question about Deaver—which was often—he would say something to the effect that he thought the charges against Deaver were "ridiculous," or that Deaver was "completely innocent." When he was asked about whether an independent counsel should be appointed in the Deaver case, Reagan said he couldn't understand why, because Deaver had done nothing wrong. My advice wasn't having much effect.

It seemed clear to me that I had to explain to the President why it was so important that he keep out of this matter—even if he wanted to help Deaver. I met with him in early May, and explained the law on the subject in detail, pointing out that Deaver could be found to have engaged in wrongdoing even if he never contacted the President himself. Contacts at the staff level about anything in which Deaver had substantial involvement while at the White House would be sufficient to violate the law. Reagan was downcast; he defended Deaver by arguing that Deaver could not have had an involvement in the matters in question that could be characterized as "substantial." I said that may be true, but it was for the Justice Department, the independent counsel, and perhaps ultimately the courts to decide. I then told him that I wanted to send a memo to the members of the White House staff, asking them to cooperate with investigators on the Deaver matter, and I asked Reagan whether I could say that the President had instructed me to send the memo. He hesitated for a moment, obviously troubled; I thought he was going to say no; but he said, "Okay, as long as you don't make it sound as if I'm participating in this witchhunt."

The troubled, loyal, and defiant man whom I saw that day is not someone who does not care about others. Of course, Deaver might be a special case, since he and the President had worked together for 25 years. Some have said that Deaver was in many senses like another son to Ronald and Nancy Reagan. Perhaps so, but my own contacts with Reagan suggested that his feelings for Deaver sprang from something deeper in Reagan's character.

One episode in particular comes to mind. There came a time during the proceedings for the confirmation of William Rehnquist as Chief Justice

of the Supreme Court that I thought the President should invoke executive
privilege. Attorney General Ed Meese did not agree, and Don Regan set up
a meeting with the President at which Meese and I could make our arguments. Executive privilege—which permits the president to withhold from
Congress and others information about the substance of his discussions
with his subordinates or advisers—is not in the Constitution, but the
courts over the years have grafted it on to the presidency more or less as an
inherent right of an executive. It is the president's privilege; only he can
claim it—even for advice given to others in his administration—but the
president can also waive the privilege if for any reason he believes its assertion will do more harm than good.

In this case, after listening to both sides, the President sided with
Meese. He would waive the privilege. He said that in his experience,
going back to the time when he was the governor of California, when
the legislature's prerogatives were challenged the members tended to
stick together; he did not want either Rehnquist's nomination, or
Antonin Scalia's concurrent nomination to be an associate justice, to be
delayed by this kind of controversy, no matter how strong the arguments in favor of executive privilege.

The President then turned to me. He said he had read the memo I
had sent him on the issue the night before and thought it was an excellent job. He continued, "However, I'm going to go with Ed. I'm sorry to
have to overrule you on this one." He said all this with such sincerity and
concern for my feelings that I remember thinking to myself, "You are the
President of the United States; God help us if you ever start making decisions based on whether someone like me will be disappointed or hurt."
It was a remarkable moment for me, and not only for the insight it provided into Ronald Reagan's concern for the feelings of others.

Reagan also seemed to keep in mind personal things about those
who worked for him. One evening, when I was in the White House residence discussing an issue with him and Mrs. Reagan, he did something
that suggested he knew more about me than I'd thought. He had just returned from a campaign trip to Maryland, where he had campaigned
for Linda Chavez, the Republican candidate for the Senate. After the

discussion was completed, he went to his desk and picked up a large campaign button that had been given to him that day, and brought it over to show me. It was the name Chavez, spelled out in Hebrew letters. Perhaps he knew I am Jewish, perhaps not. In any event, he took great pleasure in showing me the button. In turn, I told him that my son, Jeremy, who was a great fan of his, had a campaign poster hanging in his room that had the name "Reagan" spelled out in Hebrew letters. He expressed interest in this, and I told him I'd bring it in for him to see. A week or so later, I did this, and it was returned to me a few days later with the President having written a humorous message in imitation Hebrew on a portion of the poster. That he took the time to do this, instead of simply returning it without comment, says much about him.

Speaking of my children and Reagan, one of the great moments of my White House tenure occurred when two of my children met the President. It was a Friday, the day when the President and Mrs. Reagan regularly took off by helicopter for Camp David. I thought Jeremy and Rebecca would enjoy seeing the President and First Lady walk by, and the helicopter taking off. Our older son, Ethan, was busy elsewhere and could not join us. My thought was that we'd just stand in the Diplomatic Reception Room at the south entrance to the White House and watch the passing show.

As we were standing there, Reagan walked into the room. There was a fairly good-sized crowd, including Secret Service, staff, and various privileged visitors there for the same purpose we were. But when Ronald Reagan saw me with the children, he came directly over and started to chat. He said that Mrs. Reagan was still getting ready, and asked the children their names. He was dressed in his Western duds—a plaid shirt, jeans, and boots—and did not look much like the formal figure the kids saw regularly on television. Jeremy, 14, and Rebecca, 11, were awed at first, but Reagan was so engaging that they had no trouble talking with him. As the discussion went on, Reagan began to have trouble, as he often did, with his hearing aid. He pushed it around for a while and finally took it out of his ear to adjust it. The kids were wide-eyed. Then Reagan told the story of how he lost the hearing in his ear on a

movie set, and then the story of how he managed to do a remote broadcast of a Chicago Cubs baseball game after the teletype broke down (he
just kept the batter fouling off pitches until the teletype was back up).
At this point, Mrs. Reagan arrived and talked a bit with the kids. Then
we all posed for photographs (the White House photographers are always present) and off they went. You can't convince Jeremy and Rebecca
Wallison that Ronald Reagan was remote.

Reagan also had a natural and imbedded courtesy that I always
thought grew out of the same impulses that compelled him to be punctual; he simply had a high regard for the dignity and importance of
others, and did not want to be rude to them any more than he wanted
to keep them waiting. This created an awkward scene on the day in
June 1986 that the President announced the resignation of Warren
Burger as chief justice of the United States, the nomination of William
Rehnquist as his successor, and the nomination of Antonin Scalia to replace Rehnquist as an associate justice.

The announcement was a complete surprise to the press, and provoked a wild scene, as the press briefing room erupted with questions
immediately after the President completed his introduction of Rehnquist and Scalia. The plan was for the President to read a prepared statement, and take no questions, which were to be fielded by Warren
Burger. I was to follow up with background about the selection process.
But Ronald Reagan couldn't bring himself to turn on his heel and walk
out of the press room after finishing his statement. For a long moment,
he stood there, shaking his head and apologizing that he could not answer the shouted questions from the floor. Eventually, as Warren Burger
strode forward to take his place, Reagan backed away from the podium,
but one could see that he hated to be so impolite as to simply walk
away. When the press finally focused their attention on Burger, who
was willing to answer their questions, the President turned to me and
said, "Can I go now?" I assured him that he could, and he left the briefing room.

Reagan's best public humor was always self-deprecating. My favorite has always been his response to a statement from a reporter that

some people thought he was lazy and averse to hard work. "Well," Reagan said—and you can see him cocking his head a little to the side as he said it—"they say hard work never hurt anyone, but I say, why take a chance?" Then there was his remark when he spoke at the graduation ceremony for Eureka College in Illinois, his alma mater. Reagan, whose grades were only fair even at this small local institution, noted that he'd had a good time in college. Then he remarked, "I often wonder how far I could have gone if I'd studied."

He also liked to make fun of his age, especially because doubts had been raised about his ability, at 70 years old when first elected, to do the work required of a president. Many of these jokes had an underlying point that emphasized the value of his maturity. Everyone has heard his remark in the second debate with Walter Mondale in 1984: "I will not exploit for political purposes my opponent's youth and inexperience," but in May 1986, he attended a G-7 meeting in Tokyo, and was asked at the last press conference what he thought of the mischief Congress was up to while he was away. His immediate response, which brought a huge laugh from the press: "You tell them to wait until the old man gets home."

Many of his jokes have been widely reported, but Reagan delivered many very funny one-liners in less public settings. After the 1986 election, when the Republicans lost control of the Senate, Reagan held a cabinet meeting, in part to thank the members of his cabinet for their work in support of Republicans and in part to provide them with some favorable spin on what had been a disappointing election. The meeting began with a report by Mitch Daniels, who was then the political director in the White House. After Daniels completed his remarks, Reagan, with mock seriousness, said the "campaign has been very personally rewarding for me." Then he paused, and for a beat we waited. Then: "At one stop I looked out over the audience and there was a girl holding a sign that said 'Reagan's a stud.'"

Reagan's humor in private was more of the country club locker-room variety—gently off color but never truly salacious. And he used it to good effect. It was always possible to tell when a meeting with Reagan was coming to an end. If he had been listening intently before, his eyes assumed a vaguely distant look, and I knew he was now thinking of an appropriate joke. He followed the old vaudeville prescription, "Always leave 'em laughing," and in most cases he was able to come up with a story or a joke that had some relevance to the preceding discussion. Even if it didn't, his guests left with the peculiar sense of well-being that a good laugh can impart. And Reagan was a comedian who enjoyed his jokes as much as the people he told them to. Unlike Bob Dole, one of the great comics in Washington, Reagan could never keep a straight face when he delivered a punch line; he was always the first person in the room to light up.

Another example of Reagan's efforts to end meetings with humor occurred at an issues lunch in July 1986. These were attended by the President and senior members of the White House staff and were held every Monday in the Cabinet Room, which is separated from the Oval Office by a combined reception area and secretary's office. I had just given a rather long report on the judicial selection process. The President leaned over to Regan and said something I couldn't hear; then the President stood up. Saying "You all wait here; I'll be right back," he went off in the direction of the Oval Office. In a minute or so he returned with a piece of paper, which he said was a letter he'd received as governor of California from a lawyer who had lost a case involving the state. With obvious delight, he read the letter, which contained a long string of salacious invective about the lawyers who had represented the state. We were all laughing—of course at the expense of my profession. But Reagan wasn't through with me. He then told a joke about a fellow who is asking a friend for advice. He wants to propose to his girl, but he's not sure he should until he tells her about his family. What's wrong with your family?, he's asked. Well, he says, my family's kind of odd; one of my brothers went to Harvard and another has been convicted of multiple murders. You shouldn't be afraid, he's told, to tell your girl about your brother's crimes; after all, it's not your fault. By this point, of course, I could see it coming: "Oh, the crimes are no problem," said the President, "it's the brother who went to Harvard that I'm worried about." Then, as he was leaving the room, Reagan held up the letter from the lawyer, saying, "If I ever get hit by a truck, this is in the top right drawer of my desk."

When he was among friends, Reagan could be a bit of a clown. At one preparation session for a press conference, he was asked a number of questions about U.S. relations with the Soviets. He had recently had a contentious visit from Anatoly Dobrynin, the Soviet ambassador to the United States, and one of the questioners asked him to characterize the message that Dobrynin had delivered from Gorbachev. Reagan hesitated a moment, then screwed up his face and said "Sweet!" At another preparation session everyone stood up when he walked into the room. Al Kingon, the cabinet secretary and one of the designated questioners, told him as he approached the podium that this was going to be a rough session; the questioners were not going to be easy on him. Catching the drift, Reagan stepped to the podium, frowned and said, "All right, you bastards, sit down!" At another press preparation session he answered 37 questions on foreign policy, then looked out over the room full of note-taking staff: "I saw all of you writing so much; I must be in a lot of trouble."

Most people who write about Reagan comment on his sense of security about himself. He is presented as "comfortable in his own skin," or having a healthy degree of personal self-confidence. For the most part, this is true, but there were times when Reagan showed a very human concern about his undeserved reputation for limited intellectual abilities.

One example occurred immediately after the press conference on November 19, 1986, his first on the Iran-Contra matter and a difficult one. Reagan was asked whether Israel had been involved in shipping arms to Iran on our behalf, and he said no. This was not accurate; the first shipments, in fact, had been made by Israel. As soon as he left the press conference, John Poindexter, the President's national security adviser, told him of the error, and suggested that it be corrected promptly. Reagan immediately agreed, and Larry Speakes, the President's deputy press secretary, went off to write a correction. After a moment, Reagan asked where Speakes was, and was told that he had left to prepare the correction, to which Reagan said, "Well, I wanted to tell him that I hoped he would give me some credit for that correction."

In another case, Reagan brought up at an issues lunch a statement that had been attributed to Henry Kissinger and had received a great deal of attention in the press. Kissinger was reputed to have said, referring to Reagan, that he did not understand how a person of such limited intellectual abilities could function effectively as president. Reagan noted that he had received a call from Kissinger shortly after the report became public, apologizing and saying that he had been misquoted and taken out of context. Reagan said he had told Kissinger that everything would be okay, "as soon as I peel Nancy off the ceiling." It was apparent that Reagan wanted us to know that Kissinger had denied the substance of the statement.

Reagan's supposedly limited intellectual abilities have prompted some people to question whether his affliction with Alzheimer's disease was evident even then to those of us around him. Edmund Morris has written that he reviewed Reagan's diaries from beginning to end and found no degradation in the quality of his thinking. This is obviously not a scientific judgment, or even one based on close observation, but during the time I was on the White House staff I did not notice a decline in Reagan's faculties. Indeed, it seems to me that Reagan's wit—a measure in my view of his quickness of mind—his memory for anecdotes, stories and jokes, and his memory for facts, never seemed to diminish.

At the time I left the White House, at the end of March 1987, Reagan's memory was much in the news. As was well known, he could not remember whether he had authorized in advance the Israeli shipment of U.S. arms to Iran. This, plus the fact that he had changed his testimony to the Tower Board on this issue, and then admitted that he really didn't remember, brought into sharp focus the question of whether he still had full control of his faculties. Indeed, when Howard Baker and his staff arrived at the White House to take over from Don Regan, they spent a good deal of time interviewing the members of the top White House staff about whether they thought Reagan was still capable of carrying out his duties. When I was interviewed, I said that I had not seen anything that would lead me to believe that Reagan was not competent to continue as president, and I was a little surprised by the question. I did not then, and do not now, consider Reagan's inability to remember whether he approved the arms sales in advance to be anything more than a detail—blown way out of proportion by the media.

I later learned, however, that one of the people the Baker group had interviewed had said that he thought some consideration should be given to whether the 25th Amendment—which authorizes the vice president to take over the duties of the president if the president is incapable of performing his functions—should be invoked. I could not imagine who would do this, since none of the top staff, as far as I knew, saw any significant change in Reagan's behavior or capabilities during the period we had been working with him. I later learned from a member of Baker's group that it was Marlin Fitzwater, who had just replaced Larry Speakes as deputy press secretary and had not seen much of Reagan over time. But I must say, as forcefully as I can, that at no time during my year in the White House did I see any diminution in Reagan's faculties, and I believe it was the conclusion of Howard Baker's group—who watched Reagan carefully for just this reason—that he was fully capable of carrying on as president at this point and to the end of his term a year and a half later.

Reagan had wonderful political antennae and could be relied upon to sense exactly where the American people would be on any new issue, but as in the Iran-Contra matter he had his blind spots. One of these was his naïveté about human nature and his tendency to believe—until shown otherwise—that people will act rationally and with goodwill. As Nancy Reagan put it, "he assigns to everyone else his own makeup."[8]

One example of this occurred shortly after I joined the White House staff. By the time Reagan assumed office, presidents routinely made their tax returns public, and although Reagan had complied with this requirement each year of his presidency he clearly didn't like it. This gave rise to an episode that revealed not only Reagan's benevolent view of human nature but Nancy Reagan's role in keeping her idealistic husband within the practical bounds of politics.

It was the White House counsel's responsibility to manage the disclosure of the President's tax returns each year, and it was necessary—before release—to discuss the returns with the Reagans. For this purpose, I flew out to Los Angeles in late March 1986 and traveled to Rancho del Cielo, the Reagans' ranch home in the mountains above Santa Barbara. I was joined by Roy Miller of Gibson, Dunn & Crutcher, the law firm that handled many of the Reagans' personal matters. The trip took about an hour from Santa Barbara in a White House car, and I was surprised by the difficulty of the road up the mountain. It was narrow and steep with many hairpin turns. The drive, at a maximum of ten miles per hour, was an adventure in itself, and I had trouble picturing the Reagans in a private car trying to negotiate this route. Of course, when he was President they were taken to the ranch by helicopter, but when they initially bought it they could not have known this luxury was in their future.

When we reached the ranch house, Reagan came out to meet us, dressed in cowboy boots, an old work shirt, and faded jeans. He apologized for the windy and cold weather and led us inside. The ranch house was small, simple, and very rustic, with whitewashed walls and ceilings between dark wood posts, beams, and rafters. Reagan told me that when they renovated the house their contractor got the wood for the posts and beams from the scaffolding of a nearby bridge. At this point, Mrs. Reagan arrived, wearing jeans and a checked cotton shirt. I was struck by how petite and youthful she looked. After the greetings, we all sat down and began a line-by-line review of the tax returns, which both Reagans followed closely.

At one point, the phone rang and Mrs. Reagan answered it. No, she said, sorry, you've got the wrong number. I laughed to myself about what the person on the other end of the line might have thought: "Now where have I heard that voice before. . . ?"

When we finished the review, Reagan said that he was thinking of not making his tax returns public next year—in order to break the precedent for his successor. He said with some passion that ordinary Americans did not have to disclose their returns, and he saw no benefit to the public in seeing the president's returns. Although I certainly agreed with his sentiments, this idea was a political non-starter. That presidents disclose their tax returns was now firmly fixed in the public mind, and his refusal to do so would be portrayed in the media as motivated by a desire to hide something. Most important, if he took the heat for doing this—as he had, for example, in "staying the course" during the 1981–82 recession—his successor would not follow his example. Instead, it's likely he would seek to reap the political benefit that would come from promising to disclose his own returns, so that Reagan's sacrifice would have been for naught.

I was about to raise these points when Nancy Reagan spoke up. She could not bear the thought of the criticism such a step would bring, she said, and Reagan backed off. Every president, no matter how good his political instincts, needs someone to bring him back to reality on occasion, and Ronald Reagan—a president with a particularly idealistic streak—was especially in need of this kind of counsel.

Many people have remarked on the bond between Ronald and Nancy Reagan. It was truly a love story. One need only go to the Reagan Library in Simi Valley, California, and read the letters Ronald Reagan wrote to Nancy each year on their anniversary. There it is again, that wonderful flowing prose—this time in praise of the one thing other than his ideas that truly moved Ronald Reagan. The importance of this relationship was brought home to me during the Iran-Contra crisis in late February 1987. For three months, the President had been immovable in his support of Don Regan, whose ouster as chief of staff was called for almost daily by editorialists, lawmakers, Republican Party officials, and, reputedly, Nancy Reagan. This steadfastness was typical of Reagan and didn't surprise me, but I wondered how long anyone could withstand this onslaught.

Then into this volatile situation walked a man named Jack Koehler, who was under consideration to be the new White House communications director, to replace Pat Buchanan. Koehler had an adequate communications background, and although he had not been formally appointed his name had surfaced in the press.

As Claudius noted to Gertrude, when troubles come they do not come singly, but in battalions, and it happened that shortly after his name surfaced the press somehow learned that Mr. Koehler had been a member of the Hitler Youth in his native Germany. He had not mentioned this to anyone, which is perhaps understandable, since he was only ten years old at the time. But the White House—already awash in the Iran-Contra matter—wasn't in any shape to contend with this disclosure; the search for someone to blame began immediately.

Apparently, Regan had not had anything to do with the surfacing of Koehler's name, which had come from one of the President's friends. But Regan's reaction—rare for him—did not serve him well. Near the end of the daily operations meeting on February 20, 1987, the question of how to handle the Koehler controversy was raised, and Regan—who should have simply solicited advice—chose to say that Koehler's name had come "directly out of the East Wing."

Now, the East Wing—as everybody in the meeting knew—was code for Mrs. Reagan, since her offices and those of her staff were in the East Wing of the White House complex. At this, I looked across the table at David Chew. We both rolled our eyes skyward. This was a bad one. Since the daily operations meeting was virtually an open wire to the *Washington Post,* Regan had in effect just publicly declared war on the First Lady. Ronald Reagan was a loyal man, but he was also staunchly and thoroughly uxorious. Nancy was clearly the most important person in the world to him. Regan's open challenge to the First Lady, I thought, sealed his fate. Sure enough, the President's diary entry for February 22 reflects his exasperation with Regan: "*That does it.* Nancy had never met Koehler and had had nothing to do with his appointment."[9] Regan's remark was reported, of course, in the next day's *Washington Post.* That was Saturday; by Thursday, Regan was gone.

The President's treatment of Regan was out of character, and can only be attributed to Regan's publicly confronting the First Lady. Given the tremendous pressures on the President at that time, it seems that Regan's remark about the East Wing was the last straw—the President said as much in his diary entry—but I'm not so sure that the same thing wouldn't have happened at any time and to anyone else who publicly challenged this president's wife.

The U.S. presidency is the most important and powerful job in the world. The men who have reached it in the past, and the men and women who are likely to reach it in the future, are bound to have extraordinary qualities—a palpable will to power, and a willingness to make personal sacrifices that only a burning ambition could justify. Few of them could be characterized as ordinary. One could not say that Ronald Reagan was an ordinary man either, although he seemed to regard himself as such. He had extraordinary gifts—a talent for summary, the conceptual capacity to connect policy to a political philosophy at the broadest level, a vision of where he wanted the nation to go, an ability to write clearly and forcefully, a personal charm and charismatic magnetism, and a quick wit that along with these other gifts suggested a sharp intellect.

But in my experience he also reflected what is best in ordinary men and women—and frequently absent in politicians: a genuine concern for the sensibilities of others and a respect for their dignity, a genuine humility and modesty despite his high office, and a quiet, polite, and gentle demeanor at all times and to all around him. Given the demands placed on politicians in our democracy, and the extraordinary sacrifices of human qualities that are necessary to gain and hold high office, it was extraordinary that a person of his qualities and character reached the presidency at all.

CHAPTER

5

MEET THE PRESS

I've learned in Washington that that's the only place
where sound travels faster than light.
—REAGAN AT THE CONGRESSIONAL MEDAL OF
HONOR CEREMONY, DECEMBER 12, 1983

The March 2, 1987, edition of *Newsweek* had a startling cover: Ronald
Reagan, partially in shadow, his face a picture of gloom and anxiety, and
the word "COVERUP" in bold caps hovering over his head. Next to the
President's photo, these words: "To protect the president, NSC staffers say
Don Regan ordered them to conceal the early approval of the arms sales to
Iran by Ronald Reagan." Inside, the first paragraph of the cover story began: "The word was out from Donald Regan himself: 'Protect the president.' So lights burned late in a bustling paper-strewn office in the White
House last Nov. 18 as Oliver North and his colleagues in the Iran arms
deal tried to massage the record of the complex weapons-for-hostages negotiations into a chronology that would minimize Ronald Reagan's role."

I didn't know whether North's office was in fact paper-strewn, or
whether his lights burned late as he and his colleagues shredded documents, but the principal point of this article—that Don Regan had
ordered a cover-up of the arms sales—I knew to be wholly false. A few
days before, I'd had three *Newsweek* reporters in my office—the head of
the Washington office, Evan Thomas, and writers Tom DeFrank and
Margaret Warner—and told them their story was wrong. There was no

reason for Regan to order a cover-up; the President had always taken full responsibility for the arms sales. Moreover, I'd followed Regan's actions every step of the way, and his effort had always been to encourage disclosure. The only ones who had skin in this game were the National Security Council staff—John Poindexter, Oliver North, and Robert McFarlane—one or more of whom had taken Ronald Reagan's approval of an initiative toward Iran, turned it into a trade of arms for hostages, and failed to follow the procedures required by law for reporting covert actions of this kind. If there was a motive to cover up, that's where it lay.

What's more, *Newsweek*'s support for the story was flimsy at best, based as it was on a third-hand account by an anonymous National Security Council staffer.[1] But the importance of this episode is not the allegation itself; it was that a responsible news outlet would print a story such as this, accusing a major public official of what could have been a crime, with so little support and in the face of my strong denial.

Although the *Newsweek* article was only a dozen pages, it spoke volumes about the condition of American journalism at the time and, consequently, the difficulties Ronald Reagan faced generally in getting his message across to the American people. By the beginning of the 1980s, press coverage of the government, and particularly the White House, had come to be dominated by a hunt for accusations of wrongdoing, sensationalism and "inside stories." The substance of what the President was saying or doing was not deemed to be as important as the political calculations and strategies that the press assumed to be the President's underlying motivations, or those of his staff. Reagan's statements were treated simply as background for uninformed or speculative media commentary on *why* he was saying or doing what was being reported. Moreover, *accusations* of wrongdoing—even when based upon anonymous sources who might be neither truthful nor informed—seemed to take precedence in press reports over ideas or discussions of policy differences. The working assumption of the media seemed to be that the government officials were lying— or at least "spinning"—when they spoke for attribution, and that government and politics were essentially a game, in which the role of the press was to expose the strategies and manipulations of the players rather than simply report on what they were doing.

This world was wholly at odds with the objectives and ideals of Ronald Reagan. Whether or not one agreed with his policies, no one could have doubted that Reagan took the substance of politics and government seriously. Indeed, as noted in earlier chapters, Reagan saw policy as the *purpose* of his presidency, as the principal reason for gaining office; the notion that he was playing a game, acquiring power for its own sake, or manipulating the press and the public for the sake of winning some meaningless victory, would have been completely foreign to him. Yet this was the world in which Ronald Reagan found himself as he assumed office, and he and his staff had to adapt to it if he was to succeed as president.

More than with any other president in modern times, the success of Ronald Reagan's presidency depended on his ability to communicate his ideas to the American people. It was Reagan's view—perhaps his most basic premise—that the way to arrest the trend toward greater government growth was to persuade the American people that more government was not the solution to the nation's problems. However, although the media was the avenue through which this communication had to occur, its focus on scandal and trivia—on accusations of wrongdoing and presidential shortcomings—left little space for coverage of such abstractions. Indeed, the trend throughout the 1980s was all the other way as the media's willingness or ability to communicate serious ideas to the American people grew weaker and more attenuated; by the time of the 1992 election, as Professor Larry Sabato notes in his insightful study of press conduct, *Feeding Frenzy,* the average length of the soundbite allotted to the *presidential* candidates on network television was 8.4 seconds. He continues: "Short sound bites were but a tiny part of the problem. . . . What airtime the networks offer is also increasingly filled with the chattering of their celebrity anchors and correspondents, rather than the actual words and deeds of the candidates, parties and campaigns. From Labor Day to Election Day the TV reporters and anchors consumed 71 percent of the evening newscast time devoted to the 1992 presidential election campaign, while the presidential candidates were given a mere 12 percent of the time."[2]

Thus, although Reagan was raising major issues about the role of the government in the lives of Americans, and seeking to reverse trends toward bigger government that had been in place since the New Deal, his arguments were not easily transmitted to the American public. For the most part, with rare exceptions, he was required to reach the American people through a small media window, and the shades were often drawn. Although some think it is possible for a president to speak to the nation whenever he wants, this is not the case. The electronic media will cover what the president says only when it is considered newsworthy, and precious and expensive television time is frequently denied for presidential speeches or news conferences that do not meet the networks' standards of newsworthiness. Even when television time is granted, as noted by Timothy E. Cook in *Governing with the News*, the president's "ability to go directly to a national audience is limited by the increased tendency of the networks to give the opposition party equal time and journalists' 'instant analysis' immediately after the speech—interpretations that help shape the public response to its content."[3]

This is not to say, of course, that the press has an obligation to report what the president says, or that government strategies, tactics or wrongdoing should be ignored. It is a question of emphasis. Whether a presidential statement is newsworthy, and whether large amounts of time and resources should be allocated to reporting accusations of wrongdoing or commenting on political strategy, is and should remain a decision of the media alone. But it seems obvious that to the extent the media focuses on these aspects of politics and government, it is giving less space and time to the differences over policy and philosophy between the president and those who disagree with him. There is only so much newspaper space for coverage of the government, and—even more clearly—only so much time on television news for coverage of the president's statements.

There were, of course, views that competed with Reagan's, and the existence of these provided the substance for a great national debate. In reality, that debate took place—in books, in academic and learned journals, and in conferences of political scientists—but media coverage of these great issues was slight and was necessarily reduced by the relentless attention to accusations of wrongdoing in government by present or former government officials.

Regrettably, the *Newsweek* story—as bad as it was—was not an exception. By the mid-1980s, press coverage of the government, and particularly the White House, had come to be dominated by a hunt for scandal and sensationalistic stories of which the *Newsweek* story itself was a good example. Many commentators—some in the press itself—had begun to notice how frequently stories that first appeared in the supermarket tabloids ultimately made it into the mainstream media. Moreover, even where real news was involved, it was so obsessively over-reported by a howling and jostling journalistic pack that it crowded out other news of equal or greater importance. Professor Sabato's coinage for these events, "feeding frenzies," was a regrettably apt description.* Two particularly egregious examples of the way a press frenzy reduces the coverage of other more important news were the 1984 coverage of

---

*Among the more memorable press feeding frenzies before, during and after the Reagan administration were these: the Gary Hart affair with Donna Rice and the change in his name; Edmund Muskie's crying bout outside the offices of the *Manchester Union Leader* in New Hampshire; Gerald Ford's purported clumsiness (the media actually stationed TV cameras on the ski slopes at Vail to record any falls); Mike Deaver's alleged use of his White House connections for business purposes; Former Labor Secretary Ray Donovan's alleged criminal conduct while operating a contracting company before joining the Reagan administration; Joe Biden's alleged plagiarism of a Neil Kinnock speech; Jimmy Carter's "lust in my heart" remark, and his encounter with the "killer rabbit"; George H. W. Bush's alleged mistress; George W. Bush's alleged drug use, his inability to name obscure foreign leaders at the outset of his campaign in 2000, and his inarticulateness; Dan Quayle's alleged efforts to avoid military service, alleged drug use, and misspelling of potato; Clarence Thomas's alleged harassment of Anita Hill; Jack Kemp's alleged homosexuality; and of course Congressman Gary Condit's affair with the missing intern, Chandra Levy. The eight years of the Clinton administration were virtually one long press frenzy, including scandals involving the White House Travel office, Whitewater, FBI files, Gennifer Flowers, Paula Jones, Monica Lewinsky, and Marc Rich.

Apart from politicians, the press went off the deep end during the same period about Wen Ho Lee's alleged transfer of secrets to China; Richard Jewell's alleged complicity in a bombing at the Atlanta Olympic Games; O. J. Simpson, Tonya Harding, Lorena Bobbitt, Princess Diana, Amy Fisher and Joey Buttafucco, the Menendez brothers, JonBenet Ramsey, and Elian Gonzales.

There are many more examples. To be sure, all of these stories had some limited newsworthiness; the problem is that they were so obsessively over-reported that they drowned out everything else, sometimes for weeks at a time. It is important to remember that when these subjects occupy the attention of the press, something else—most likely real news and real policy conflict—is not being reported.

Democratic vice presidential candidate Geraldine Ferraro's finances, and the 1988 coverage of Republican vice presidential nominee Dan Quayle's alleged efforts to avoid military service. These were genuine news stories, to be sure, but the hint of scandal or wrongdoing that was associated with the charges against Ferraro and Quayle caused them to overwhelm other stories about the presidential campaigns of which they were a part. As Professor Sabato notes: When "Geraldine Ferraro was the focus of an investigation concerning her family finances in August 1984 . . . the *Philadelphia Inquirer* assigned a dozen employees to the story full-time, and the *Washington Post* and the *New York Times* five each. . . . Dan Quayle was the subject of ninety-three network evening news stories over the twelve days of the frenzy about him in August 1988—more coverage than twelve of the thirteen presidential candidates had received during all the primaries combined. . . . Quayle alone garnered three-quarters of all the evening network time devoted to the presidential campaign during his August dog-days tribulations. By comparison, the Reagan-Gorbachev summit meeting in December 1987 registered considerably less network news interest."[4]

Moreover, the press seemed to prefer "meta-news"—stories about the news rather than the news itself. In covering elections, for example, the press often focused on the horserace elements, rather than what the candidates were saying. These stories were much easier to write, did not involve the arduous work of understanding policies and programs, and fit well with the general press attitude that policies and ideas are only part of a political game. Professor Sabato records that

of seven thousand print news stories surveyed between Labor Day and Election Day 1988, 57 percent were horserace items and only 10 percent concentrated on real policy issues. On television network news shows during the 1988 primary campaign, two and a half times more horserace pieces aired than did policy-issue ones. Reporters love the horserace and not policy for many different reasons. Most journalists are generalists, unfamiliar with the nuances and complexities of many issues and therefore unprepared to produce stories on them. Then, too, the horserace fits many reporters' rather cynical view of politics: Elections are but a game, not a contest of the power of competing ideas.[5]

It was not always thus. "Veteran newsmen," writes William Hachten in his book *The Troubles of Journalism,* "say there used to be a 'fire wall' at responsible news organizations—such as *The New York Times, The Washington Post, Time, Newsweek,* and *CBS News,* and a few other media—between serious reporting and mere sensationalism and entertainment. Some feel that wall has almost disappeared or at least has too frequently been breached in the competitive scramble for audiences, circulations, and profits. . . . Certain kinds of lurid stories come along that seem to cause some of the most reputable news organizations to forget the fire wall and compete with 'bottom feeders' (i.e., supermarket tabloids) for juicy tidbits about the travails of some celebrity or public figure well known to television viewers."[6]

The *Newsweek* story on the alleged Iran-Contra cover-up by Regan should convince fair-minded people that the "firewall" had melted away by the mid-1980s. Instead of reporting news, the press now seemed to favor scandal-mongering and dramatic charges based on weak or anonymous sources. Rather than reporting what political figures were saying, the press focused on mistakes in the way they said it. Ronald Reagan himself noticed this phenomenon, and commented on it in his autobiography: "It bothered me . . . that, from time to time, some of the press seemed anxious to catch me making a mistake. . . . Some in the press corps seemed to make a special effort to play 'gotcha' with me, especially during a press conference. If they wanted to question our policies or our approach to solving a problem, fine. But isn't it a little petty to point out every time a *t* isn't crossed or an *i* isn't dotted?"[7]

The decline in press standards seems to have begun with the revolt of the educated classes against the Vietnam War. Hostility toward the government's Vietnam policies among the elites was reflected in the press, which was and is dominated by this class. Ultimately, the media refused to accept the government's interpretation of events, an attitude seemingly vindicated by the publication of the Pentagon Papers, which showed that the Johnson administration was not truthfully reporting events in Vietnam, even to Congress. Although this was a serious blow to the relationship between the government and the media, the most significant damage was done by Watergate, which showed reporters that they could become celebrities—rather than the obscure and underpaid scribblers they had always conceived themselves to be—if they could uncover a good government scandal. In 1993, Thomas Patterson, a writer on the role of the press in presidential campaigns, accurately described this phenomenon: "The poisonous effect of Vietnam and Watergate on the relationship between journalists and politicians has not dissipated. The antipolitics bias of the press that came out of the closet two decades ago has stayed out."[8]

Nowhere is this better demonstrated than in the consistent press assumption that campaign contributions are the key influence on the policy positions of officials. In reality, it is the reverse; campaign contributions go overwhelmingly to officeholders who support policy positions with which contributors agree. This is as it should be; in a democracy, voters have the right—even the obligation—to assist the election or re-election of officials who follow policies with which the voters agree. But the virtually uniform view among reporters that politics is corrupt and politicians are untruthful leads them to seek and describe corrupt motives for relatively simple policy preferences. Thus, the press will regularly cite campaign contributions from oil interests when reporting that Republicans want to drill for oil in the Arctic National Wildlife Refuge, not the fact that Republicans generally want to increase the nation's oil supplies as a matter of policy. Similarly, stories about Democrats opposing tort reform will note that they receive campaign contributions from trial lawyers, not that Democrats generally believe government should act to protect consumers. This is not to say that campaign contributions don't have some influence, but that—because of its bias against politics and politicians—the press sees and reports as significant only one limited element of the complex subject of government policy development.

The combination of cynicism about the government's truthfulness or motives and the great potential rewards for both reporters and the media organizations that employ them changed the relationship between the press and the government. Most of the phenomena we see today—pack journalism, scandal mongering, focus on trivialities and personalities, reporting on the strategies of candidates and officeholders rather than what they and their opposition are actually doing or saying—is fallout from this changed attitude toward government.

Even in the 1980s, the need for "inside" or scandal stories sometimes led reporters and newspapers to devote enormous resources to matters that were worth, at most, a single story. One particularly memorable episode occurred relatively early in my White House tenure, beginning with a call from the *New York Times*. Two of its reporters, Martin Tolchin and Stuart Diamond, were following up on accusations that Mike Deaver, after he had left the administration, had used his influence in the White House to set up a meeting with President Reagan for Kim Kihwan, an economic adviser to the President of South Korea.

This investigation was begun in the midst of a huge press flurry about other accusations involving Deaver, particularly that he had violated the ethics laws by contacting the White House concerning matters he had worked on while he was the deputy chief of staff to President Reagan. Initially, one might ask whether what Mike Deaver was doing after he left government was really news, and whether mere accusations against him were worth the prolonged attention of the *New York Times*. To be sure, if Deaver had been in substantive contact with the White House during the year after his departure—if in other words, the accusations proved true—he could have violated the government's ethics laws. That would certainly be news, but the enormous press outpouring on what were merely *accusations* against Deaver was totally out of proportion to the true significance of the story. Deaver, after all, was no longer a government official, and there was no indication—even if the accusations were

true—that anything he had done after leaving the White House had had
any significant effect on government decision making.

In this case, the *Times* allegation—based on reports from anonymous "State Department officials"—was that Mr. Deaver "played a key
role in arranging the meeting" between the President and Mr. Kim.[9]
The *Times* reporters had gone to Asia to develop this story and, by the
Times account, had interviewed "100 Government officials, business-
men and intelligence officials in Seoul, Tokyo, Washington and New
York." In the midst of this huge effort merely to find out whether a *former* government official had possibly violated ethics laws, the White
House was asked for comment.

I decided to take the *Times* investigation seriously—especially because, if it turned up evidence of an effort by Deaver to influence the
President or others in the White House, I would have to re-emphasize to
the President the rules concerning contacts with Deaver and other former
White House staffers. In the course of my own investigation, I found that
the meeting between Reagan and Kim had been set up in response to a cable from our ambassador in Korea. I saw the cable and the memorandum
from the National Security Council staffer—based on the cable—stating
that Mr. Kim had a message from President Chun of Korea that the Korean President wanted delivered personally to President Reagan. Mike
Deaver's name was never mentioned. It seemed reasonably clear that if the
President of Korea wanted the President of the United States to see his
emissary, and such a meeting was recommended by our ambassador in Korea, there wouldn't be any need for a Mike Deaver to set up the meeting.

All of this information was given to the *Times* reporters. Clearly, it
called into question whatever little significance their story now had. The
ethics laws forbade Deaver to contact the White House on matters of his
private business for a year after leaving office, but my investigation showed
that Deaver had not been involved with the White House in connection
with this meeting. Case closed, right? That's not how the *Times* saw it.

Shortly after getting the information from me, the *Times* went
ahead with its story, relying for support on its unnamed State Depart-

ment sources, and on a statement from our ambassador in Korea that he had talked to Deaver about the matter. The fact that Deaver had talked to our ambassador about a meeting was irrelevant. Under the ethics laws, Deaver was clearly allowed to do this. He was also allowed—if he did so—to advise the South Korean Government that if they wanted to get a message to the President they could do it by contacting our ambassador. The story had significance only if Deaver had actually contacted the White House. What I told the *Times* explicitly negated this idea. But without any White House contact Deaver was doing what almost every former government official in Washington ends up doing entirely legally at one time or another—advising people how to deal with the White House, Congress, or the bureaucracy. As the *Times* story put it: "A two-month study by the *New York Times* of Mr. Deaver's activities in Asia has turned up new details on how a former high White House official was able to use, in his private business dealings, knowledge and contacts he had gained in government." Stunning. That might have been worth a story in Mike Deaver's college alumni magazine, but not an exposé—a two-month study, involving 100 interviews—in the *New York Times*.

The effect of the change in press focus, from reporting on what government or the president was doing to reporting scandal and personality trivia, is seen in polling of the American people between 1958 and 1997 on the following question: "Do you think that quite a few people running the government are a little crooked, not very many are, or do you think hardly any of them are crooked at all?" The results, recorded in *What's Wrong*, by Everett Carll Ladd and Karlyn Bowman, show that the "Quite a Few" responses rose from 24 percent in 1958 to 50 percent in 1997, with a big jump occurring in 1974 at roughly the time of Watergate; significantly, the "Hardly Any" response declined during this period from 26 percent in 1958 to 8 percent in 1997.[10] In other words, the American people's view of the honesty of public officials has declined substantially as the media has focused increasingly on government scandal rather than the substance of what government is doing.

Of course, it is possible that government officials are actually more dishonest today than they were 50 years ago—and hence that the press attention to this question is justified. But this is highly unlikely. The more likely interpretation of the data is that the media's coverage of scandal, by devoting more space and time to that issue than to the substance of government policy and programs, has created the impression among the American people that many or most government officials are corrupt.

Another way of assessing the impact of the media emphasis on scandal would be to look at whether the American people think government is attuned to their needs. Not surprisingly, these data also show that Americans' confidence in the quality of their government has been declining steadily since 1973, around the time of Watergate. Between 1973 and 1994, the number of people who agreed with the statement, "Most public officials [people in public office] are not interested in the problems of the average man" increased from 59 percent to 75 percent, while the percentage who disagreed declined from 41 percent to 25 percent.[11] It is highly unlikely that in this 20-year period the government actually became less responsive to the problems of ordinary Americans, but there is no doubt that Americans have come to think so.

Ironically, all of this scandal mongering has not done the press any good either. The American people apparently recognize that they are being ill-served by reporting that fails to cover the substance of what government is doing, or the real disputes over policy that lie at the heart of politics. Between 1979 and 1997, the Gallup Poll recorded a decline in those who have a great deal of confidence in the press from 51 percent to 35 percent, and a rise in those who have very little or no confidence from 13 percent to 22 percent.[12] Combined with the data on Americans' attitude toward government, these poll numbers reflect an increasing cynicism, paralleling the post-Watergate cynicism of the press itself.

Thus, as Ronald Reagan began his presidency, he and his staff were required to solve two quite different problems. The first was to find a way to communicate directly with the American people, avoiding the filter of the press. The second—far more difficult—was to develop a way to keep the attention of the press focused on the President's agenda, rather than the scandal and accusations of wrongdoing they would have preferred to report.

The stakes couldn't have been higher for the President. In Richard Neustadt's analysis, a president's power to achieve his goals, whatever they may be, depends on his reputation, and his reputation depends in large part on the image communicated by the media. "More than ever," writes Martha Joynt Kumar, "the media play a powerful role in establishing a president's reputation and impact. Reputation is not just titillation, but a fungible resource used by a president to reach his political goals. Further, how a president is portrayed is a critical factor in his success building and consolidating support. Unfortunately, just as the reputation stakes have increased, the president's ability to control how he is perceived has decreased. The news media have actually reduced presidential opportunities to talk directly to the public while opponents have found the means to get more coverage."[13]

The solution to the first problem—finding a way to avoid the press filter in communicating with the American people—was relatively simple. Shortly after he assumed office, the President began a series of regular Saturday morning radio addresses in which he discussed the major issues of the day. Since radio time was less valuable than television time, most radio stations were willing to carry the President's message, as well as the response of his Democratic opposition. Although this gave the opposition a voice they would not otherwise have had, the opportunity to speak directly to the American people was of far greater value to the President. Although each of these addresses was ostensibly concerned with one or more of the issues that were then before Congress or widely discussed in public, Reagan also used them to make the broader philosophical points that were the core elements of his presidency.

Thus, in a radio address on April 9, 1983, Reagan took up the subject that would be on many taxpayers' minds a few days later, making many of the points about government's appropriate role that were central to his philosophy:

In just a few days, the date many of us dread more than any other will be upon us—April 15th, deadline for filing income tax returns.

Like Federal employees, taxpayers also work for the government, they just don't have to take a civil service exam. Here in America, land of opportunity, governments at all levels are taxing away 40 percent of our nation's income. We've been creeping closer to socialism, a system that someone once said works only in heaven, where it isn't needed, and in hell, where they've already got it.

We know that the secret of America's success has been our drive to excel, a spirit born and nurtured by our families. With their dreams and hard work, they've built our nation, made her great, and kept her good. Everything we've accomplished began in those bedrock values parents have sought to impart throughout our history—values of faith in God, honesty, caring for others, personal responsibility, thrift, and initiative.

But families cannot prosper and keep America strong if government becomes a Goliath that preys upon their wealth, usurps their rights, and crushes their spirit. For too many years, overgrown government has stood in your way, taking more and more of what you earned, no matter how hard you tried.

Make no mistake, the thousands of small businesses and the workers in steel, autos, and housing who have suffered so badly from the recession didn't lose their jobs by chance. . . . By 1981 double-digit inflation and excessive regulations had driven up the price of their products. Record interest rates made it too difficult for their firms to borrow money to modernize their equipment, and record tax increases sharply increased the price of their labor in the marketplace.[14]

In another address, on May 14, 1983, he celebrated Small Business Week with this:

True wealth is not measured in things like money or oil, but in the treasures of the mind and spirit. Oil was worthless until entrepreneurs with ideas and the freedom and faith to take risks managed to locate it, extract it, and put it to work for humanity. We can find more oil and we can develop abundant supplies of new forms of energy if we encourage risk-taking by thousands and thousands of entrepreneurs, not rely on the government to horde, ration, and control. The whole idea is to trust the people. Countries that don't, like the U.S.S.R. and Cuba, will never prosper. . . .

We came to Washington confident that this small business spirit could make America well and get our economy moving again. Well, it's working. And we want to keep on using that special principle of giving by putting America's destiny back into the people's hands, providing you new incentives to save, invest, and take risks, so more wealth will be created at every level of our society.[15]

The same core idea reflected in this address—returning power to individuals—occurs again and again in Reagan's radio addresses, along with the other issues Reagan chose as the principal objectives he would seek as president: free trade, military strength, reduced taxes, less regulation of the economy, and restoring the confidence of the American people. In this way, through these weekly statements, Reagan was able to evade the media's filter and deliver his message directly to a national audience. It is doubtful that these ideas would have reached the American people as often or as fully if Reagan had simply relied on the media to report them. A president's philosophy is not "news," nor are statements, made previously, that are intended to persuade the American people to his point of view. Over time, however, Reagan's relentless effort, coupled with the power of his ideas and convictions, succeeded in changing the one factor that Reagan believed was the key to achieving the purposes of his presidency: the attitude of the American people toward the role of government.

Finding a way to reach the American people directly was relatively easy. Much more difficult was addressing what Martha Joynt Kumar called the president's reduced ability to control how he is perceived. To do this it was necessary to keep the attention of the press focused on the President's agenda rather than their own. Stories in the press frequently set the daily agenda for the White House. A report in one newspaper elicits questions from a dozen more, and the White House staff is soon swamped with inquiries and demands for more information while the story is in play. In this sense, then, the *Washington Post* can have more to say about what the White House staff does on any given day than the president himself. To avoid the appearance of chaos, and the loss of control over events, it is necessary for the White House to take control of the news agenda.

The way the press treated the Iran-Contra story—and its effect on the functioning of the White House staff—illustrates the importance of this objective. As will be discussed in detail later, because of the secrecy with which the arms sales to Iran were carried out, after the departure of North and Poindexter the White House had no better information than the press about what had actually occurred, and it was impossible either to confirm or deny many of the stories, or to correct inaccuracies. Each day was spent tracking down rumors and accusations that appeared on the evening news the previous day or in the newspapers that morning. As information was furnished to investigators, more accusations were leaked, creating a never-ending cycle.

In the fullest sense, then, during the Iran-Contra crisis, the White House was working off the press's agenda, and for four months—from early November 1986 to early March 1987—virtually nothing was done in the White House that did not relate directly or indirectly to the Iran-Contra matter. It's a good thing there were no foreign or domestic crises during this period. On the other hand, maybe there were—and nobody noticed.

To be sure, there was plenty for the press to cover. The arms sales had been opposed by both the Secretary of State and the Secretary of Defense; the sales appeared to violate the President's own executive order against selling arms to terrorist nations, and—because the sales were not reported to Congress—the provisions of the Arms Export Control Act; in a B-movie story line, a former national security adviser had gone to Tehran—to meet with the people who had kept our diplomats hostage for 444 days—with a cake, a key, and a Bible; two hostages had been released, but the releases were not clearly related to the arms sales;

the first White House statements referred to dealing with Iranian "moderates," but knowledgeable sources denied that there were any in or near power in Iran; although the President readily acknowledged that he established the policy that authorized the arms sales, he could not remember approving particular transactions; and the government of Israel was somehow implicated—at least at the beginning—but it was not clear whether its motives were to help itself or the United States. Finally, the discovery of a plan to use a portion of the proceeds of the arms sales to support the Contras suggested extra-constitutional action reminiscent of Watergate.

But even allowing for all this raw material, the coverage of the Iran-Contra matter was excessive—unprecedented before or since. Between November 4, 1986, when the first stories appeared, and the end of January 1987—when I stopped counting—there were 555 Iran-Contra stories in the *Washington Post* alone, and 509 in the *New York Times*. That's an average of six stories every day in the *Post* and almost that many in the *Times*. There was one day when the *Post* had more than 20 separate Iran-Contra stories, and many days when both papers had ten or more. And this tally did not include editorials and commentary by regular op-ed writers for the *Post* and *Times*, most of whom wrote of little else for four straight months. Of course, the *Washington Post* and the *New York Times* were only two of the newspapers that covered the Iran-Contra story in detail. The *Los Angeles Times*, the *Wall Street Journal*, the *Washington Times*, the *Baltimore Sun*, and all the news magazines competed with the *Times* and *Post* and with each other for the most extensive coverage and the most sensational stories.

Nevertheless, as subsequent investigations would show, the arms sales were at most a failed and perhaps mistaken policy. There was no cover-up involving the President—or Regan or the White House—after the departure of North and Poindexter. Whether there were any clear violations of the laws covering the arms sales has never been established, and there were no prosecutions for these matters. Instead, people were convicted of offenses like lying to Congress or accepting illegal gratuities—none having to do with the arms sales themselves, the support of

the Contras, or the failure to report to Congress. Iran-Contra, then—
when one compares the outcome to the press attention it received—
may have been the biggest press frenzy of all time.

Although the absence of reliable information about what actually
happened in the arms sales or the diversion of funds exacerbated the
problems of the White House, and made the Iran-Contra affair somewhat *sui generis* among presidential-level scandals, the consequences for
the functioning of the White House and the President's effectiveness
during this period were sufficiently serious to demonstrate the importance of maintaining the news initiative.

The Reagan White House strategy for doing this was relatively simple; it relied on the perception that the press was fundamentally a business and required raw material to continue producing its product.
While many reporters longed for the opportunity to expose wrongdoing or scandal, their newspapers and news shows needed a story every
day. Their first priority, therefore, was to produce copy by the evening
deadline. Thus, as a practical matter, keeping the news initiative was
simply a question of whether the White House provided the story or
the press provided one of its own. In a process analogous to making
sure the lions were well fed before cleaning their cage, the Reagan
White House acted on this principle by making sure that each day there
was a story involving the President or his administration.

When I joined the White House staff in April 1986, over a year after
Don Regan had replaced James Baker as chief of staff, this strategy—
which was begun at the outset of the first Reagan administration—was
still in place. Every evening, the top White House staff would gather in
the office of Dennis Thomas to discuss what the news event would be the
next day. The President's calendar was the first stop. Did he have a speech
or an event that would be newsworthy? If not, was there something that
the President could do or say that would put him on the evening television news shows and in the morning papers? This was good public relations, of course, but it had a more serious purpose: when reporters were
writing stories about what the President was doing, they weren't writing
stories that would obscure his message with the scandal *du jour*. Later ad-

ministrations abandoned this policy and paid the price. The first Bush White House, in particular, looked chaotic and without direction as it chased after press stories instead of getting its own message out.

Although the White House strategy was modestly successful in avoiding this problem until the Iran-Contra affair came along, it could not fully avoid the fallout of the post-Watergate environment. The Watergate story was driven by anonymous sources, embodied in the famous "Deep Throat" of the Woodward and Bernstein articles, and this seemed to validate the idea—previously resisted by scrupulous editors—that anonymous sources could be cited as the sole support for a news story. Because sources that refuse to be named are as likely to be lying as telling the truth, there was no way after this shift in standards to prevent the manipulation of the press by anonymous sources, or—worse—the manipulation of the news by reporters in search of sensationalistic stories.

In retrospect, it is easy to see how a lowering of attribution standards flowed logically from a change in the attitude of the press toward the government. Once reporters and editors became suspicious of the government's motives, and dubious about whether they were being told the truth, anonymous sources could seem more credible than those who allowed their names to be used. After all, anonymous sources—like Deep Throat—could be whistle-blowers, remaining anonymous because they feared retaliation by their superiors for telling the truth. Indeed, because anonymous sources told more sensational stories, they seemingly came to be preferred to the government spokesmen and others who allowed themselves to be named.

Academic commentators have also noticed this change. Martha Joynt Kumar has written that "because today's news organizations have lowered their standards of proof and attribution of sources," a president's opponents have gained particularly good opportunities to define him in negative terms. She continued: "Larry Sabato observed the problem as it affected presidential candidates: 'The press itself has aided and abetted the lowering of the evidentiary standard held necessary to make a charge stick.' Further, he remarked that 'In addition to the publication of rumor and the insinuation of guilt by means of innuendo, news out-lets are willing to target indiscriminately not just ethical problems, but possible problems and the perception of possible problems.' With oppo-sition groups and individuals ready to provide grist for the news mill, presidents have difficulty shaping their own image."[16]

The strong preference of reporters for anonymous inside material has resulted in the unseemly process of reporters actually asking for leaked information. In this, they reduced themselves to supplicants, suborning disloyalty to the president. When I got to the White House as a senior official, I was visited by a number of reporters from the White House press corps who asked that I keep them in mind when I had something to leak. I felt sorry for reporters who had to ask me and other White House insiders for leaks. In effect, they were begging for handouts; it couldn't have been satisfying work. Some reporters went further with some of my colleagues than they did with me, saying quite openly "if you take care of us, we'll take care of you."[17]

In Don Regan's book, he recounts a discussion between his execu-tive assistant, Tom Dawson, and *Washington Post* White House corre-spondent David Hoffman. Dawson, new to his job in the spring of 1985 along with others who came over to the White House with Re-gan, was told by Hoffman that it would be in the interest of the new staff to be cooperative with the press. Hoffman noted that because the former chief of staff, Jim Baker, had "cooperated" he got the benefit of the doubt when the Debategate scandal erupted. This affair, another of the great media frenzies arising out of the possibility of wrongdoing by important people, involved fixing responsibility for the theft of the briefing book used by Jimmy Carter to prepare for his 1980 presiden-tial debate with Reagan. But, Hoffman continued, because Bill Casey, the chairman of Reagan's 1980 campaign and later the director of the Central Intelligence Agency, had not been cooperative, "we were tough on Casey."[18] This anecdote is entirely credible to me, since I myself was told by Hoffman that a piece the *Washington Post* was do-ing on John Poindexter, then the President's national security adviser, would be negative because Poindexter (who distrusted the press in any event) had refused to be interviewed.

Reporters have also thought it was within their power to manipulate events and officials in order to get a story, rather than wait for the story to occur. On one occasion, I was talking with David Hoffman about why the *Post* would not report the White House view on some of the stories he and other reporters had been receiving as leaks from the Hill. One example was the frequent report that Lt. Col. Oliver North, the principal staffer on the Iran-Contra matter, had met with and briefed the President on what he had been doing. This story was totally false. We had reviewed all the President's meetings and telephone logs and found that he had never met alone with North and that North's only meetings with the President had been in large groups where he was probably a notetaker. Nevertheless, the stories that North had met with the President were reported regularly from anonymous Hill sources, with never a reference in the *Post* to the contrary evidence reported by the White House. Hoffman, responding to my complaint, told me that the *Post* would not report the White House view until the President held a news conference and opened himself to questioning on the subject of Iran-Contra.

Lest I give the incorrect impression that all members of the White House press corps behaved this way, I'd like to mention Gerald Boyd, who was the White House correspondent for the *New York Times* while I was White House counsel. Boyd was a tough and honest reporter, whose primary interest was accuracy for himself and his newspaper. On several occasions, before the *Times* went with a story on the Iran-Contra matter that was based on anonymous sources, Boyd would call me for some indication of the story's accuracy. From time to time—when I had the necessary information, or could disclose it—I was able to show him that there was documentary or other evidence to cast doubt on what a *Times* reporter had been told. In some of these cases, other newspapers—not as careful—published these stories, and Boyd was then apparently criticized by his colleagues for his caution. I was happy to note, however, many years later, that none of his insistence on journalistic standards impaired Boyd's career. He is now the managing editor of the *New York Times*.

Nevertheless, the experiences recorded above—like the *Newsweek* cover-up story and the *Times* non-story on Deaver—are replete with elements that should cause concern among responsible journalists. The willingness of reporters to threaten or punish those who do not cooperate in providing inside information—indeed the obsessive focus on inside information and unsubstantiated accusations of wrongdoing—suggests that the press has lost a vision of its proper role. The publication by *Newsweek* of an allegation that Regan led an Iran-Contra cover-up—published with virtually no support—was a reckless act that can only have come from a serious decline in press standards for accuracy. And the *New York Times's* overblown and pointless story on Mike Deaver shows that even the most highly regarded press outlets had begun to allocate their resources toward sensationalist stories rather than substantive news.

What is to be done? It is a cliché—and true—to say that a vigorous press is necessary for a democratic system to function, and in any event the U.S. Constitution will not allow significant tethering of the press. But it does seem that when the press thrives on scandal instead of substance, and publishes accusatory or false information without any significant concern for the reputations of those it writes about, the quality of democratic government can also be degraded. To say that the press should be vigorous and aggressive is not to say that it should function without restraint. Indeed, the opposite is probably true. Rights imply corresponding responsibilities, and many members of the press have not yet shown that they understand this equation. Because of the immense discretion they have been granted, reporters should be under more, not fewer, strictures to act responsibly.

Journalism is a profession, but it is a profession that is unusual in one major respect—it does not have a universally accepted code of conduct or other standards that define proper or professional behavior and are enforceable in any formal sense against the profession's practitioners. There may be informal standards, or courses in proper conduct taught in journalism schools, but reporters who do not abide by these standards are not disciplined, and cannot even be cited for their violations by any recognized professional disciplinary group. This separates the journalistic profession from architects, lawyers, doctors, and accountants. The result is that as standards spiral downward, there is no place at which anyone can call a halt or say "now you've gone too far." There is no bottom.

Professional standards are not a quaint tradition; there is a reason they exist. Professionals such as doctors and lawyers have power over lay people because of their expertise. Lawyers, for example, are expected to advise clients to proceed in ways that are in the client's—not the lawyer's—best interests. Thus, a lawyer is expected by his or her professional standards to tell a client when litigation would not be cost-effective, even if the lawyer would profit from it. Doctors, particularly surgeons, are expected to tell their patients when surgery is unnecessary, even though the surgeon might profit from the work. Professional standards, accordingly, are employed to prevent abuses of power.

The press also has power—in some ways more power than doctors and lawyers. Reporters, for example, have the power to destroy reputations—a power that has been enhanced by Supreme Court rulings that virtually immunize reporters against liability when they are making statements about government officials or other "public figures." Over time, the concept of "public figure" has expanded, so that some courts have held that a person is a public figure if he injects himself into a public debate of some kind—for example, by writing an article. In these cases, the public figure has to prove that a false and defamatory story was published maliciously; a reporter's gross negligence is not enough. Destroying a reputation is no small matter for the people to whom it occurs, and many people refuse to serve in government—or allow their names to be considered for government positions—for fear that a reckless press will negligently and thoughtlessly destroy a good name they have spent a lifetime developing. Yet there is no restraint on reporters that is comparable to the professional standards that lawyers, doctors, and other professionals must meet.

Writing in his autobiography Ronald Reagan said: "[A] free and aggressive press corps is essential to the health of our democracy. If the press does not tell us, who will? But with that freedom comes a special responsibility to be accurate and fair. The press should remember the great impact its words can have on a person's life. Sadly, the words *questioned about* sometimes translate into *guilty of* in the minds of readers and listeners. That does not mean that reporters shouldn't do their job. It just means they should be careful."[19] Too often, journalists are not.

To be sure, the government can and does exhibit arrogance and abuse its power, and one of the restraints on this behavior is a free press. But government is also subject to other restraints—such as the separation of powers, the Bill of Rights, and a system of laws enforced by independent courts—while the press is subject to none. Overt outside restraints on the press are not warranted and probably not constitutional; the only effective prescription is likely to be a code of professional conduct, enforced by the press itself.

Ironically, in the midst of the Iran-Contra frenzy, Governor Mario Cuomo of New York made a speech in which he called for the press to police itself if it is to avoid government or court action that will erode its freedoms. His modest proposal was rejected by the *New York Times* in a subsequent editorial, but the Governor—an avowed liberal—was correct to point out that all liberties have limits, and the press cannot expect that it will remain the only group that can say what it wants, about anyone it chooses to victimize, and still claim to be a responsible profession, performing an important public service.

As much as Ronald Reagan was the Great Communicator, getting his words before the American people was always an uphill struggle in the press environment described in this chapter. In another age, the press might have been interested in publishing and writing about the great issues raised by Reagan's ideas, and the great debate about the role of government that these ideas provoked. But in an age when the greatest rewards in journalism seemed to go to those who could produce the most sensational stories, this was not to be. Nevertheless, because of Reagan's persistence and conviction, and his willingness to pursue his case relentlessly, day after day, during his eight years in office, some of his message got through. There was indeed a change in the relationship between the American people and their government, and—because of the strong comeback of the U.S. economy when Reagan's ideas were adopted—a recognition in the United States and around the world that the way to achieve growth and prosperity was through freeing the market from excessive government control.

CHAPTER
6

OF LOYALTY, LEAKS, AND THE WHITE HOUSE STAFF

Semper Fidelis
—U.S. MARINE CORPS MOTTO

*We've found that the White
House is the leakiest place I've ever been.*
—RONALD REAGAN, APRIL 9, 1986

On April 1, 1986, Don Regan—who was in California with the President—set up a conference call with the top White House staff. The participants, if not in California, were either in Washington or scattered around the country; the purpose of the call was to assess where we were and develop an agenda for the months ahead.

Things had been going well for the 15 months Regan had been chief of the White House staff, and he began the call with praise for everyone involved in the successes thus far. The President, he said, had weathered a number of difficulties and political controversies—here Regan was probably referring particularly to the Bitburg crisis—and had achieved a great deal of what had been on his domestic policy agenda from the outset of his presidency. The economy was growing strongly, inflation was under control, and tax reform was gaining the credibility and momentum that would see its enactment later that year as the Tax Reform Act of 1986.

Moreover, the President's popularity was at a high point, with a favorable/unfavorable ratio of 62/29 in the Gallup Poll—nearly the highest of his presidency. Regan and the officials whom he had recruited to the White House in January 1985 and thereafter were justified in feeling some sense of achievement for what they had accomplished. The overall goal for the next few months, Regan said, would be to foster continued growth of the economy, move the President's legislative program, and reduce the deficit; the major issues he cited were tax reform, Contra aid, defense procurement reform, Social Security cost of living allowances, catastrophic health insurance, welfare reform, and the upcoming economic summit. He then asked everyone individually for their views and plans, and closed by saying that, based on what he'd heard, he would prepare a list of priorities for the next few months.

On the telephone that day were the President's senior advisers and principal staff, most of whom headed offices within the White House. They included Dennis Thomas, who was in effect the deputy chief of staff, without the title; David Chew, staff secretary; Alfred Kingon, cabinet secretary; Will Ball, assistant to the president for legislative affairs; Larry Speakes, deputy press secretary;* Mitch Daniels, assistant to the president for political affairs; Pat Buchanan, director of communications; Mari Maseng, head of the Office of Public Liaison; Jack Svahn, head of the Domestic Council staff; Bob Tuttle, the President's appointments secretary; and Tom Dawson, Regan's executive assistant. As White House counsel, I was also listening in, although it was one of my first days on the job.

Also on the call were the heads of the principal bureaus and agencies that are part of the Executive Office of the President, including Jim Miller, the director of the Office of Management and Budget (OMB),

---

* After James Brady was shot during the March 1981 assassination attempt on the President, he retained the title as the President's press secretary, even though his wounds made it impossible for him to function in that role during the balance of the Reagan administration; the President's chief press spokesman, accordingly, was the deputy press secretary.

Beryl Sprinkel, the chairman of the Council of Economic Advisers, a representative of the Vice President's office, and Admiral John Poindexter, the President's national security adviser and head of the National Security Council staff. All these offices were regularly represented at the daily operations meeting, the 8:00 A.M. senior staff meeting at which Regan presided and the latest events and plans for the day to come were discussed and decided.

In theory, the White House staff in the Reagan administration should have had a great deal of power. In conformity with his management style, the President delegated extraordinary amounts of authority to his staff, and relied on his staff to set an agenda for action, establish his schedule, formulate and pursue his legislative program, and monitor the policy and program development process as specific initiatives worked their way through the cabinet councils—the principal policy-development vehicles in the Reagan administration.

Paradoxically, however, because of the unique nature of his presidency, as outlined in earlier chapters, Reagan's White House staff had considerably less power than the staffs of Reagan's predecessors and successors. Because Ronald Reagan led through his speeches, and for the most part did not take a direct role in the development of either particular policies and programs or the strategies and tactics associated with getting them enacted into law, the White House staff was not heavily involved in carrying out directions from the President to his cabinet officers or allies in Congress. Moreover, Reagan's desire to reduce the role of government in the economy, to reduce taxes and trade restrictions, and to give the American people confidence in their future did not require that his White House staff or his administration develop and pursue a comprehensive agenda of legislative initiatives.

Accordingly, while the White House staff worked to assure that the President was able to get his message out, and to respond to the day-to-day demands on the White House, it did not attempt to direct or coordinate the activities of the departments and agencies of the Executive Branch the way overall control was exercised in, say, the Nixon, Ford, or Carter administrations. In general, the cabinet departments were left free—within the policy framework outlined by Reagan in his philosophy and his speeches—to develop their own policy and programmatic initiatives.

Indeed, the Reagan administration was as close to real cabinet government on domestic policy as any administration in the modern era. Although many presidents have talked about instituting cabinet government, few have ever done so. After the first few cabinet meetings, presidents realize that cabinet members usually represent the institutional positions of their departments, and understand little about the broader political considerations that are the president's principal concern. Unlike cabinet members in parliamentary systems, the heads of the major departments in the U.S. Government are generally not chosen from among politicians, and don't represent political constituencies. As a result, their advice on political questions—the key questions for a president trying to balance a number of competing demands—is often not very useful to the president. Full cabinet meetings then become rare events, staged more often as morale-building exercises and media events than for truly substantive purposes.

Once again, however, because the Reagan presidency was so different from other presidencies, it opened the prospect for greater cabinet involvement in policy and program development. With the President's philosophy as a unifying theme, the cabinet departments could—at least in theory—develop policies and programs that were consistent with the President's policy objectives. The cabinet council system, instituted at the outset of the administration, seems to have been developed with exactly this goal in mind. The cabinet councils, made up principally of the cabinet-level departments and agencies in the Reagan administration, were divided during Reagan's first term into subject areas such as economics, trade, domestic policy, and energy and the environment—with departments and agencies participating only in those councils where their particular jurisdiction or expertise was implicated. When a consensus was achieved, or a set of options developed for the President, the cabinet council would meet with the President and solicit his approval. In the second term, after most of the President's major domestic initiatives had been achieved, Regan reduced the significance of the cabinet councils by merging all of them into two larger and more diffuse groups, but they still functioned as policy and program development vehicles.

Although cabinet government—where the president's program reflects the objectives of the major departments of his administration—is an attractive idea to some, it has significant deficiencies. The most important of these is the randomness with which initiatives for the administration are developed. The motivating factor is not the president's political needs—the desire to keep ahead of the press and to be seen as working in the interests of the American people—but the far less important and pressing needs of the departments and agencies for changes in policies and law. Although it is not politically prudent for a president to leave his legacy in the hands of so inherently passive a process as this, that is where the policy development initiative rested in the second Reagan administration.

It is not clear whether the April 1 conference call—in which Regan sought suggestions for policy initiatives from the White House staff—was an effort to retake the initiative in domestic policy development, but if so it was not likely to succeed. By the second Reagan administration, the White House Domestic Council staff—which had been designed and developed in the Nixon administration as an institutional domestic policy staff for the president—had atrophied into a small group that mostly shepherded and commented on cabinet council proposals. In a sense, this continued a trend that had begun after Nixon left office, but the strong desire of the Reagan administration to make a reality of cabinet government had accelerated the decline of the Domestic Council staff as the president's own instrument for designing and developing policy. Indeed, the White House staff that Don Regan directed was largely concerned with process—communications, legislative strategy, getting papers to the President in an orderly way, and keeping tabs on what was going on in the cabinet departments and in the cabinet councils.

As a result, there were few new policy initiatives in the second Reagan term, even allowing for the disruption caused by Iran-Contra. Indeed, it might have been easier for him to make his way through the

Iran-Contra minefield if he had had some important domestic initiatives to take to the country. Don Regan might have changed this with an active program of recruitment and staff enhancement, and I among others recommended frequently that he do this, but it is not clear in retrospect that it would have resulted in significant new domestic policy initiatives. By his second term, Ronald Reagan had largely achieved his principal domestic policy objectives; his focus now was on foreign policy, and particularly arms control and reduction. The task now on domestic policy was to play defense, to protect and institutionalize what had already been accomplished. The President himself would have had little enthusiasm for new initiatives—although, as was his pattern, he would have endorsed those initiatives developed at the cabinet or White House staff level. Without the President's enthusiastic support, however, there was little impetus for Regan to embark on significant enlargement of the domestic policy staff.

On a practical political level, the absence of a strong policy group in the White House can also have significant adverse effects on the quality of a president's response to legislative initiatives, and even the quality of the political advice he receives. Legislative strategy, and advice to the president about legislation he is required to sign or veto, depends on a fairly thorough understanding of what is in the bills Congress is moving toward the president's desk. Although cabinet departments and OMB keep watch on legislation that has an impact on their operations or their budgets, their institutional interests frequently distort their advice to the president. Cabinet departments have stakes in legislation that reflect side deals with lawmakers unknown to the White House, and even OMB has an outlook on budget and management questions that can color its advice.

The difference between the institutional views of the cabinet departments and the president's own political interests is a matter seldom discussed by students of government, but can be a substantial problem for a president. His decisions have to be based on rather broad political considerations, and sometimes he may not realize that the advice he is getting from his cabinet officers reflects the institutional views of their departments and agencies rather than his political interests. For this reason alone it is important for the president to have a strong domestic policy staff, even if he prefers to rely on his cabinet departments for most of his policy initiatives. The Reagan White House, at least in the second Reagan term, was very weak in this area, and hence vulnerable to the institutional interests of cabinet departments.[1] That's why a president needs his own domestic policy staff just as he has his own national security staff and his own counsel. This was one of the reasons for the establishment of the Domestic Council staff in the Nixon administration. In its zeal to effectuate cabinet government as fully as possible, those who designed the structure of the Reagan administration lost sight of this fact, and thus reduced the quality of the advice on legislation that the President needed.

At the time Don Regan convened the April 1 conference call, none of these problems were of major concern. The Reagan White House was functioning as smoothly as it had ever operated during the President's six years in office, and for this Don Regan deserved much of the credit.* Moreover, during Regan's tenure, the President achieved a complete overhaul and reform of the U.S. tax system, began a series of discussions with Mikhail Gorbachev that led to major disarmament agreements, and reached the highest levels of popularity in his presidency. From January 1986 until just before the Iran arms sales became public, the President's approval ratings averaged 63 percent in the Gallup Poll, ranging from a low of 61 percent to a high of 68 percent in the 11 samples taken through November 1986.

Less than four months later, however, Regan was virtually chased from his White House office, after delivering a resignation letter to the President that consisted of a single terse sentence. He had learned through CNN only moments before that he would be unceremoniously replaced as chief of staff by Howard Baker, and only a few days earlier the *Washington Post* had said in an editorial that he was "arguably the worst White House chief of staff ever." How this happened to Don

---

* At just this time, in fact, the President joked at the annual White House correspondents dinner, "You know, I do follow what you write. One of you recently wrote a piece questioning why things seem to be going so well for me lately. Well, it's just a case of letting Reagan be Regan."

Regan is a tale rich with the hazards of holding a high position in Washington—especially on the White House staff—then and now.

The pressures on the White House staff are many, but the most direct and continuous is pressure from the press for inside or leaked information. As noted in the previous chapter, some reporters can be so aggressive in seeking "inside" stories that they threaten members of the White House staff with unfavorable coverage if they don't cooperate. Usually, however, the press confines its efforts to rewarding the cooperative rather than punishing the uncooperative. This creates something of a conflict of interest for the White House staff, since the rewards offered by the press can be significant in Washington.

If a member of the White House staff is a consistent anonymous source, he or she will often receive favorable attention in the press. There will be admiring stories in the Style section of the *Washington Post* and favorable references to the competence and sagacity of the staffer in news stories. Indeed, a careful reader of the *Washington Post* and *New York Times* should be able to figure out who is a good inside source—and who is not—by the way the press describes the people around the president.

"Tips and leaks," writes Larry Sabato, "are the chief currency of investigative journalism, and most frenzies could not be sustained without them. All skilled journalists cultivate sources, and most recognize the dangers inherent in the undertaking, such as 'sweetheart' arrangements whereby a frequent tipster (perhaps a political consultant) is immune from critical coverage or guaranteed an enviable quota of kudos in print."[2]

A good illustration of this process is the following item, which appeared in the *New York Times* late in 1986, and from which I have removed the names of the subject and other possibly identifying material:

> In what some Washington observers see as a setback to [a high-level official] at a time when he needs a smartly functioning and politically savvy staff to run the store . . . a key aide . . . has decided to leave.
>
> Although [he] keeps a generally low profile, he is credited with being one of [the official's] most astute and able aides. White House

insiders say it was [the aide] who was largely responsible for [the official's recent success].

The piece goes on in this vein for several more paragraphs, extolling
the virtues of the aide as he was about to enter the private sector. There
are several things to note about this article. There are no names supporting any of the statements, which are attributed to "some Washington observers" and "White House insiders." One would have supposed that
since the subject of the article was so good at his job, and was to be so
missed by his boss, the reporters could have found someone—maybe
even the grateful boss—who would attach his or her name to this praise.
The second oddity is that the praise is so unalloyed—"smart," "savvy,"
"low profile," "astute," and "able" are the words used in just the first two
short paragraphs—a stark difference from the usual give/take coverage in
which the departing aide's failures are cited along with his or her good
works. The piece seems more like product advertising than journalism,
and while it is not certain that the departing staffer was in fact the source
of leaks, the *Times* article has all the appearances of a classic case.

Thus arises the conflict of interest for the White House staff, between
their loyalty to the president and the opportunity for self-advancement
in Washington. Considering the amount of attention paid to the White
House by the press, a reputation burnished by favorable press references
can have significant tangible and intangible value. One's stock in Washington rises. Good sources, or those who are perceived because of favorable
press notices to have power, get invited to the dinner parties, the openings,
the press club speeches, and the like. People solicit their advice, and provide pieces of information that are useful in their jobs and in social relationships. Perhaps more important, when they leave government, the
celebrity status they have achieved often leads to lucrative board member-
ships, high positions in significant educational or cultural institutions, and
high-paying private-sector jobs. Thus, by compromising the president's
interests a bit, one can do quite well on the Washington scene, and in the
world at large later on. Perhaps most important, when problems arise, the
good sources get the benefit of the doubt, and sometimes much more.

The result is that leaks to the press are endemic at the White House. Indeed, the day after Don Regan's April 1 conference call with the White House staff, the *New York Times* carried a fairly detailed account of what was said. New to the staff, I was appalled that someone on that call—all of whom were the top staff to the President—would disclose its details to a reporter, and amazed that anything could be accomplished in such an environment. Clearly, press access to what is happening at the top levels of government can be important and valuable in a democracy. But premature or distorted disclosure can also interfere with the development of policies and programs, or the planning of future efforts. Apart from their assistance to the president's political opponents, leaks in advance of a policy or program announcement also prevent the president from achieving the important element of surprise. For example, if the president is developing a new energy policy initiative, the disclosure in advance that a new policy is under consideration immediately sets off speculation about what the program will or should contain. By the time the new program is formally announced, half the public will think it's too limited and the other half will think it goes too far. The initial press coverage, accordingly, is likely to be about the program's deficiencies as seen from these varying perspectives rather than what the president was trying to achieve.

In a very real sense, politics is about whose ox gets gored—who wins and who loses when the president makes policy choices—and thus there is virtually no decision by the president for which there is not a vigilant and well-informed opposition ready to act in defense of its position. Accordingly, when disclosure reveals to political opponents where the White House will place its priorities over the next few months, it enables them to marshal their own forces. When disclosure identifies specific programs in the planning stage or specific individuals as proponents of particular positions, it enables opponents to focus their fire or to plan their opposition more effectively. At the working level, the results of press leaks are decidedly adverse. The fear of leaks generally means meetings are smaller, fewer views are considered, there is less candor in the room, and people who should be working together tend to distrust one another.

The effect of leaks on communication among the staff is illustrated by my experience with the Deaver matter—in which Mike Deaver was accused of violating the government ethics laws. At one point in the controversy over Deaver's post–White House activities, I mentioned at the daily operations meeting that the FBI was broadening its investigation of Deaver to cover five additional accusations, and I would shortly be sending out a memo advising the staff to search their files for the documentation the FBI would be seeking. Obviously, this information was necessary for those in the room, who included the top White House staff and representatives of the major White House offices, such as the Vice President's office, the Office of Management and Budget, the National Security Council, and the Council of Economic Advisers—all organizations that Deaver might have contacted if the accusations were true. That afternoon, to my surprise, I received a call from a *Washington Post* reporter, who wanted to know what was in the memorandum I was planning to send. In other words, someone in the room—one of the President's top staff—felt free to disclose to the press the fact that the FBI was investigating new charges against Deaver, even though this might have compromised the investigation. After this experience, I limited my discussion of sensitive issues in the daily operations meeting, and thus reduced the useful information my colleagues received. Since others undoubtedly did the same, the value of this daily meeting of the White House senior staff was inevitably reduced.

Thus, leaks to the press—events about which the general public is only vaguely aware, and probably does not even recognize as out of the ordinary—have a significant impact on the functioning of the White House. Not only do they aid the president's opponents and reduce the amount of communication and consultation within the staff, but they divert the staff from what they might otherwise be doing to advance the president's agenda. Leaks, because they generally contain information that is controversial or inimical to the president's interests, require immediate response. They sent the staff off to do repair work, to get the facts, to decide on how to respond. In these diversions, as explained in the previous chapter, the White House is following the press's agenda and not the president's.

To my surprise, I found during my time on the White House staff
that these unauthorized disclosures were the dominant outside influence
on how—or indeed whether—the White House staff could perform its
regular daily functions. As Vice President Rockefeller's counsel during
the Ford administration, I had attended senior staff meetings as the Vice
President's representative; there were occasional leaks from those meetings, but nothing like what was happening in the Reagan White House.

Leaks also prevent candor in advising the president, potentially reducing the quality of his decisions. Certainly, members of the president's cabinet should feel free to provide him with their views without
fear of public criticism. That indeed is the rationale for executive privilege—a concept the courts have read into the separation of powers in
order to assure insofar as possible that the president can receive the candid advice of his advisers. But in an environment where leaks are common, the protection afforded by executive privilege is significantly reduced, and those who express dissenting or unpopular views of various
kinds are subject to exactly the kind of candor-suppressing criticism
that executive privilege was intended to prevent.

The debate over drug testing for federal employees was a good example of this. As the Cabinet Council on Domestic Policy moved toward
the final decision memorandum for the President, a major question was
how extensive would be the testing program proposed for current government employees. There was a good deal of pressure from the Justice Department and members of the White House drug policy staff for a tough
and far-reaching program, and some opposition from cabinet members
and others, including myself, who were concerned about constitutional
and privacy questions. Although these were all legitimate concerns, those
who favored extensive testing were often said to be hostile to federal employees, and those who opposed an invasive program were criticized as
soft on drug abuse. In a community dominated by federal employees, accordingly, entering either side of this debate was fraught with hazards. At
the end of a very contentious meeting, Ed Meese and Larry Speakes im-
plored those present to keep the substance of the discussion within the
room, so that the views of the participants on either side would not be

spread across the press. However, within an hour of the meeting's end, the press office notified me that the *New York Times* had a fairly complete report of the positions of the principal participants.

An even more troubling and ironic case than the leaks from a cabinet council meeting or staff conference call occurred shortly after I joined the White House staff. In a series of instances in the spring of 1986, national security classified information found its way into the press, and the leaks were considered serious enough to warrant a meeting with the President in the secure NSC conference room known as the Situation Room to discuss a response. There was an extended debate about how to find the sources, including the possibility of setting up a special FBI group to pursue suspected sources immediately after a disclosure occurred. But even the establishment of an interagency study group on this question was leaked, and the administration had to beat a hasty retreat from what was characterized as another Nixon plumbers operation. It would have been amusing if it weren't so sad. The only reasonably effective mechanism was to establish a "need to know" system among the staff and the cabinet, where the only people invited to meetings were those who absolutely had to be there. And this is no way to run a government. The President himself noted the need to know strategy: "We've found that the White House is the leakiest place I've ever been," he told the press in April 1986, discussing the rescue of U.S. students in Grenada, "So, you'd be surprised how few people know that we were planning that operation."

The fear of leaks also interferes with the process of consultation and disclosure between the White House and Congress. An example is the strenuous effort to prevent leaks associated with the bombing of Libya in April 1986, where there was concern that a leak might jeopardize the mission or the lives of the airmen involved. Under the War Powers Resolution, passed by Congress over a presidential veto during the Nixon administration, the president is required to consult with Congress before placing U.S. troops in jeopardy. Although the Executive Branch challenges the constitutionality of the act, it attempts to act "consistently with" the act rather than in compliance, and thus makes some effort to consult with Congress when the act would require it.

In order to avoid the possibility of leaks in connection with the attack on Libya, a bizarre arrangement was conceived in which key leaders of Congress were brought to the White House to participate in a briefing about the Libya raid while the bombers were actually in the air on their way to Libya. Thus, the "consultation" contemplated by the War Powers Resolution occurred in a literal sense, but at so late a stage that the congressional leaders were not really in a position to offer any advice. In fact, the briefing did not actually end until the bombing had begun, and there is some reason to believe that this timing—which prevented any contact between the congressional leaders and the press until the Libyans actually knew they were under attack—was deliberate. Unfortunately, in light of the leaks that were routinely occurring at the time, this White House stratagem seemed fully justified when American lives were at risk.

Another example of a successful effort to avoid leaks was the process, in June 1986, through which the President selected a new chief justice and a new associate justice of the Supreme Court. It began with a visit to Reagan by Warren Burger, then the chief justice, in late May. Burger told the President that he intended to retire. He wanted to devote more time than his current role permitted to the Commission on the Bicentennial of the Constitution, of which he was the chair, and he thought this was a good time—before the 1986 elections—to get his successor in place. The next day, we began the process of assisting the President with the selection of a nominee for chief justice.

It was the President's hope to do the necessary vetting and make the selections before the vacancy at the Court became known. There were several reasons for this. Once the fact of a Supreme Court vacancy was disclosed, the speculation and pressures on the President would be enormous. Groups for and against particular candidates would mobilize, and the usual semi-hysterical concerns from single-issue groups would crowd out any reasoned discussion in the press. In addition, during the frenzy that would ensue, much of the other business of government would be lost in the noise. The President wanted Supreme Court justices who believed in judicial restraint and strict construction of the

Constitution—a philosophy in which the courts do not substitute its own judgment for that of the elected branches of government—and was going to choose from a relatively small group of federal appellate court judges, all of whom had longstanding records with which to assess their judicial philosophies. A long and contentious public debate about potential candidates would not throw much light on this question. The most likely outcome would be to lengthen the time that opponents would have to organize opposition among their constituencies, in the media, and in the Senate. Accordingly, we decided to limit as much as possible the number of White House and administration officials who knew about the Supreme Court vacancy.

Nevertheless, it was clearly necessary to bring in the Attorney General, and on May 29, in an Oval Office meeting, Ed Meese was briefed on what had transpired in the meeting between the President and Burger. We discussed some potential candidates, one of whom was clearly Associate Justice William Rehnquist, and there was further discussion of potential candidates for associate justice if Rehnquist became chief justice. When Judge Antonin Scalia's name was mentioned in this context, the President was quite interested, and asked whether Scalia—who was then a judge on the federal Court of Appeals for the District of Columbia Circuit—was of Italian ancestry. I said that he was. Clearly, Reagan wanted to be the first president to nominate an Italian-American to the Supreme Court, but there was a lot of vetting that had to be done before we reached that point.

The vetting of potential candidates was initially begun at the Justice Department. However, when I found that the Justice lawyers were slow in sharing their views, I asked two members of my staff—Chris Cox and Alan Raul—to take over the task. This they did quickly and discreetly, providing me with valuable assessments that went to the President before he made his selections.

Indeed, I was fortunate to have recruited all nine lawyers who made up the White House counsel's staff during my tenure. They were among the finest lawyers with whom I've ever had the privilege to work, and I doubt that the White House counsel's office has ever been staffed, before or since, with a group of such consistent quality. The office was organized

along functional lines, and each lawyer had a number of areas of special-
ization and various White House offices to advise as clients. Jay Stephens,
my deputy, worked directly with me on all matters I was handling, and
was also in charge of liaison with the Justice Department. Jay is now the
general counsel of Raytheon Corporation, having been a U.S. Attorney
and Associate Attorney General of the United States. Chris Cox, who was
senior associate counsel and is now a congressman from California and a
leader of the House Republicans, generally handled foreign policy and
constitutional matters; Alan Raul, now a partner of a major international
law firm in Washington, handled litigation issues and questions about
election law and presidential travel; Dean McGrath, who is now deputy
chief of staff to Vice President Cheney, was the specialist in defense issues;
Mike Shepherd, now general counsel to the Bank of New York, was the
specialist in executive privilege issues and financial regulatory matters;
Arnold Intrater, now counsel to the chairman of the Federal Housing Fi-
nance Board, handled administrative and personnel questions and advised the White House Office of Administration; Bob Kruger, who is
now the general counsel of the Business Software Alliance, was a utility
fielder of constitutional issues, among others (we all joked, after the drug
testing issue arose, that Bob was our "fluids" man); Peter Keisler, now a
partner of an international law firm in Washington, handled budget issues among many others; and Vicki O'Meara, Executive Vice President
and General Counsel of Ryder System, Inc., was our expert in environ-
mental matters, among other specialties. Because of the tremendous
workload in clearing officials for appointment to administration offices,
all of the lawyers handled ethics issues and the vetting of nominees for
presidentially appointed positions. The office would not have run as
smoothly as it did without the extraordinary organizational skills of Dianna Holland, my executive assistant, and our two amazing secretaries,
Charlene Zerkle and Nancy Scott-Finan.

After a couple of weeks of staff work at both the White House and
the Justice Department, the President decided that he'd like to meet with
Rehnquist and Scalia. If Rehnquist did not want the Chief's job, I think
the President would have nominated Scalia for that position. In any

event, the President wanted to see them both, and that presented some logistical problems in light of the effort to maintain the secrecy of the project. How would we get these two into the White House to see the President without their being spotted by the White House press corps? It's one thing for the Chief Justice to visit the President; he had a position that would make a meeting natural, if unusual. But if Justice Rehnquist or Judge Scalia were seen, the press would have known something was up, and that would have been the end of the leak-free vetting process. A good reporter can usually find a source if he or she knows that there are questions to be asked. The key to our success this far had been the fact that none of the White House correspondents had any hint that a Supreme Court resignation was in the offing. Fortunately, both Rehnquist and Scalia, on separate days, were brought in to see the President without waking the sleeping watchdogs in the press room.

By June 17, the President was ready to make the announcement. He would nominate Rehnquist for chief justice and Scalia to replace Rehnquist as an associate justice. Still, no one outside the small group at the White House and the Justice Department who had been working on this matter knew that the Chief Justice was planning to retire. The announcement was scheduled for 2 P.M. in the White House press room. At about 11:45 A.M., Regan called the top staff together in his office—Larry Speakes; Pat Buchanan; Dennis Thomas; David Chew; Will Ball, the President's assistant for congressional relations; Tom Dawson; and myself. I was delighted that no one except Regan, Dawson, and I knew that in about two hours the President would make one of the most important announcements of his presidency, but somewhat concerned that I'd had to keep this information from my colleagues for almost a month. However, no one seemed to mind, and someone noted that this was the first time he could ever remember the President making an important announcement that had not been leaked to the press in advance.

But there were still two hours to go, and now the press would have to be alerted. Speakes was going to issue an advisory that there would be a special announcement by the President at 2 P.M. Regan asked all those present to maintain confidentiality until that time. As soon as this notice went out, all the phones in the White House lit up, as reporters tried to learn from their sources what this announcement was going to be about. Fortunately, most of these sources did not know either—and couldn't even speculate—so the usual dynamic that produced leaks was not in operation.

At 2 P.M., with the press assembled and speculating madly, the President, followed by Burger, Rehnquist, and Scalia, entered the press room. There was an audible gasp when the three jurists appeared. The President made a brief statement, and turned the podium over to Burger, who explained what would happen next and answered the barrage of questions. When Burger was finished, I briefed the press on how the selection process had worked. Most of the reporters knew what Rehnquist's views were, but Scalia was a bit of a mystery. Of course, the principal question was whether Scalia would support *Roe v. Wade*, the Supreme Court decision that established the right to abortion and, if not, what would happen to the Court's position on this issue. (One reporter, approaching the issue as gingerly as possible, asked me what would be the complexion of the Court after Scalia was confirmed. "Ruddier," I said.)

These examples demonstrate that it is possible, although very difficult, to avoid leaks—even about vitally important matters. Two things appear to be required: discussions must be kept within a small group, and the press must not know that there are questions to be asked. Unfortunately, if these two rules are not observed—and of course neither is infallible—it is not possible to avoid damaging leaks. The siren song of the press—the personal advancement they can offer individual members of the White House staff—is simply too appealing to those who have a weak sense of loyalty to the president.

While cooperation with the press can bring good things to a White House staff member, lack of cooperation can bring the reverse. If a high official is not particularly cooperative, when the hard rain falls there is no cover. This, ultimately, was Don Regan's problem. When Regan wrote his book about his time as White House chief of staff, it contained no quotes from the President. Regan generally took careful and thorough notes in meetings with the President—so in many cases he had the quotes—but because of his respect for the presidency and the discretion required by his own role as chief of staff he would not quote the President directly. This says a great deal about Regan. He lived by a code, and—as an ex-marine—at the top of this code was loyalty. All through the Iran-Contra matter, he was blamed for problems that he did not create and could not resolve. The press carried leaks from the Hill, from the Tower Board, and from other current or former "insiders," accusing Regan of everything from incompetence to carrying on a cover-up, yet he never defended himself with anonymous source stories. Those stories, which were common from the offices of chiefs of staff before and after him, improved the reputations of the leakers but inevitably diminished the President's. To Regan, this would have been disloyalty; it would have violated the code.

There are many examples of Regan's loyalty, but one sticks out in my mind. As noted in earlier chapters, once Ronald Reagan was convinced he was right, he was difficult if not impossible to move. And in the Iran-Contra matter he believed he had made the correct decision to seek an opening to Iran, even though it involved arms sales. Accordingly, although the President could have ended much of the Iran-Contra controversy—as President Kennedy had done with the Bay of Pigs fiasco in Cuba—simply by admitting he'd made a mistake, he refused to do so. The American people do not expect the president to be flawless. They understand and readily forgive occasional mistakes. What they won't forgive is being treated like children, or being lied to, or—just as bad—being asked to accept as true an incredible story. As it developed, the American people just would not believe that Ronald Reagan had not traded arms for hostages, and the more he insisted that he had not done so, the angrier and more resentful they became. It was thus very much in Reagan's interests for him to say he'd made a mistake, and those who counseled him to do so were doing him a favor.

Of those who pressed the President to say he'd made a mistake, Regan was probably the most persistent. On one occasion, when the President's Saturday radio address was being prepared, and the subject was the Iran-Contra matter, Regan had a sentence in which the President said he'd made a mistake inserted in the draft. The President, however, struck out the line; he'd agree to say that "mistakes were made," but re-fused to say that he'd made them. Dennis Thomas later told me that Regan "had fallen on his sword" in an effort to get the President to change his mind on this question.

Needless to say, it would have done wonders for Don Regan's repu-tation—and might have saved his job—if the press had reported that he was counseling the President to admit he'd made a mistake. Not only would Regan have shown that he had some political savvy—or at least understood what the press wanted—but he would also have provided some of the much sought-after evidence that the President was the source of his own troubles. Regan undoubtedly knew this, but loyalty apparently prevented him from saying it, even on terms in which his name would not be disclosed. After all, while this would improve Re-gan's image, it would cast the President in an unfavorable light. Rather than run for cover, Regan went on the record to defend the policy that was then under fire. In an article in the *Washington Post* of November 22, 1986, Regan—referring to the President's decision to reach out to Iran through the arms sales—was quoted as saying: "Should we have done it? . . . In retrospect, yes. We were able to build on a relationship that Nixon set up with mainland China; someday perhaps some presi-dent will build on that relationship we've started with Iran." By going on the record to defend the President's policy, Regan confirmed in the minds of the pundits and Republican leaders that he was politically tone deaf, and thus incapable of helping the President out of his Iran-Contra predicament.

Contrast this with the leaks of the White House insiders in 1982, who were not just telling the President he should raise taxes, they were also telling the press what they were telling the President. There were per-sistent anonymously sourced stories out of the White House to the effect that the President was just not listening to reason on this subject. Those of us who were Treasury officials at the time never knew who was respon-sible for these reports—which painted the President as stubborn and be-nighted—but we had our suspicions. We now know from David Stock-man's book that virtually the entire senior White House staff was in on the effort to get the President to agree to reverse his economic course. As Richard Neustadt would have noted, stories like this ultimately weaken the president's ability to accomplish his objectives by reducing the respect with which he is held within the Washington community and among the American people. Although it might be argued that those who wanted the President to change his views were justified in communicating with him through press leaks rather than directly, these disclosures fed the press perception that Ronald Reagan was out of touch with economic reality and weakened his position with the American people and in Congress. From April through December 1982, while the press was reporting "inside" stories about Reagan's alleged economic illiteracy, public approval of how the President was conducting his office never exceeded 45 percent in the Gallup Poll, and was always lower than his disapproval level. Stories like this are not a way to improve the president's chances of success, but they do wonders for the reputations of those who are providing this information to the press.

The cost to Regan of defending the President on Iran-Contra was severe. Of course, acting as the president's chief of staff is bound to be a high-wire act, and part of the job is taking the blame that people don't want to lay on the president himself. But even allowing for this, Don Regan was probably the most unfairly maligned person ever to hold the position. According to a later White House press summary, there were stories that Regan had participated in a cover-up of the President's role in the Iran arms sales in the *Washington Post* on January 31, February 13, and February 22, 1987; in the *Los Angeles Times* on February 21; in *USA Today* on February 23; in the *New York Times* on February 23; and in the *Newsweek* edition of March 2. In addition, there were stories that Regan manipulated the President's testimony to the Tower Board in the *Washington Post* on February 19, *USA Today* on February 20, the *Los Angeles Times* on February 20, and the *Time* edition of March 2. Finally, stories that Regan was concerned about himself and not the President appeared in the *Los Angeles Times* on February 20, the *Washington Post* on December 5, 1986, and February 22, 1987, on the United Press International wire on February 23, and in the *Wall Street Journal* on February 23.

As one who was there at the time, I can say that all of these stories were false. From the beginning, Regan urged the President to disclose all the facts; he was not responsible for the President's change of testimony to the Tower Board, and certainly had no interest in getting the President to do so; and—as shown by Regan's on-the-record support of the President while he was urging that the President admit a mistake—the only fair view of Regan was that he held the President's interests above his own.

To the press, however, Regan could do no right. He was criticized for not managing the Bitburg controversy effectively, although it was the President's desire to keep his promise to Helmut Kohl that made the problem intractable.[3] Then he was criticized for creating a huge public relations offensive after the collapse of the arms-reduction talks in Reykjavik, even though that offensive turned the public's perception of the incident from a policy failure to a political success.[4] He was criticized by conservatives for being insufficiently ideological, and by others for actually "letting Reagan be Reagan." Finally, when the Iran-Contra crisis erupted, he was criticized for not managing it effectively, although—like Bitburg—the crisis was probably prolonged by the President's firmly held conviction that he had not made a mistake in authorizing the arms sales and would not say that he had.

This is not to criticize the President. As noted above, his steadfastness in support of his convictions enabled him to stay the course on an economic policy that ultimately changed the direction of the United States and the world. He was entitled to be stubborn where he thought he was right, and in most cases he was. But I do mean to praise Regan for never abandoning the President when it was very much in his interests to do so. When the lowest point of Ronald Reagan's presidency came during the Iran-Contra affair, the President was fortunate to have had a chief of staff who willingly took the heat.

Before I became general counsel of the Treasury in 1981, I had never met Don Regan—other than in a short interview many months earlier. He had a reputation in New York and on Wall Street as a maverick, and indeed he had been largely responsible—as the chief executive of Merrill Lynch—for the elimination of the treasured system of fixed brokerage commissions in the securities markets. This was a major step, which ulti-mately had the effect of bringing more traders into the market, increas-ing liquidity, and stimulating the explosive growth of share values that almost half of all Americans enjoyed during the last quarter of the twen-tieth century. He also had a reputation for toughness, a quick temper, a demanding nature, and impatience with mistakes by his subordinates.

Those of us who worked with Regan when he was secretary of the treasury between 1981 and 1985 have nothing but praise for his qualities as an executive and as a person. The nonpolitical civil servants at Treasury remember the Regan period as a kind of golden age, when morale was high and there was a sense of community and élan. This was in part a re-sult of the unification of purpose created by the President's philosophy, but part was also Regan's doing. He was the kind of executive who brought his subordinates into his thinking, who gave them responsibility, and re-warded them with recognition and—even more important in Washing-ton—access to him and to the other important figures in the government. Just about every morning that he was in town, Regan held a staff meeting attended by all the Treasury officials at the assistant-secretary level and above. These meetings were good examples of Regan's management and leadership style. Everyone had a chance to talk, and there was plenty of hu-mor. The information shared among all of us was passed down to our staffs in most cases, and made everyone feel a part of the administration.

Thus, when Regan polled the White House staff during the April 1 conference call about their plans and thoughts for the coming months, he seemed to be following the same inclusive process he had followed as treasury secretary. The imperious, arrogant Regan was not in evidence, nor did I ever see it during the time we served together in the White House. Regan had a temper, to be sure, but it was the kind that flashed for a moment, and then was gone. An Irish friend once told me a joke about an illness called Irish Alzheimer's: the victim remembers nothing but the grudge. Regan, although Irish, did not have this disease. There must have been times when he was disappointed with staff work the rest of us produced, but he never let that carry over to later events. This, plus his inclusiveness, inspired strong loyalty among those who were at the Treasury during those years, and we all still get together with him and his wonderful, outspoken wife, Ann, in biennial reunions.

This Don Regan was not the person portrayed in the press when he was White House chief of staff. There are exceptions, of course, but in general the White House press tends to accept and propagate stereotypes. In *Feeding Frenzy,* Larry Sabato describes this phenomenon as "subtext." The press concludes, with little evidence and a good deal of elitist prejudice, that they know all they need to know about an official, and from that point on they search for and publicize all examples that tend to validate this picture.[5] Any observer of politics is familiar with this process: President Ford was said to be physically clumsy, so pictures of his falling, even on the ski slopes, were eagerly sought; Vice President Dan Quayle was thought to be rich and shallow, so he was referred to as J. Danforth Quayle to emphasize his patrician origins, and when he misspelled "potato" during a school visit the incident was widely and gleefully publicized; most recently, George W. Bush was regarded by the press as a lightweight and a dummy, so his slips of the tongue and misuse or mispronunciation of words became a prominent element of the coverage he received during the 2000 campaign. The false idea that Ronald Reagan was intellectually challenged and merely a performer for his staff is another example of subtext in the Sabato sense, and one of the reasons for this book.

Regan—a former marine, a wealthy former Wall Street boss with a reputation for toughness—was bound to be stereotyped by the press as imperious, arrogant, and self-aggrandizing. That's what rich CEOs are like, right? And sure enough, that was the book on Regan. Thus, shortly after I arrived at the White House, I heard Leslie Stahl of CBS—who had been covering Regan for about a year and a half—tell a national television audience that Regan insisted that the White House staff call him "Chief." I'm sure she believed this—the same false story had earlier appeared in the *Washington Post*—but she couldn't have checked it with anyone either. The senior staff at the White House called him Don, as had the staff at Treasury.

One of the most pervasive press stories about Regan was that he controlled everything that happened in the White House, and insisted on loyalty to him rather than to the President.[6] To be sure, many on the White House staff reported to the President through Regan, but officials like the President's national security adviser, the director of OMB, and the chairman of the Council of Economic Advisers, were completely independent of Regan and relied on him principally for scheduling time with the President. Those who were assistants to the President technically held the same rank as Regan and also owed their loyalty to the President. Although this did not happen often, where Regan's interests and the President's diverged, the President's interests were those the staff kept uppermost in mind. During the Iran-Contra crisis, for example, Regan complained from time to time that no one was defending him—implicitly that I and other members of the staff were not speaking up for him in dealing with the press. He was right about this. Despite the fact that we all knew that Regan was pressing the President to say that he had made a mistake in selling arms to Iran, no one told the press, even though that would have helped Regan establish greater political credibility with the Washington community. The White House staff, including those closest to Regan, never revealed this effort because to report it would have diminished the President. In his heart of hearts, Regan understood this; he couldn't bring himself to do it either. But this was a demonstration of a fact of life in every administration: the senior White House staff owes its loyalty to the president, and not to the chief of staff.

A particularly dramatic example of this was the report that Mitch Daniels gave Regan in late November 1986, after the full scope of the Iran-Contra scandal had taken hold. Daniels, on his own, as an assistant to the President and White House political director, had polled Republican Party officials all over the country and found them unanimously in favor of ousting Regan as the President's chief of staff. If Daniels had been working for Regan he would not have conducted the poll, since its likely outcome was clear, and if he feared retaliation from Regan he would not have reported the results to Regan or to the President.

With the advent of the Iran-Contra crisis, the limits of Regan's authority became clear, especially with respect to the President's national security adviser, Vice Admiral John Poindexter, who was also head of the National Security Council staff. From the beginning of Poindexter's tenure, it had been agreed that he would have the same access to the President as his predecessor, Robert McFarlane. This meant that he reported to the President and not the chief of staff, and could see the President whenever he wanted. In practice and as a matter of courtesy, Poindexter would ask Regan for time on the President's schedule, but he had no obligation to do so.

When, as White House counsel, I first began looking into the legal issues associated with the Iran arms sales matter, I did so at Regan's request. Poindexter, however, refused to give me any information, and I went back to Regan to see if he could get Poindexter's cooperation. Regan later reported, after a discussion with Poindexter and the President, that he could not get Poindexter to provide any of the information I required, and told me to try to gather this information from whatever other sources I could assemble. Obviously, if Regan had some authority over Poindexter, this would not have occurred, but he did not.

Regan's problems with the press were only one element of his difficulties. The job of chief of staff to the president is too much for one person to do alone. There is simply not enough time in any day for one person to sit in on meetings with the president, handle the president's calendar and travel schedule, develop and implement a legislative strategy, manage press relations, mediate cabinet squabbles, attend to the First Lady's priorities, field calls from and hold meetings with House members, senators, and cabinet members, and address the myriad problems that arise with actual and potential nominees to administration or judicial offices. In addition, in the Reagan White House, the list was even longer, since the President delegated a substantial amount of authority to his staff and preferred to lead the nation through speeches rather than direct involvement with Congress. So the chief of staff, and those involved in the legislative process, as also required to cut the deals on the Hill that were necessary to move legislation.

Nevertheless, while Regan held this extraordinary portfolio of delegated authority, he was loyal to the presidency as well as the President.

By this I mean that despite all the decision-making power delegated to him by the President, Regan never suggested in my presence that he was the ultimate authority on any issue. When a decision was made or an agreement reached, Regan would call the President, brief him, and get his assent, despite the fact that Regan could have treated the general delegation of authority he had explicitly or implicitly received from the President as a sufficient mandate to proceed on his own.

One of the jobs of the chief of staff is to say no—no to people who want to meet with the president, no to people who want to interview him, and no to ideas that their proponents think will, if adopted by the president, revolutionize his administration and his relationship with the American people. Saying no to important people makes enemies, but it is possible to ameliorate these resentments by meeting or talking personally with those who have been, are, or will be disappointed. It also helps to lend a sympathetic ear, raise a glass, pat a shoulder, and ask after the wife and kids. In Washington, this kind of stroking is done during working hours through meetings and telephone calls, and after working hours at dinners and other gatherings. Regan didn't have time during working hours to do these things, and didn't like to attend social events in the evening.

The solution would have been to have a number of deputies who are trusted to handle these matters. The troika system in the first Reagan administration—with James Baker as chief of staff, Mike Deaver as his deputy, and Ed Meese as counselor—worked well for Baker and the President because Deaver and Meese were both perceived as close to and able to speak for the President. A senator or cabinet member might be satisfied with a meeting with Deaver or Meese if he couldn't see the President or Baker. In the current Bush White House, there are deputy chiefs of staff, as there were in the Ford and Clinton administrations, who could fill in for the chief of staff when he is—as he should be—with the president. When Howard Baker succeeded Regan, he immediately appointed a deputy, Ken Duberstein, who also had an extensive network in Washington and the clear authority to speak for Baker and the President.

Regan allowed himself no such support, and he and the President suffered for it in several important ways. It is clearly necessary for the

chief of staff to attend the president's substantive meetings with outsiders. The president's positions and commitments are often articulated
in these meetings and the chief of staff has to be able to interpret what
was said for himself and make sure that the president's promises and
wishes are carried out. But while Regan was in these meetings—assidu-
ously taking notes[7]—no one was minding the store. Dennis Thomas
could have been Regan's deputy and with this title might have been able
over time to take many burdens off Regan's shoulders, but Regan never
took the step of formally authorizing a deputy. Nor did he bring into
the White House—until the arrival of David Abshire during the Iran-
Contra crisis—any senior respected "wise men" who could have served
as eyes and ears for the President and himself.

Indeed, Abshire is the exception that proves the rule. A soft-spoken,
discreet, and intelligent veteran diplomat, Abshire became a central figure in mediating among the players in the Iran-Contra drama inside
and outside the White House. By the time he arrived, in early January
1987, so many people had gone on record calling for Regan's ouster that
Regan could no longer easily deal with outsiders as the President's chief
of staff. He was now a part of the story, with interests seen by many
outsiders as distinct from and in some cases hostile to the President's. It
was Regan's hope that Abshire would take over the management of the
Iran-Contra crisis, while Regan would continue to manage the White
House. The President's position with the American people was being
badly damaged by the paralysis that the Iran-Contra affair had produced within the White House staff, and it was necessary to get the
President out around the country and to show that he was still functioning as chief executive.

This hope was not entirely realized, although Abshire did exem-
plary work. The Iran-Contra crisis had to continue until all the facts
could be made available from an objective and credible source. But
Abshire steadied the ship. His credibility with the press and with
Washington power brokers on the Hill and elsewhere moderated the
storm, but the overwhelming number of demands from the investigating bodies, and the leaks that flowed from the satisfaction of those de-

mands, made it impossible even for Abshire—with his staff and the White House counsel's office working full time—to keep up.

Nevertheless, Abshire's presence on the White House staff during this period showed how valuable a person of his quality and background could have been. If he or his like had been appointed earlier in Regan's tenure as chief of staff—not just after the Iran-Contra crisis had spun out of control—the Washington perception of the White House and of Regan might have been different.

In this respect, some of Regan's critics are correct.[8] Regan reserved to himself too much of the chief of staff's authority, did not delegate enough to his subordinates, and in the end failed to do the little things—like returning phone calls and meeting with senators and other power brokers—that count so much in Washington.

Whether Regan did not do these things because he was turf-conscious and unwilling to share his access to the President with anyone else—or because he simply failed to see the importance of schmoozing and stroking egos—is difficult to assess. I incline to the latter view. Before he became White House chief of staff, Regan's experience in Washington was limited to his four years as secretary of the treasury. He had done quite well in this position, without having to spend large amounts of his time making the powerful feel important. Moreover, at Treasury, Regan had left many of his responsibilities to his deputy secretary, Tim McNamar, suggesting that Regan was not as turf-conscious as he was portrayed. Finally, Regan might never have understood that the focus on the president is so stark—in the media and among those who are accustomed to having their views taken seriously—that the White House chief of staff confronts an entirely different and important constituency. In slighting this constituency, he seemed to many to be remote and arrogant, and when it was his time in the barrel—during the Iran-Contra crisis—he had few people other than the President himself who would come to his aid.[9]

It was also not helpful to Regan that he was perceived as the person who, in January 1987, sidetracked a large pay raise for Congress that had been recommended by a special presidential commission.[10] If Regan had recognized the importance of congressional goodwill to his own reputation—or had recognized that the pay raise was of major importance on the Hill—he might have let it go through. It would not have been the first time that public support was purchased with taxpayer dollars. But he seemed to believe that with the Iran-Contra matter already buffeting the President, the last thing the President needed was an angry backlash from the public on this issue, too.

Despite the organizational problems recorded in this chapter, the record of the White House staff under Regan deserves a second look by historians. Ronald Reagan achieved his highest level of popularity for a sustained period while Donald Regan was his chief of staff. At the very least, this suggests that Regan was not the "worst White House chief of staff ever" in the words of the *Washington Post* editorialist. The "first draft of history" prepared by the press in this case was more distorted than usual by the bitterness of the Iran-Contra episode, the refusal of Regan and the staff to blame or belittle the President, and the media's unquestioning acceptance of a stereotype about Don Regan that he and other members of the White House staff did little to dispute.

CHAPTER 7

IRAN-CONTRA:
THE COVER-UP[1]*

I'm not smart enough to lie.
—RONALD REAGAN, JULY 1980

It was election day, November 4, 1986, when the Iran-Contra story first landed on the White House. As usual, near the end of the daily operations meeting, Regan asked Larry Speakes, the President's deputy press secretary, to talk about what news stories were likely to raise questions that day. Speakes was typically laconic as he noted without comment a bizarre report in the *Washington Post* that Bud McFarlane, the President's former National Security Adviser, had been in Tehran to negotiate for the release of American hostages who were then being held by a radical Islamic group in Lebanon.[2] Given that Iran still seemed to regard the United States as the Great Satan, one might have thought Speakes's report was a joke, but he wasn't smiling. In addition, according to the story, the United States had provided arms to Iran to obtain the release of David Jacobsen, a former hostage in Lebanon whose return to the

---

* See endnote 1 for a full discussion of the executive privilege and attorney client privilege issues associated with the disclosures in this chapter.

United States had been celebrated in a public ceremony at the White House only a few days earlier.

John Poindexter, the President's current national security adviser, was absent that day, but his deputy, Alton Keel, was in his seat. After referring to the *Post* article, Speakes let the matter hang there—not asking explicitly for a comment—although he looked down the table at Keel, sitting at the far end. Keel said that we always "no comment" this kind of "speculation" and recommended, unhelpfully, that Speakes use that formulation to answer any press questions that might arise. But then he added that the report was "nonsense."

Thus began—on this note of candor—the greatest crisis of Ronald Reagan's presidency, and an episode with which his critics have sought to define him. During the four months that it continued, the Reagan administration was essentially brought to a standstill. Ronald Reagan, who just prior to its onset enjoyed the highest approval ratings of his presidency, watched these ratings plummet to levels he had not seen since the severe recession of 1981–82. In retrospect, despite the enormous outpouring of press coverage—555 separate stories in the *Washington Post* and 509 in the *New York Times* in just three months—the Iran-Contra matter was simply another of the great press frenzies that periodically afflict American politics. There were investigations by a joint committee of Congress, a special review board appointed by the President, and an independent counsel, but when it was all over the results did not warrant all the shouting and tumult, let alone the disabling of a president in a dangerous world.

The congressional investigations criticized Reagan for trading arms for hostages; the special review board criticized his management style; and the independent counsel indicted and convicted the two most prominent malefactors—John Poindexter, the President's national security adviser, and Oliver North, a member of the National Security Council staff—but not for the arms sales, for failing to report to Congress, or for the diversion of funds to the Contras. None of the investigations ever found a cover-up in the White House after North and Poindexter departed, but it certainly was not for want of looking. At most, Iran-Contra was a foreign policy blunder. Unlike the Bay of Pigs fiasco and Vietnam, no one for whom the United States was responsible was killed or even endangered as a result. It is hard to resist the conclusion that the whole episode was another example of the destructive American tendency to criminalize political or policy disputes.

Nevertheless, the Iran-Contra affair says a great deal about Ronald Reagan, and the strength and significance of his convictions. As the crisis continued, the White House staff came unanimously to the conclusion that the President should tell the American people that he had made a mistake by not properly supervising his national security staff. To us, this was an easy call—reminiscent of Kennedy's successful *mea culpa* after the Bay of Pigs. But to Ronald Reagan it was not that simple. It violated a management principle and a style of governing that he considered central to his success. It took me a while to recognize this, and I doubt that many others have yet understood it. For many people, and most politicians, it may not be credible to say that they willingly absorbed punishment because of their adherence to something as seemingly inconsequential as a management principle, but Ronald Reagan was not like most people or virtually any other politician. He believed in principles, and he stubbornly adhered to them. In most cases, this accounted for his success—as described elsewhere in this book—but in the Iran-Contra affair it prolonged the crisis. The chapters that follow are an account of what happened as the Iran-Contra crisis unfolded.

The foreign policy initiative that became known as the Iran-Contra affair had its origins on July 18, 1985, when President Reagan was in Bethesda Naval Hospital recovering from colon cancer surgery and received a visit from his then national security adviser, Robert McFarlane, accompanied by Don Regan. McFarlane told the President that he had been approached by representatives of the Israeli Government with information that it might be possible for the United States to open a political dialogue with Iran, a strategically important country with which the United States had had bitter relations since 1979, when Iranian radicals had invaded the U.S. Embassy building in Tehran and taken U.S. citizens hostage.

According to McFarlane's account in his book, *Special Trust,* at the hospital meeting he outlined for the President a plan under which the two countries would offer reciprocal gestures of good faith: the United States would agree to let Israel sell U.S. arms to Iran, which was then at war with Iraq, and the Iranians in turn would obtain the release of six U.S. citizens who were then being held hostage by radical elements in Beirut, Lebanon. The United States would replenish Israeli stocks through additional sales to Israel.* Regan and McFarlane agree that the President did not approve arms sales at this point but expressed interest in the idea of a strategic opening to Iran and authorized McFarlane to explore it further. The President's diary entry for the McFarlane visit said simply "Bud [McFarlane's nickname] came by—it seems 2 members of the Iranian govt. want to establish talks with us. I'm sending Bud to meet them in a neutral country."3 No reference to arms sales.

In his book *Perilous Statecraft,*4 Michael Ledeen, a consultant to the National Security Council and an early intermediary between the Israelis and McFarlane, states that from the beginning Israeli arms sales to Iran were on the table, but he notes that there was some ambiguity about their purpose. They could have been seen as a way to achieve some reconciliation with Ayatollah Khomeini, the hitherto rabidly anti-American religious leader of Iran, or as a way to strengthen the hand of the groups in Iran who wanted to moderate the regime's anti-American stance. That there were such groups was documented in a *New York Times* article of November 4, 1986, based on Mideast diplomatic sources, which discussed in detail a power struggle then going on in Iran between those who favored a continuing hard line toward the United States and those who wanted a more moderate stance.5 In any event, the U.S. gesture of a willingness to permit Israeli arms sales to Iran was to be reciprocated with the release of the American hostages in Lebanon.6

---

* Robert C. McFarlane, *Special Trust* (New York: Cadell and Davies, 1994), pp. 17–31; Regan, *For the Record,* pp. 20–21. McFarlane's account, which contains far more detail than the testimony he provided to congressional investigating committees or the Tower Board, states that he first broached the idea of a hostage release to Reagan on July 3, 1985; the idea that a shipment of arms by Israel might be involved—as a gesture of good faith by the United States—was not raised with the President on July 18.

The lack of clarity about who said what to whom in the hospital meeting would come back to haunt the participants, especially the President. Apparently, McFarlane never prepared a written *aide-mémoire* of the President's decision to open a dialogue with Iran, or any subsequent decision to permit arms sales, and as a result the original purpose of the President's policy became subject to interpretation by those who subsequently carried it out. Here, the President's leadership style, in which he delegated extraordinary amounts of authority—a style that had worked well for six years as president and before that as governor of California—began to work against him. McFarlane, it seems, handed off the "action," as they say in government, to Lt. Col. Oliver North, an active-duty marine and a member of the National Security Council staff. North appears to have been a particular favorite of McFarlane, an ex-marine himself.

North was no by-the-book marine and no run-of-the-mill NSC staffer. He had a well-deserved reputation as something of a swashbuckler, and a habit of enhancing his reputation for derring-do with stories that could only be described as fantasies.[7] There is no way of knowing what McFarlane said to North in giving him this new responsibility, or what North thought he heard. McFarlane later described the initiative as an opportunity for a dialogue with Iran, but it seems likely that North saw the Iran operation as another exciting adventure—this time an opportunity to free the hostages in Lebanon—rather than as some highfalutin strategic initiative. If so, he was likely to have described the operation in these terms to the CIA, which produced an initial presidential finding that portrayed the arms sales as a trade for hostages and was subsequently destroyed by Poindexter.[8]

Thereafter, on August 20, 1985, the Israelis shipped a quantity of U.S.-manufactured TOW missiles (TOWs are shoulder-launched, wire-guided anti-aircraft missiles) to Iran. There is some question whether the President approved this shipment in advance, or whether the Israelis simply proceeded under the impression that the President had approved. McFarlane, after some initial vacillation, finally contended that the President had approved in advance, but while the investigations of the Iran-Contra matter were going on could neither recall nor document when that occurred.* Regan—who attended virtually all the President's morning briefings with the national security adviser—recalled that the President was "surprised" to learn of the shipment. Later, we learned that Israel had sent a second shipment of TOWs in September.

Ultimately it did not matter whether the President approved in advance or afterward; the legal and practical consequences were the same. As a political matter, however, the important question was the motivation for the sale. The President contended from the beginning that he had approved arms sales only as an initial step in a strategy intended to begin a political dialogue with Iran. However, the written record, and the testimony of participants in the arms sales and the negotiations with Iran, make reasonably clear that the strategic elements were quickly discarded in favor of a flat-out effort to obtain the release of the hostages by shipping arms to Iran. The absence of a written record from McFarlane—a significant lapse by a top government official and former military officer who dealt regularly with the President—left the President pitting his recollection of what he approved against a formidable record of what had actually happened. In this contest, the President's credibility suffered.

Whatever the motivation, the arms shipments were fraught with legal difficulties. In August 1985, when the first shipments occurred, the Arms Export Control Act (AECA) required that Congress be notified before any sale of arms that exceeded $14 million. The AECA also covered sales by countries, such as Israel, that had acquired the weapons from the United States. However, Congress had not been notified in advance of the August 20 shipment by Israel, or at any time thereafter. Nor had it been notified of several shipments of arms that occurred after August 20. The AECA, however, was not the only applicable law.

---

* In *Special Trust*, McFarlane provides a detailed account of an Oval office conversation with the President on August 3, 1986, at which the President approved the arms sales by Israel. To my knowledge, this recollection was not made available by McFarlane to any of the investigating authorities. In 1986 and 1987, McFarlane said he could not recall when the President had approved.

Under the National Security Act the President could send or sell arms to anyone as part of an intelligence "covert action," but prior to any such shipment he was required to make a "finding" that the sale was in the national interest, and to report the sale to Congress "in a timely manner" after it had occurred. Again, no report was ever sent to Congress, with respect to this or any subsequent sale, and—at least with respect to the arms sales that occurred in 1985—the President had not made a written finding before the arms were shipped by Israel.

Except for Regan and Keel, none of these facts were known to anyone at the November 4, 1986, daily operations meeting, and few of us thought that the wild story about McFarlane visiting Tehran could possibly be true. For an event that was to have such significance over the next few months, its introduction into the morning staff meeting had no immediate impact. Regan went on as though nothing unusual had occurred. At the end of the meeting, he announced that whatever the outcome of that day's election the President would continue with his agenda, which consisted then of three main elements: budget process reform (both the President and Regan were interested in establishing a new budget process, perhaps including a capital budget); a more productive America (efforts to improve productivity in the service sector and the general health of the U.S. population); and strengthening defense so as to bargain more effectively with the Soviets. With the exception of the last item, this agenda reflected the President's overall success at that point in getting his more important priorities adopted. As significant as they are, budget process reform and the general idea of improving productivity and health were not the things Ronald Reagan sought the presidency to achieve.

The next day was taken up with analyzing the implications of the Republicans' loss of the Senate—although now there were more detailed articles on McFarlane's visit to Tehran in the *Los Angeles Times* and the *New York Times*. It wasn't until Thursday, November 6, that the White House staff—or at least that portion not concerned with foreign affairs or national security—began to reflect any sustained interest in the Iran arms sales story. The subject arose again during the daily operations meeting, when Larry Speakes noted that he was getting an increasing number of press questions on the matter. This time Poindexter was present and responded by saying that one of the hostages who had been released, David Jacobsen, had been severely beaten by his captors when it was thought he had given some kind of signal during a press interview. Therefore, Poindexter went on, the safety of the other American hostages depended on our keeping the media out of this story. This approach raised my suspicions, and I wrote in my diary: "It was very difficult to tell whether this was in fact the reason for not speaking about it, or whether there might be reluctance to talk about a controversial policy decision." The arms sales issue was already looking to me like a bureaucratic blunder, and I was on the lookout for a cover-up effort.

There was a cabinet meeting that afternoon, to review the election results, hear the President's views on his agenda for the rest of his term, and receive a budget briefing. The Iran arms sales issue had not by this point attracted enough attention that any of the cabinet members mentioned it during the formal part of the meeting. There were briefings from Mitch Daniels, the President's assistant for political affairs, and by Jim Miller, the director of the Office of Management and Budget. Regan outlined the President's agenda in much the same terms that he had discussed it the previous day in the daily operations meeting.

The President then talked about what was in prospect for the next year in dealing with Congress. He outlined a tough strategy in which he said—always looking for the bright side—that he would now feel free to veto bills because he no longer had to compromise with a Republican Senate. He told a story about California—a favorite diversion in all circumstances—describing a time when the speaker of the Assembly came to see him, as governor, and raised his hands in surrender, pleading with Reagan to "stop those letters." The President was saying he would take his case to the voters: "[O]ur allies have to be the people." In retrospect, the optimism of that moment is an ironic commentary on what was just ahead.

Early on the following morning—November 7, a Friday—I ran into Larry Speakes as I entered the West Wing of the White House. Speakes asked me whether the President could violate his own executive order. An interesting question, I thought, and asked him what this was about. Speakes told me that arms sales to Iran appeared to have violated a Reagan executive order against the export of arms to terrorist states. I told Speakes that I did not think the President was legally bound to observe his own executive orders, but I would check on this and get back to him. As it turned out, I could not give Speakes a definitive answer that morning—the issue was far more complicated than the simple question of whether the President could violate his own executive order. A preliminary review of the law indicated that the facts about what had actually occurred were very important, and I went to talk with Regan about what had happened.

Regan told me without hesitation that we had been dealing with Iran for quite a while, and had sold them small amounts of arms, obtaining in the process the release of three hostages. He said the shipments had been made to a faction within the Iranian government, and that infighting among the various factions in Iran had resulted in the disclosure of these transactions. I said I was not certain about the legality of the activity under the Arms Export Control Act, which restricted the shipment or sale of U.S. arms to foreign countries, but Regan said that the Attorney General had been involved in the discussions of the matter from the beginning, so he was reasonably sure that everything was done legally. At the time, I did not know when the sales of arms had occurred, and was concerned about an amendment to the AECA, signed into law in August 1986, that prohibited all arms sales to terrorist states unless the proposed sale was reported in advance to Congress. In the executive order Speakes had asked me about, the President had declared Iran to be a terrorist state. I asked Regan when the Attorney General had given his opinion, and Regan estimated that it had been about 18 months earlier. I then asked whether the opinion had been reviewed since the adoption of the new and tighter restrictions in the AECA. Regan said he did not know, and suggested that I talk to John Poindexter about it.

Poindexter was a quiet and precise naval officer who was out of his depth in the world of politics. Having graduated first in his class at the Naval Academy, Poindexter was an excellent example of the limited value that raw intelligence brings to government. It's good to have intelligent staff people around—people who can master details, recognize patterns, and analyze issues—but the key quality necessary for a senior government position is judgment, and there are no tests for this. Again and again studies have shown that the most successful members of society—from business to law to the military—are not necessarily those who graduated at the top of their classes, but those who have the various qualities of personality, people skills, and judgment that are required for operating in complex environments. John Poindexter, for all his brilliance, lacked these qualifications.

Responding to my questions, Poindexter was not forthcoming. In fact, he told me in that first meeting that some of the arms destined for Iran had been sent by Israel without the President's authorization, and pulled back for that reason at the request of the President. I did not know it then, but this was a false story, part of the initial effort by Poindexter, North, and McFarlane to cover up the facts concerning the involvement of the U.S. Government in the arms sales. I may have had the dubious distinction of being the first person outside this little group to be lied to about the President's role in the Iran arms sales matter. When I asked for additional information about the arms sales, Poindexter told me that Attorney General Meese was the legal adviser on this matter, and all legal issues had been and would be handled by him. He would not provide me with any further information.

The irony here is that there was no need—from the President's point of view—to obscure his role in approving the arms sales or the involvement of the U.S. government. The President himself never denied that the arms sales were his policy, but he insisted that they were motivated by his desire for a strategic opening to Iran and not by an effort to trade arms for hostages. It is true that the legal requirements of the AECA and the National Security Act—which called for reports to Congress—may not have been complied with. This was troublesome, to be sure, but in practical terms this lapse was not the fault of the President. Although it is certainly the President's responsibility—in an ultimate sense—to see that such laws are observed, he is not expected to know when various technical reporting requirements have been triggered. That is the job of his staff. Then, too, the Attorney General was involved in the discussions of the Iran arms sales initiative at several points, and the President was entitled to rely on the government's chief law enforcement officer to see that all legal requirements were met.

In any event, it was not the President or the U.S. Government that Poindexter was trying to protect; it was McFarlane, North, and himself. As would no doubt come to light if disclosure continued, the arms sales initiative had perhaps been a policy mistake, but it was certainly an immense operational blunder. Large amounts of arms had been shipped to Iran, but since the shipments began only two hostages had been released and two more had been taken; the Beirut radicals were still holding six U.S. citizens. There had been no significant dialogue begun with Iran, although that was what the President said his policy had been about. The United States, in the person of McFarlane, North, and Poindexter, had been outwitted and scammed by the Iranians. Moreover, in the course of this debacle, the staff had failed to comply with the law, placing the President in a politically embarrassing position. And there was more. No one other than McFarlane, Poindexter, and North yet knew that some of the proceeds of the arms sales had been diverted for the support of the Contras.

It is here that we confront the hazards associated with Reagan's management style—his willingness to delegate substantial authority to subordinates and to await their reports. If no reports came, he had no mechanism in place to follow up. Worse still, he did not have the suspicious nature that might have impelled him to question his national security adviser about what exactly was happening in the policy he had approved, and whether—for example—the strategic opening he said was the basis for his policy was in fact coming into view. A president who reposes such trust in subordinates must have very trustworthy subordinates. In the vast majority of cases during the Reagan administration, his subordinates did not fail him. In this case, they did.

Even more serious, as it turned out, was the lack of knowledge on the part of the President and Regan about what had actually happened in the arms initiative as it proceeded. This, too, was the result of the substantial delegation of authority that the President had given to his national security advisers—first McFarlane and then Poindexter.

Apparently, the President was told very little of substance about the arms sales after his initial delegation of authority. This seems clear from Don Regan's limited recollection. Although the President might not have had an interest in or memory for details, Regan did, and Regan had sat in on virtually all of the President's morning briefings from his national security adviser. Accordingly, even if the President's recollections were weak, Regan's recollections were likely to have been a reasonably good reflection of what the President was actually told. Subsequent discussions with Regan, including those associated with preparing him for his House and Senate testimony, revealed that he had very little knowledge about how the initiative was actually carried out. He was aware of the significant events—the initial shipments in August and November 1985, the President's signing of a finding in January 1986, the release of two hostages, McFarlane's visit to Tehran—but not operational details such as the number and quantity of the subsequent shipments, or North's many meetings with Iranian intermediaries. Moreover, the Iran arms sales initiative was so closely held that few people at the NSC or the CIA knew more than superficial facts about it. Thus, when North and Poindexter eventually left the White House—and subsequently refused to testify or talk about how the arms sales had been conducted—the President and the White House staff were left without any reliable information with which to respond to questions or inform the American people.

It is something of a mystery why the arms sales were never reported to Congress. The ostensible reason was that the National Security Council staffers in charge of the matter—first McFarlane and North, and later Poindexter and North—feared leaks from Congress. But this fear—sometimes well-grounded—does not seem rational under the circumstances. After the arms sales became known, both Poindexter and North argued that no further details should be disclosed. Disclosure, they said, would endanger either the hostages or the people we were dealing with in Iran, who were said to be "moderates" somehow in opposition to the hard-line regime of Ayatollah Khomeini. But from the beginning of the initiative, North was dealing directly with representatives of the Iranian government, and McFarlane actually went to Tehran in May 1986, to do the same. It is impossible to believe that the so-called hard-liners did not know of McFarlane's presence in Tehran, or why he was there. Moreover, because the Iranian Government knew all about these dealings, it is absurd to argue that the U.S. Congress should not have been told. If the hostages were really going to be endangered by a disclosure of the arms transactions, their lives had already been placed in the hands of the Iranians.

After getting stonewalled by Poindexter, I returned to Regan's office to ask for his assistance in persuading Poindexter to provide me with the necessary information. Regan, however, did not have the authority to get Poindexter to cooperate. Only the President could direct Poindexter to disclose anything about what had happened in this matter, and he was listening with concern to Poindexter's arguments that leaks of information from the U.S. Government would endanger either the Iranian moderates or the hostages, or both.

It is from this point, November 7, 1986, that I date the beginning of a cover-up of the Iran-Contra matter in the White House, and where Poindexter's effort to protect himself and his NSC colleagues threatened to draw the President into participation. High government officials such as the president are wholly dependent on the facts they receive from their subordinates when they make their decisions, and self-interested staff are thus able to manipulate their superiors by manipulating the facts. Although this seldom happens in matters of such magnitude, it was now happening to the President.

In the days that followed, Poindexter and North would use the alleged plight of the Iranian moderates and the hostages to beat back efforts by Regan and others to obtain full disclosure of what had happened. As it turned out, if there was a "moderate" faction in Iran, it was perhaps opposed to, but not in any sense in danger from, the Khomeini regime. Indeed, it seems clear that the Khomeini regime—having received a visit in May 1986 from Robert McFarlane himself—was fully aware of what was going on. However, once the arms sales were disclosed, the so-called moderate group in Iran was transmuted into something like an active, underground opposition—at least as described by Oliver North. Indeed, in my first encounter with North on this subject—when he and I were working with others on a speech for Reagan on November 13, 1986—he said, in the melodramatic style that was his trademark, that there would be "heads on stakes" in Tehran if, as a result of this speech or other disclosures, we compromised the existence of the Iranian moderates.

On Monday, November 10, the President met with his senior advisers—Secretary of State George Shultz, Secretary of Defense Casper Weinberger, Regan, Poindexter, and Edwin Meese—in order to prepare a statement on the developing Iran arms sales matter. According to Regan's notes, at the conclusion of the meeting the President said that any statement should avoid detail "because of long-term consideration of people w[ith] whom we have been talking about the future of Iran." [9] As this statement shows, the President believed at this point that there were "moderates" in Iran who would be endangered by excessive disclosure of our dealings with them.

I was disappointed to see that the brief statement by the President that came out of the meeting said that "no laws were broken." I was not at all sure this statement was correct, was angry that the President had been put out in front to endorse what seemed to me at this point to be a monumental blunder on the part of his national security staff, and worried that the President was being drawn deeper into a defense of the indefensible.

On November 11, Veterans Day, I wrote a memo to Regan outlining the difficulties I saw in the President's legal position. I reviewed the problems as I then saw them under the AECA and the National Security Act, including the fact that there had been no reporting to Congress, as seemingly required. I recommended to Regan that the President waive executive privilege with respect to all requests for documents or testimony from investigating bodies. My view was that if violations of these statutes occurred, it was the fault of the staff rather than the President, who could not reasonably be expected to know the technical reporting requirements involved. While the President would have to take responsibility for the mistakes that had occurred, it would not in my view be seen by the American people as an error of such magnitude as to jeopardize his presidency. On the other hand, an effort to withhold documents or testimony showing that laws had been broken was a far more serious matter. Indeed, at that point I regarded the efforts of Poindexter and North to limit disclosure by citing the danger to the hostages or the moderates as little more than efforts to protect themselves. As I got deeper into this matter, that view became stronger.

As White House counsel, in common with all my predecessors, I had been a strong advocate of executive privilege, and had argued on several occasions that the President should invoke it in response to certain demands for documents from Congress. However, executive privilege, like any privilege, can be waived by the person who holds it—in this case the president. And it is appropriate to waive the privilege—as many presidents have done—when invoking it would do more harm to the presidency, or the president then in office, than waiving it. In this case, it was my recommendation that the President waive the privilege, since I foresaw a long series of investigations looming before us, and believed that the President would be hurt far more by an appearance that he was covering up wrongdoing than by disclosure of any of the lapses that may have occurred. Fortunately, after North and Poindexter left the White House the President waived executive privilege for all matters relating to the Iran-Contra affair.

The overall judgment that the danger of a cover-up was more serious than the consequences of admitting a violation of law was borne out by subsequent events. None of the official investigations and reports that eventually reviewed the actions of the President and the administration—the joint committee of Congress, the independent counsel, and the Tower Board—attached great significance to the President's failure to notify Congress as required by law. The principal focus of all these reports was on the President's failure properly to manage the NSC and on the possibility that there had been a coverup of the facts within the White House.

In the early days of the developing Iran arms sales crisis, however, it was far from certain that the President would waive executive privilege and agree to full disclosure. Although Regan was pressing for this, Poindexter was opposed. He continued to argue to the President that anything more than limited disclosure would be dangerous to the moderates in Iran and our hostages, and in any event, he said, the whole controversy would soon blow over. As demonstrated by the President's statement at the November 10 meeting, Poindexter's arguments were having an effect. When I met with Regan on November 12, he acknowledged that he had not been able to get Poindexter to agree to talk with me or get the President to commit to more complete disclosure. "The President is listening to John [Poindexter] on this one," he said.

By November 13 the explosion of press interest in the Iran arms sales matter had become so great that some additional White House response was necessary. I joined a meeting in Regan's office that included Poindexter, Thomas, Buchanan, Keel, Chew, Ball, and Speakes. Regan had just returned from the Oval Office and had gotten approval from the President for a speech to the nation that evening. Poindexter objected to moving so quickly, but Regan said that the longer we waited the worse things would get. Regan thought the speech should contain specific assurances to Congress that all information they required would be made available to them, but Poindexter disagreed, arguing that a recent briefing of congressional leaders was all that was necessary.

Buchanan, Keel, Chew, and I were designated to work on the President's statement, and we were soon joined by Oliver North, although it was unusual for North to participate in discussions at this level. As far as I could recall, I had never met him before, but I had first heard North's name from Tony Dolan, then the President's chief speechwriter. We were chatting one day shortly after my arrival at the White House, and Dolan asked me whether I'd encountered Ollie North. I said I hadn't and Dolan smiled. "Well," he said, "Ollie's going to cause you enormous problems someday." I've respected Dolan's sagacity ever since.

Indeed, North's tendency to exaggerate and fantasize did cause enormous problems for the President as the crisis deepened in the months ahead. The President's contention that he had approved only a strategic opening to Iran, and not a trade of arms for hostages, was constantly under challenge in the press, and no doubt contributed to the erosion of his credibility with the American people. One of the key difficulties for the President was separating himself from North, who had unquestionably been attempting to trade arms for hostages. North, however, had told those he dealt with outside the White House that he met regularly with and briefed the President about his activities. This was not true. White House records showed that although North had been in meetings in the Oval Office it was always with a group, and in these cases he was a junior staffer and unlikely to have said a word. Yet North had spread far and wide accounts of his close connection to the President, and the media were only too happy to assume that Reagan was fully informed by North of all North's activities.

A typical article was one that appeared in the *New York Times* on December 3, entitled "North Told Group He Met Reagan Often." The article begins, "Lieut. Col. Oliver L. North, the ousted White House aide, told a church delegation in February that he personally briefed President Reagan twice a week on terrorism and Central America," and quotes a member of the group as saying that "'North says he sees Reagan twice a week, half on this problem [Central America] and half on terrorism.'" Then the *Times* quoted a "senior Administration official involved in Central America" as saying, "'Ollie was very, very close personally to the President—Reagan thought of him almost as a son. . . . He briefed him often. Several times he helped write Presidential speeches. Everyone who knew anything thought of him as a plenipotentiary for Ronald Reagan." This was all sheer fantasy, and could only have come from North himself. The effect was to make it seem as though the President was much more closely connected to the arms sales, and later to the diversion of funds to the Contras, than any facts would warrant.

The drafting group for the November 13 speech met in Chew's office. We worked through a first draft and sent it to the President. The text explained the Iran initiative as an effort to open a dialogue with

Iran, to bring an end to the Iran-Iraq war, to eliminate state-sponsored terrorism, and, finally, to bring about the release of the hostages held in Lebanon. The arms shipments were meant to show that U.S. negotiators were operating with the authority of the President, and that the United States was trying to start a new relationship with Iran. The Iranians were told that, for their part, the most significant step they could take would be to use their influence with the kidnappers to obtain the release of the U.S. hostages. This had been the President's consistent position since the arms sales were first disclosed, and remained so throughout the subsequent controversy.

As we continued to work on the speech, we got back from the President his handwritten comments, including this opening, "I know you've been reading, seeing, and hearing a lot of stories the past several days attributed to Danish sailors, unnamed observers at Italian ports and Spanish harbors, and especially unnamed government officials of my administration. Well, now you're going to hear the facts from a White House source, and you know my name." We all enjoyed the Gipper's jaunty addition, and it went into the text as the President had written it.

As we approached the final draft, Keel said he wanted to insert a sentence to the effect that "all laws had been complied with." I objected, saying that it was not yet clear that this was true, and I did not want the President making statements to the American people that we did not know to be true. At this, Keel exploded, telling me among other things that this is what the President and the Attorney General wanted and what the President said in his prepared statement of November 10, and that I should not be disagreeing with the Attorney General's opinions. Since the President's statement of November 10 did in fact contain the sentence about no laws having been broken, I was in a weak position to object. Buchanan, the keeper of the draft, put in Keel's sentence over my objection.

The magnitude of Keel's error became apparent later that afternoon, when I was finally able to get in touch with Ed Meese. He said that Chuck Cooper, the assistant attorney general in charge of the Justice Department's Office of Legal Counsel, was working on the matter for him and would provide me with the information I wanted. Cooper was an extraordinarily bright and diligent lawyer, who—as far as I could tell—played things completely straight. I was happy to know he was exploring the President's legal position. When I called Cooper, he said he was working on the issue. We agreed that the AECA was a problem, but could be trumped by the provisions of the National Security Act, which gave the president the authority to engage in covert actions—subject only to the president making a "finding" that the action was necessary and reporting it to Congress. Unfortunately, at that point, we did not know whether the President had made the finding required under the Act, and we were reasonably sure that there had been no report to Congress. This meant we might have to rely for support on the president's general constitutional authority—not a politically strong position.

At this point, I asked Cooper how long he had been working on this problem, and he replied "about a day." I asked whether anyone else at Justice had been working on it, and he said he did not think so. In other words, the Attorney General's opinion, on which Poindexter and Keel had so heavily relied—if it was ever really given in any formal sense—was not the result of a careful examination of the law at the Justice Department. The emperor, apparently, had no clothes, and I was in the unenviable position of having to point this out.

My first concern was the President's statement that all laws had been complied with; to me, this represented the first major step by the President down the path to a cover-up. Once the President goes on record in this way, all the forces of the administration are marshaled to prove him right. The President himself may feel compelled to justify this position. Certainly those who were responsible for whatever violations occurred would use the President's statement to justify what they had done. We already had one written statement by the President making this assertion, and that had been used as leverage to get a similar statement into a speech to the American people. We were on a very slippery slope, and it was getting steeper and greasier.

I hurried down to Regan's office to see whether the President's speech text could be modified, but it was too late. The text had already been given to the President and was widely available in the White House. The removal of the statement that all laws had been complied with would, needless to say, attract a lot of attention and would almost certainly be leaked to the press. We had to hope that whatever theories we could eventually develop to sustain the President's position would be credible; there was no longer any possibility of separating him in the minds of the American people from a statement that was likely to be false. I told Regan I was disgusted with a process in which we had been assured falsely that the operation had been carried out within the requirements of the law, in which no one was permitted to inquire into what had been done and on what basis it was legally authorized, and in which the President was now put out in front to assume the blame.

Although I didn't know it at the time, the text contained at least one other false statement, as the President—unwittingly—was again used for the protection of the NSC staff. The speech noted that the arms were shipped in small amounts, and could all have fit inside a single cargo plane. The apparent purpose of this statement was to bring the sales within the $14 million ceiling that some believed could be made without reporting to Congress. Here again was an effort to minimize the significance of the activity, which the top NSC staff—but not the President—knew to be untrue.

The President's speech on November 13 resulted in an enormous outpouring of press reports and commentary the next day. Multiple articles in all the nation's major newspapers—there were four each in the *Washington Post* and *New York Times* alone—raised the controversy to a new plateau, with many of the articles noting that the President had said, "The actions I authorized were in full compliance with the federal law." Some press accounts followed this statement with a paragraph like this from the *Wall Street Journal* of November 14: "But the president didn't address technical legal issues that still are far from being settled—including whether he was required to inform congressional leaders of his activities before undertaking them." The next day I ran into Richard Wirthlin, the President's pollster, at a White House meeting. Wirthlin told me he had heard stories that the President had directed Bill Casey, director of the CIA, not to report the Iran initiative to Congress—although this report was never confirmed—and that in Wirthlin's view the Iran initiative was assuming the proportions of Watergate. Somewhat ominously, he asked me what "high crimes and misdemeanors" were.

The White House response continued to be controlled by the NSC staff into the following week. Despite Regan's efforts, we were hamstrung without the facts, and these were withheld from all of us. At a meeting on Monday morning, November 17, in Dennis Thomas's office, Keel essentially refused to comply with requests for information and seemed perfectly comfortable telling the President's top White House staff "we won't do that" in response to suggestions for actions that would improve the President's position. He seemed wholly confident that those in the room really had very little to say about how this matter would be handled. This was perfectly true. None of us had any more authority than Regan, and as long as the Poindexter story about the danger to the hostages and the moderates was accepted by the President, Regan was not able to overcome Poindexter's opposition to further disclosure.

Meanwhile, press interest was building to frenzied levels. On November 16, there were eight Iran-related articles in the *New York Times*—not including editorials and op-eds by regular columnists—and several in the *Washington Post.* The evening newscasts, which take their cues from the *Times* and *Post,* were focusing on little else.

Nevertheless, the NSC "stonewall" continued the following day in another forum. I had assembled the general counsels of all the agencies that had anything to do with the Iran matter, including State, Defense, CIA, Justice, and the NSC. The purpose of the meeting was to see if we could agree on a common set of legal theories to support the position the administration would have to take on the Iran initiative when hearings and briefings began on the Hill. We went through the known facts and tried to fit them into the statutory structure. Shipments of arms before August 1986 had to be reported to Congress only if they exceeded a value of $14 million; after August 1986, because of an amendment to the AECA, shipments of arms to terrorist states—which included Iran, according to a presidential executive order—were prohibited entirely unless reported to Congress in advance. Thus, we had to know when the various shipments had occurred, and their approximate value.

Further, even if the administration had not complied with the AECA, the shipments could be justified, we agreed, by a presidential finding prior to the shipment. As far as we were aware, there was a finding—although none of us had seen it—in early January 1986. There was one major loose end; the existence of a finding had to be reported to Congress in advance of the activity to which it related, but in extraordinary circumstances the covert action could be reported after the event, "in a timely manner." In the case of the Iran initiative, there had been no reporting at all.

One of the advantages of a meeting like this was that it enabled all of us to share our knowledge of what had occurred. At the time, we had been operating on the assumption that all the arms sales had occurred in 1986. Since the President had signed a finding in January 1986 authorizing the sales, they could be justified under the National Security Act—apart from the fact that they had not been reported to Congress as the NSA required. But as the discussion at the meeting continued, someone noted that the records of his agency recorded at least one shipment of arms in September 1985, before any finding had been signed by the President. None of us—with the probable exception of Paul Thompson, the NSC's general counsel—then knew that the first shipment, by Israel, had occurred in August 1985. Chuck Cooper, the assistant attorney general who had been developing a theory based on the January 1986 finding, looked shocked. He now had no theory that would support the earlier shipment.

This disclosure demonstrated the importance of knowing the facts, and we asked Paul Thompson for a chronology of events. Thompson said he would ask Poindexter, but he doubted that a chronology would be made available. Abe Sofaer, the State Department's legal adviser and a former federal judge, was outraged by this response. He told Thompson with some heat that he could not imagine how the NSC staff could deny the facts about this matter to the lawyers for the other members of the NSC—State, Defense, Justice, and the CIA—let alone the Counsel to the President. Nevertheless, Thompson refused, saying he had been directed to do so by Poindexter.

That afternoon, there was a briefing for the President in preparation for a news conference that had been scheduled for the following day, November 19. The President did reasonably well on the domestic issues he would have to respond to, but when it came to the many questions about the Iran initiative he gave the worst performance I had seen since coming to the White House. The President clearly knew very little about the entire Iran arms sales program, and Poindexter and Keel kept interrupting his answers with additional facts and corrections. It was close to disastrous. The contrast between the President's knowledge of the Iran matter and his knowledge of aspects of his domestic and other foreign policies and programs was so stark that I wondered how much he could have been briefed on as the Iran initiative developed. Even a cursory briefing would have left some traces in his recollection, but from all appearances he knew about as much as I did—which was not much.

Reagan knew how ill-prepared he was; when the briefing ended he said, "Now I have a question. . . ."; we all stopped and waited . . . "Do I have to go through with this press conference?" Our laughter, and his, was a bit hollow. Tomorrow would not be a good day.

After the briefing, there was a small meeting in Dennis Thomas's office to discuss the President's opening statement for the press conference. A draft was passed around, but it contained little that was new. Dissatisfaction with the draft provoked discussion of a new approach: perhaps the President should simply say he had made a mistake in selling arms to Iran. This was the first time that this idea had been discussed seriously, and I thought it made a great deal of sense. The precedent would be Kennedy's admission that he had made a mistake in approving the Bay of Pigs fiasco—an event far worse in every respect than the Iran arms sales. Kennedy's confession let the steam out of the controversy. This strategy would have worked for Reagan. The American people clearly respected him; he had had six years in office in which he had carried on the presidency successfully and with dignity. One mistake, even a big one, would be easily forgiven. Unfortunately, however, this approach went nowhere at this point, and I was soon to find out why.

As the time of the November 19 press conference approached, I spoke with Attorney General Ed Meese about how the President should handle questions about the legality of his actions. By this time I knew—and I presume Meese knew—what a difficult problem this was. It is true, of course, that a president's failure to report to Congress when he is required to do so by law is a serious matter, but in reality the reporting requirement was a technicality that the President could not be expected to know about. Lawyers and laws have always made distinctions between violations of law that are *malum prohibitum* (wrong because prohibited) and those that are *malum in se* (wrong in themselves); reasonable and moral people are expected to know what is *malum in se,* but not necessarily what is *malum prohibitum.* While ignorance of the law is no excuse, there is always a lighter punishment for violating a rule that is *malum prohibitum,* and the reporting requirements of the AECA and the National Security Act certainly fall into this category.

Nevertheless, the President had to have a cogent answer to a question about whether he complied with these laws, and at this point his answer would be what he had said in his statements of November 10 and 13—that no laws had been violated. Given what we now knew, I did not believe that the President should say that again in his news conference. Searching for a way out, I called Ed Meese and suggested that the best answer for the President would be to cite the Attorney General as authority, simply saying the AG had advised him that all actions that he had taken with respect to the Iran initiative were in compliance with the law. This would leave the AG with the hot potato of finding and articulating the justification. Despite what he must have known by then was a dicey situation, Meese readily agreed. He said he had never given any written opinion on the subject, because he was afraid it would be leaked, but that he was very comfortable with the advice he had given and could easily defend it. I wondered, thinking about Chuck Cooper's befuddlement, where Meese had come up with his advice, but I was delighted that Meese would not abandon the President in his time of trial.

At the President's final briefing before the press conference, he was slightly better than he had been the day before, but still not sharp on Iran matters. When he fumbled a question on the legality of the arms shipments, I told him that the right answer to all questions on this subject was that he had been advised by the Attorney General that all actions he had taken were in compliance with the law. This was true, since the Attorney General had been in the original November 10 meeting where the President's most senior advisers agreed on a presidential statement that said just this. If pressed, he should refer all questions to the AG.

It was difficult to believe that the President was going to walk into this nationally televised event—perhaps the most crucial of his presidency—as unprepared as he was about the Iran arms sales. By this time, I had seen enough of Ronald Reagan to know that when he was engaged in a policy issue—even one that did not particularly interest him—he understood the principal issues, and he could summarize the position he wanted to take. Iran, for some reason, was different. It was not because the policy was not debated; in fact, it was strongly opposed by both the Secretaries of State and Defense, who seldom agreed on anything else. I suspect the reason is that the debate among his advisers in 1985 was at a very high policy level while the questions he was facing at this early stage of the controversy in 1986 were about the details of how it was carried out. Ronald Reagan never cared much for this kind of detail, probably never asked, and in the Iran arms sales matter was almost certainly never told. Now he was being forced to master a mind-boggling set of details about who shipped what, when, and why.

In the event, the press conference did not go as badly as the rehearsals. The President made one major error—denying that it was Israel that had made the first shipment of weapons to Iran at the behest of the United States. Although the original guidance from Poindexter had been that Israel was not to be named as the third-country supplier, the fact of Israel's involvement had become widely known in Washington. The President's denial was known to be incorrect, and it was necessary to issue a correction immediately after the conference.

However, in the strange way that chance intervenes in human affairs, this episode gave rise to a major break. When the President denied that Israel was involved in the shipment of arms to Iran, the reporter who had asked the question—Andrea Mitchell of NBC—followed up with, "But Mr. President, your own chief of staff, Donald Regan, told us yesterday that it was Israel." The President was clearly surprised, and said that he had not heard this but would find out what Mr. Regan had said. After the conference, Regan vehemently denied to all within earshot that he had identified Israel as the third country, and assembled a group in the Roosevelt Room—the West Wing's principal conference room, just across the hall from the Oval Office—to go through the transcripts of his briefing to prove that he had not said such a thing. In fact, no reference to Israel was ever found.

While this meeting was going on, however, Oliver North entered the Roosevelt Room and went over to talk with Alton Keel. Both of them then came over to show me what was written on a single sheet of paper that North had in his hand. It looked like a series of dates, with a brief summary of activity on each date. There was a reference to August 1985 and a statement that Israel had shipped TOW missiles to Iran without U.S. approval. I think they wanted to show me this because it would demonstrate—if true—that since Israel had acted without our approval we had actually not sent arms to Iran before the President had made a finding. I thought this was interesting, but I was far more interested in what the paper had been excerpted from. To me, it looked like a chronology of events for the Iran initiative. The next morning, before the daily operations meeting, I told Regan that I thought I had been shown a page from a chronology the night before and told him he should ask Poindexter for a copy. Regan did this, and the following day, in an envelope marked "Top Secret," he handed me the copy of the chronology he had just received from Poindexter. If Regan had not called for a review of the transcripts—which brought North into the

Roosevelt Room with a page from the chronology—neither Regan nor I would have known that a chronology existed. What we did not know was that a copy was also given to the President, with troublesome results later on.

At the daily operations meeting on the morning after the press conference, there was a great deal of discussion about why the President was in so much trouble over the Iran matter. Speakes suggested that the American people just did not like our dealing with Iran. To me, this was part of the explanation, but only a part. I wrote in my diary for that day that it was not public hostility to Iran that was the problem, "it is simply a case of the people not believing the President's contention that we did not trade arms for hostages. This controversy will not end until the Pres. admits he made a mistake and allowed arms to be traded for hostages or he fires Poindexter and others, or both."

In midafternoon, there was a meeting with Richard Wirthlin to go over his most recent polling data. It showed a sharp drop in the country's estimation of the President's handling of foreign affairs, a smaller downward shift in his overall approval rating, and an 11-point loss in the number of people who thought he was trustworthy.

Later that day, Chuck Cooper and Paul Thompson came by my office. I had asked to see Cooper, who was continuing his legal analysis at the NSC's offices, and his visit with Thompson was in response to my call. Both lawyers had just been involved in a review with Poindexter and CIA Director William Casey of the testimony Casey was to give the following day before the Intelligence Committees of the Senate and House.

We began a discussion of how Casey should respond to the question about the legality of the August 1985 sale of TOW missiles to Iran. We went through a few possibilities, but nothing worked very well with what we then thought we knew of the facts. At this point, I received a call from Abe Sofaer, the State Department legal adviser. He was quite upset. In his view, the President had not told what Sofaer believed to be the truth at the press conference the previous evening, and Sofaer hoped that this was only because the President had not been properly briefed. He then asked me whether I knew about an Israeli shipment of HAWK

(Homing–All-the-Way- Killer anti-aircraft) missiles to Iran in November 1985. I said I did not, although I had a vague recollection of having been told by Poindexter in my first meeting with him on the Iran initiative that a shipment of HAWK missiles had been called back because the President hadn't authorized the sale. I asked Cooper and Thompson whether they were aware of this sale, and they said they were not.

Sofaer then said that Secretary Shultz had a recollection that, at some time during the November 1985 Geneva summit meeting with Soviet leader Mikhail Gorbachev, McFarlane had told the President that a shipment of HAWK missiles was on its way to Iran, and after it arrived all the hostages would be released. I relayed this to Cooper and Thompson, both of whom looked somewhat shocked. I did not know at the time that Casey's testimony—at North's suggestion—had been changed just a little while before to say that no one in the U.S. Government knew of the Israeli HAWKs sale at the time it occurred. Clearly, if Shultz's recollection was correct, Casey's testimony was false. Although Cooper did not know who was correct, he had the good judgment to see that the challenged statement was removed from Casey's prepared testimony the next day.[10] In any event, the discovery of the HAWK shipment, and its attempted concealment by North, was a crucial turning point in the course of events at the White House.

I learned later, in reading Sofaer's deposition to the select committees of the Senate and House investigating the Iran-Contra matter, that he had first called the Justice Department with his concerns, and was told by Arnold Burns, the deputy attorney general—who said he was reporting only what the AG had told him—that the Attorney General was aware of Shultz's report but "knew of certain facts that explained all these matters and that laid to rest all the problems" Sofaer had in mind.[11] This response, fortunately for the President, did not satisfy Sofaer, and he decided to call me.

The discrepancy between Casey's draft testimony and Sofaer's revelation had an immediate effect. Cooper asked Thompson to find out whether North and McFarlane agreed with Shultz's account, and Thompson reported back that both North and McFarlane stood by the story that

Israel had shipped the HAWK missiles in November 1985 without U.S. knowledge. Cooper, not knowing whom to believe, probably reported this to Meese and recommended that Meese (who was at West Point for a speech) return to Washington to work out the differences in the stories.[12] This is likely to have been the genesis of the Attorney General's investigation, during which Justice Department lawyers found in North's files a plan to divert some of the Iran arms sales proceeds to the Contras.

I first heard about the Meese investigation in a meeting with Regan the next day, November 21. He told me he had just met with the President and Meese, and the Attorney General had been assigned to investigate the facts surrounding the Iran arms sales. Although I was concerned that the Attorney General's loyalty to the President might reduce the usefulness of his report as the objective record of the facts I thought we needed at that time, I was pleased to have any presidentially authorized investigation that would get information out of the NSC staff.

It was then that Regan handed me a copy of the NSC chronology he had just received, still in its "Top Secret" envelope, and asked me to review it for him. He noted that on the following Monday, November 24, there would be a meeting of the National Security Planning Group (NSPG)—the Secretaries of State and Defense and the President's other senior national security advisers—and he wanted me to suggest what questions he should ask. Even with my relatively limited knowledge of the facts at that point, I could tell that the chronology was, in many respects, a misleading account. Among other things, it said that the President had not approved the initial Israeli shipment of arms to Iran, but did not detail what the United States had done after this supposedly unauthorized act; on the question of the HAWKs, the chronology said they had been called back by the President, because the shipment was unauthorized—although we now had indications from the State Department that this was untrue. After the President signed a finding in January 1986—which would have made subsequent shipments of arms arguably legal—he disappeared completely from the chronology's account. This part could well have been accurate, however, because it suggested that the President was never briefed thereafter.

That evening, a Friday, I sent Regan by courier an unsigned and undated memorandum on my views of the chronology, and met with him the following Monday morning, November 24. Over the weekend, Regan had gone through the chronology and my memo, and agreed that it was simply an "apologia." He asked me to review it again before the NSPG meeting that afternoon for inconsistencies with what I knew or had been told. Regan then asked me what I thought should be done at this point. I said that Poindexter and North should resign from the NSC staff, and that the President should appoint a commission of inquiry to look into what had happened. I also said that the President should make a statement of some kind to the effect that he had not authorized some of the things that had been done in his name and on his authority. I was referring here to the November HAWK shipment, which seemed to have been structured as an explicit exchange of arms for hostages. This transaction, I said, if it occurred, cast doubt on the whole basis for the President's policy. This did not mean that the President was being untruthful—only that he was not aware that the policy he had originally approved had degenerated into a trade of arms for hostages.

Later that afternoon, as I was headed toward the Oval Office to request a change in the President's scheduled meeting with a visitor the next day, I saw Regan and Meese coming toward me. Both looked very grim. As I passed, going the opposite way, Regan put his hand behind his back and signaled for me to follow them into his office. When Meese left, Regan asked Dennis Thomas and me to step inside. Then, uncharacteristically for these informal meetings, he shut the door. As we stood in front of his desk, he said "a situation is developing now that looks like Watergate." For the first time since the Iran arms sales had come to light, Regan looked genuinely worried about what was happening. Something had occurred that convinced him we were now dealing with facts or events that went well beyond managing a political or public-relations problem.

Before telling us anything, Regan asked us both to promise—swear, really—that we would not tell anyone what he was about to impart. He then said that Attorney General Meese had done an investigation over the weekend and found evidence that some of the money Iran paid for the weapons it received might have been funneled by North to the Contras through a Swiss bank account. I asked whether the President or Poindexter had known about this, and Regan said that Poindexter had known generally about it but the President had not. Regan asked me whether what he'd described was illegal, and I said that it might depend on whose money it was. If the payments should have gone to the U.S. Government for shipments of arms after January 1986, then it was almost certainly illegal; if the money should have gone to Israel for the shipments before January 1986, then the answer was somewhat less clear. In any event, Dennis Thomas and I both said that Poindexter had to resign.

As he usually did when a problem arose, Thomas immediately began making a list of what had to be done, including a statement by the President about what happened and why he was dismissing Poindexter. The three of us then discussed the appointment of a special review board of some kind, which would look into what happened and how and why the national security policy implementation process had failed. Regan told us to draft a statement for the President, and we went to my office, closed the door, and began working on both a statement that included the reasons for dismissing Poindexter and North and a structure for the special review board that we thought the President might announce at the same time. In four or five hours, we had something we thought was satisfactory. Sometime between our departure from his office and the early morning of the following day, Regan obtained the President's approval to ask for Poindexter's resignation.

I arrived at Regan's office about 7:00 the next morning and found Thomas, Chew, and Dawson already there. We sat down around Regan's conference table and he distributed a three-page document outlining the steps he thought should be taken at this time. I didn't know whether Thomas had already shown him our draft of the previous evening. Regan's plan was not too different from ours, with one major exception: it left out the review board and assigned the Attorney General to do the investigation. I argued strongly against this on three grounds—the Attorney General's investigation would inevitably become a criminal inquiry, when the real question was what had happened as a management or administrative matter to the President's policy on Iran; the Attorney General, who had a deserved reputation as a protector of the President, would not be regarded as objective; and, finally, his conclusions, if they absolved the President of blame as we hoped they would, would be regarded as a whitewash. If we had any chance to avoid a full-scale congressional inquiry into the arms sales and funds-diversion matter, it would only be through the appointment of a review board that fair-minded people would regard as unbiased and independent. Dennis Thomas agreed with me and the special review board idea—which ultimately became the Tower Board—went back into the action plan.

At about 7:30, we were notified that Poindexter had stopped by the Justice Department on his way to the office, and at 7:50 that he had arrived at the White House. Regan went down the hall to tell Poindexter that he had to hand in his resignation that morning. Regan returned about 8:00 and said that Poindexter had been completely calm when told that he had to resign. According to Regan, he asked Poindexter whether he had known about the diversion of funds to the Contras, and Poindexter acknowledged that he had, but had done nothing about it. He felt sorry for the Contras, he said, and was angry at House Speaker Tip O'Neill for denying them aid. The detailed account of this meeting in Regan's book,[13] which accords with what Regan told us when he returned from Poindexter's office, has the ring of truth, both in the way Regan asked the questions, and in Poindexter's answers, which did not have the "buck stops with me" bravado of the testimony he eventually gave to Congress.

Poindexter's response to Regan's question about the diversion of funds made clear that there was no point asking him whether he had told the President, and Regan did not do so. However, Poindexter's statements to Regan, together with Regan's reaction after returning from the Oval Office with Meese the previous afternoon, are to me convincing evidence that the President was never informed of and did not approve a plan to divert a portion of the Iran arms sales proceeds to the Contras. As noted above, when Regan asked me and Dennis Thomas to join him in his office after Meese left, he said that something was developing that "looks like Watergate." This is not the reaction of someone who had heard about the diversion of funds before that afternoon. Yet Regan had sat in on virtually all meetings between the President and Poindexter, including virtually all morning national security briefings. Perhaps the President might not have seen the significance of a Poindexter statement—if one had been made—that a portion of the proceeds of the funds received from Iran had been set aside for or made available to the Contras. Clearly, however, since Regan regarded the information imparted by the Attorney General that afternoon as so significant that it might rise to the level of Watergate—that is, potentially threaten the President's very continuation in office—he would certainly have recognized the significance of a Poindexter statement about the diversion of funds.

In addition, Regan's visit with Poindexter on the morning of November 25 was very brief. Poindexter was of course aware that he was being asked to resign because of the disclosure of the diversion of funds. If Regan had previously been told about the diversion, one can imagine that Poindexter would not have gone quietly. He would have said something like, "Well, Don, why am I being asked to walk the plank when you knew about it, too?" This would have necessitated a complicated conversation in which Regan would have had to explain why Poindexter alone would have to bear the humiliation for the sake of the President. This is highly unlikely to have happened, in my view, in the brief time Regan spent with him that morning.

Over against this, we have nothing but speculation—statements to the effect that Poindexter or North would not have taken it upon themselves to do such a thing on their own. People who take this position have never met Oliver North. Near the end of the Tower Board's inquiry, the board's staff came upon a tape of a meeting between North and a senior Iranian in a location in Germany, in which North vividly described for the Iranian a walk with Reagan through the woods at

Camp David where, among other things, Reagan, according to North, expressed admiration for the Islamic Revolution in Iran. When the Tower Board staff played this tape for Reagan, he began to understand the dimensions of the problems caused for him and his administration by North's fantasy life.[14] It was also North who promised to the Iranians, and eventually delivered, top-secret U.S. photo reconnaissance showing the Iraqi defenses. No one ever admitted giving him the authority to do this. In 1991, North published a book entitled *Under Fire: An American Story,* in which he speculated, with no evidence whatever, that Reagan knew about the diversion of funds to the Contras. His assertion was based solely on his view that "Ronald Reagan knew of and approved a great deal of what went on with both the Iranian initiative and private efforts on behalf of the contras and he received regular, detailed briefings on both. I have no doubt that he was told about the use of residuals [profits from the arms sales] for the contras, and that he approved. Enthusiastically."[15] Needless to say, North could not have known what briefings, if any, Reagan received, and his statements must be taken as yet another falsehood in the fabric of deceptions he created around the Iran-Contra affair. I have never understood why North— who can so easily call Ronald Reagan a liar—has been treated as a hero by the same people who profess to admire Reagan. No, North was no ordinary Lieutenant Colonel. If he had been, the Iran-Contra story would have been very different.

Shortly after Regan reported on his conversation with Poindexter, the Attorney General and Chuck Cooper arrived at Regan's office. Cooper and I went off to make final changes in the action plan containing the proposal for a special review board and the draft statement about the diversion of funds that had been prepared for the President to deliver that morning. We returned about 10:00 A.M. with completed drafts, and Regan read them aloud to the group that had assembled, including Meese, Thomas, Buchanan, Chew, and Speakes. Changes were made in the statement, principally to go more easily on Poindexter than the draft Cooper and I had prepared. I don't know the reason for this, but I suspect that it was because the President continued to have sympathy for Poindexter, and Regan's account of Poindexter handing in his resignation seems to confirm that the President was genuinely sorry rather than angry.[16] This was not my view. I believed then and believe now that if Poindexter and North had not been forced out of the NSC they would have been able to continue the cover-up that was then under way—with disastrous consequences for the President.

In this sense, the Attorney General's discovery in North's files of a memo that suggested there had been a diversion of funds to the Contras was a lucky break for Ronald Reagan and the country that wanted to believe in him. It is important to recognize, however, what a near thing this was. If Abe Sofaer had not called me when Chuck Cooper and Paul Thompson were sitting in my office, and if I had not then brought to their attention (even though at the time I did not realize its significance) the huge discrepancy between Casey's draft testimony and McFarlane's report at the time of the Geneva summit about the HAWK sale, there might never have been an Attorney General's investigation. In that case, the North diversion memo might not have been found or might have been shredded with the rest of North's files, and Poindexter and North might have been able to continue their effort to withhold the facts from Congress and the American people. Under these circumstances, the President—misled by claims that disclosure would endanger the hostages or the "moderates" in Iran—might have been unwittingly drawn into a Watergate-style cover-up, with similar results for him and the nation.

Nothing, however, seemed to worry Ronald Reagan. After meeting with leaders of Congress that morning, and announcing to the press that a plan to divert funds to the Contras had been discovered, the President joined the Supreme Court for lunch and—to all appearances—had a wonderful time. The juxtaposition of the President's enjoyment of the Supreme Court lunch with the serious events of the morning will always be something of a mystery to me, but it was the beginning of a pattern that the President would follow throughout the trying months to come.

Despite everyone else's worries about the future of his presidency,[17] the President appeared to remain unconcerned. He seemed not to be following the events in any detail, and—except in one instance—he made no special effort to guide his staff's efforts or to control the direction of events. It was rather like a person learning that he had to undergo surgery. There was not much to be done about it; he would simply put himself in the hands of the experts, and ultimately it would come out all right. As I speculated at the outset of this book, I believe this attitude was the result of the fact that at this point in his presidency Ronald Reagan had achieved almost all of what he had set out to do, and did not believe that the Iran-Contra scandal that now threatened to engulf him really threatened anything that he had already achieved. This is further evidence that Reagan was a unique president and politician—a man devoted to his ideas rather than himself. That is my assessment; whether it accurately reflects what Ronald Reagan was thinking, we will never know.

CHAPTER 8

IRAN-CONTRA: IN THE DARK

Christmas in Washington that year [1986] was a difficult time for all of us. As we waited for the Tower Board to complete its investigation . . . Nancy . . . wanted me to be more critical of North and Poindexter for hiding things from me—but I said that I was the one responsible for the Iran initiative, that we still didn't know all the answers, and that it wouldn't be fair to do that.

—RONALD REAGAN,
Ronald Reagan: An American Life

With the departure of North and Poindexter, the problem facing the President changed substantially. He was no longer in danger of participating in a cover-up—in my view the most significant danger of all—but he had to restore his credibility with the American people, in part by explaining fully what had happened and why. This proved to be more difficult than might be expected. Although the White House staff now had access to Poindexter's and what was left of North's files, and could now begin to assemble a rough picture of what had happened in the Iran-Contra matter, our information was far from complete.

As was his custom, the President had delegated responsibility to the two national security advisers who had been in office while the arms sales policy was in force—first Robert McFarlane and later John Poindexter—and they, in turn, had delegated operational responsibility to Oliver North. Neither McFarlane nor Poindexter appears to have reported regularly to the President, and other than a series of false chronologies that were part of the cover-up, they prepared no written overall summary of what had occurred. As a result, after the departure of North and Poindexter, the President and the White House staff had no reliable sources of information who could bring all the pieces together into a coherent whole. We were literally in the dark, unable to answer even basic questions about what had taken place, and when.

The only way to prepare a complete account would be through an investigation, including testimony of witnesses and a review of an enormous trove of documents containing the operational details. The White House staff did not have the time or resources for this, and even if it did, the credibility of the result would have been called into question. Because of the suspicion with which the press then regarded anything the White House said on this subject, any substantial misstatement in a White House account would have been cited as evidence of deception and a cover-up.

Thus, unlike any White House scandal in my recollection, we were wholly dependent on finding independent sources to investigate and report what had actually happened. And since these bodies—committees of the Democratic-controlled Congress, for example—had little incentive to move quickly, the President would continue to be pummeled in the press until we had a definitive account on which to rely. Accordingly, the first step was to assure that a review board of independent but well-known figures was promptly appointed, to investigate the entire Iran-Contra matter and report to the President and the American people on what had actually taken place. However, getting the board the broad mandate it needed proved to be more difficult than might have been expected.

In a meeting with Regan on the afternoon of November 25, right after the lunch with the Supreme Court, Ball, Thomas, Dawson, and I consulted on the selection of the members of the presidential review board that the President had called for in his public statement that morning. Former Republican Senator John Tower was Regan's choice to head the board; someone suggested former Senator and Secretary of State Edmund Muskie—a Democrat—and Regan added Brent Scowcroft, a former national security adviser. Regan called the President, who gave his assent immediately, and Will Ball did some checking on the Hill that turned up no problems with any of the choices. Regan then called Tower and asked him to serve. He agreed with some reluctance, as did Muskie and Scowcroft.[1] All of them asked what the board was going to be empowered to do. I had a fairly clear idea about this, having framed the board with Dennis Thomas as a vehicle for getting the facts out as quickly as possible, but the details of the board's mandate had not been settled.

Indeed, there was another view—that the board was only to make recommendations concerning how the NSC staff was to be organized and was to behave in the future, without reviewing the mistakes of the past. Regan seemed to favor this approach, apparently fearing that the board would otherwise criticize the President's Iran policy. Limited in this way, however, the board would be useless for the major purpose I thought it was intended to serve—to discover and report what had happened in the Iran-Contra matter before the inevitable and partisan congressional investigations were commenced.

By early on November 26 Dennis Thomas and I had drafted a statement for the President that empowered the board to look into the *implementation* of the President's policy on Iran and the diversion of funds to the Contras. When Regan saw the statement, he was visibly uncomfortable; he did not want the board to be reviewing the President's policy. I argued that the purpose of the board was not to review whether the President had adopted the right policy, but how his policy was implemented. This would be the only truly objective review of this question, since the Justice Department would be concerned with criminal activities and Congress would be concerned with its foreign policy prerogatives. I said that if we did not have this investigation, the only story ever told about the Iran-Contra matter would be the account provided by the Democratic-controlled Congress and in the press through leaks from the Hill.

I thought I had convinced Regan, who left with the President for Santa Barbara later that morning, but in the afternoon I received a copy of the statement the President issued. To my dismay, I found that the word "future" had been inserted in the original draft language in such a way as to suggest that the board would have authority only to report on how things should be done in the future, not how they had been done in the past. I called David Chew, who was with the President and Regan in Santa Barbara and who told me the word had been inserted in the statement by the President and Regan before they departed. It appeared that I had lost the argument for a true review board.

Later that day, I received a call from Will Ball, the President's assistant for legislative affairs, with the news that Senator David Durenberger—a Republican and chairman of the Senate Intelligence Committee—wanted to call McFarlane, Poindexter, and North as witnesses in his committee's investigation. Ball asked whether we had any problem with that. Obviously, the first problem was executive privilege. McFarlane and Poindexter had directly advised the President. If they were called as witnesses, and chose to speak, the President had the right to claim a privilege that would prevent them from divulging what they had advised him. Early on, I had told Regan of my view that I did not think the President should claim executive privilege with respect to any of the Iran arms sales matters; of course, this view also extended to the Contra matters and the diversion of funds. I had never heard directly from Regan about whether the President had agreed to waive the privilege, so I told Ball that while I thought the President would agree to waive executive privilege, we would have to check with Regan to determine finally whether the President concurred.

I reached Regan on Saturday, November 29. He confirmed that the President would not assert executive privilege. I then raised the question of the scope of the Tower Board inquiry, and found Regan leaning strongly toward a narrow assignment for the Tower Board. He didn't want the board to inquire into the President's policies, or to interfere with the Justice Department investigation that Meese was heading. I had to start from the beginning: the fact that the congressional committees would get into this anyway, that Meese's report would have no credibility because he was so close to the President, and that this was the only investigative group likely to draw its conclusions without politics in mind. Regan listened patiently to my arguments for the third or fourth time and continued to give ground. By the end of the conversation—although he was still insisting that the board's mandate not extend to a review of the President's policy—he agreed that it could look into the facts of the Iran-Contra matter from beginning to end.

The following Monday, December 1, the President, Regan, and I met with the members of what was now called the President's Special Review Board (informally, the Tower Board after its chairman). The President gave them their charge. The talking points I had worked up for him were very broadly worded, and Regan called on me to amplify this language for the board. I made clear to the board that they were free to investigate all aspects of the NSC's processes, including how the President's policy on Iran was implemented.

All day, there were press stories that one or another Republican officeholder or party official had called for Regan's resignation. Considering the number and sources of these stories, it's amazing to me that Regan lasted as long as he did. Mitch Daniels, the assistant to the president for political affairs, had privately polled large numbers of Republican Party officials and told Regan that without exception they thought he should resign. Regan apparently had only one important supporter. His name was Reagan. I supposed that the President was as puzzled as I about what exactly Regan had done to deserve this treatment, and indeed he wrote in his autobiography: "A lot of people wanted me to replace Don Regan. They said he had supported the Iran operation and hadn't been on top of things when it started to get into trouble. But I felt that, whatever blame there might be in the Iran-Contra affair, it wasn't his."[2] Lou Cannon attributes the attack on Regan to the "accumulated hostility of Republican congressional leaders, who had long resented his nonconsultative style, his disdain for politics, and his displays of ego."[3] I'm inclined to agree with at least part of this assessment, although it was hard to imagine congressional leaders being shocked by displays of ego. It should be noted, however, that Cannon did not cite any substantive error on Regan's part—only his failure to ingratiate himself with powerful members of Congress.

That evening, I received a request to go to Regan's office. There, I was told the *New York Times* had a story that Robert McFarlane, in nonpublic testimony before the Senate Intelligence Committee, had said that Regan knew of the diversion of funds. I later learned from Bernie McMahon, the committee's staff director, that McFarlane had testified only that he could not imagine North and Poindexter authorizing a diversion of funds without approval "at the highest levels" of the White House. At my request, the use of Regan's name in the *Times* story was eventually killed by a call from Senator David Durenberger, the committee chairman, but the "highest levels" language remained, suggesting that both Regan and the President knew.

Of course, McFarlane had no direct knowledge of who might have known about the diversion of funds. His statement was pure speculation, but tendentious leaks of this kind were what we could expect as the congressional investigations began.

During this period, stories based on similar speculation were routinely reported in the press, even though they involved a serious accusation by a clearly biased observer against the President or, sometimes, Regan. On December 7, 1986, for example, the *Washington Post* ran a story on page 1, extensively quoting Democratic House Speaker O'Neill, hardly a non-partisan observer, as follows: "My personal opinion is, I honestly believe the president knew [about the diversion of funds to the Contras]. . . I've talked to generals since this thing happened, I've talked to colonels, lieutenant colonels, and [to] each one of them I say, 'Can you conceive of Lt. Col. [Oliver L.] North accomplishing this by himself?' They laugh. . . . They say . . . no lieutenant colonel would ever have done that on his own. . . . He had to have authority from somebody higher up than himself." Then the *Post* story continues: "O'Neill, interviewed Thursday in his Capitol office, said the information also went higher than Reagan's departed national security adviser,

Vice Admiral John M. Poindexter. 'They had to run it by someone higher up in the White House,' he said."

On the other hand, when Senator David Boren, the new Democratic chairman of the Senate Intelligence Committee, which at that point had been investigating the Iran-Contra matter for almost three months, told a *Time* magazine conference in late January that he did not think the President had intended to trade arms for hostages—a key question then in dispute—the *New York Times* put the story in the bottom left corner of page 7.

Meanwhile, it appeared that Attorney General Meese was moving toward recommending the appointment of an independent counsel to investigate the Iran-Contra matter. Things were so bad that we actually hoped this would happen. The idea was that once an independent counsel had been appointed, the press coverage would die down while the investigation continued. The President could get on with his presidency. This seems absurd and unrealistic now, in hindsight, but at the time we thought of the possible appointment of an independent counsel as a glimmer of good news.

By early the next day, December 2, we received word that Attorney General Meese would in fact be recommending the appointment of an independent counsel, and the President decided to make a statement that combined both the appointment of the Tower Board and the appointment of an independent counsel. In this statement, delivered at noon on December 2, Reagan expressed hope that with the Tower Board and an independent counsel investigation under way, the American people would soon have all the facts about the Iran-Contra affair. However, this idea was immediately picked apart by press speculation that Attorney General Meese, in his request for an independent counsel, would attempt to limit the scope of the counsel's activities. Shortly after the Attorney General's recommendation went forward, the special panel of the United States Court of Appeals that handles such requests appointed Lawrence Walsh, a Republican and a respected former prosecutor. There were no apparent restrictions on his investigation. Walsh quickly assembled a staff, and we were soon receiving document requests from his office, too.

By December 3, a consensus had developed among the White House staff that the President should say he had made a mistake. The previous day, the *New York Times* had published a poll showing that the President's approval rating had dropped 21 points—from 67 percent to 46 percent—in a single month. The poll indicated that while the President was regarded as generally honest—and a good deal more honest than most other politicians in Washington—the American people simply did not believe that he had not traded arms for hostages or that he did not know that funds from the sale of weapons to Iran had been used to support the Contras. This poll confirmed internal White House polls that showed similar erosion of the President's standing with the public since the onset of the Iran-Contra scandal. It seemed that the more the President protested, the less the public believed he was telling the truth. The staff diagnosis, which I strongly shared, was that the President would not recover his public support until he admitted that he had made a mistake by allowing his policy to become an arms-for-hostages swap. Accordingly, preparations were begun for a Saturday radio address that would deal with the Iran-Contra matter, possibly to include a statement by the President that he had made a mistake.

The first draft, in my view, did not go far enough. In it, the President apologized for the confusion and disappointment that had resulted from his policies but did not take responsibility for any mistakes. By the next day, a new draft had been developed in which Regan had penciled in a statement by the President that he had made a mistake in shipping arms to Iran and in not informing Congress. Discussions among the staff and doubt that the President would say he made a mistake resulted in dropping any reference in later drafts to the failure to report to Congress. But the President ultimately refused to say that he made a mistake of any kind, only that "mistakes had been made" in the implementation of his policy. It was a start—the President had for the first time recognized a distinction between the policy and its implementation—but it was a long way from what I and others thought was necessary to restore the President's credibility and put the controversy behind him.

On Friday, December 5, the *New York Times* published a story that the President had approved the first Israeli shipment of arms to Iran before it had occurred. The *Times* story was based on McFarlane's testimony, given behind closed doors to the Senate Intelligence Committee several days before, and was thus a leak from either the committee or McFarlane. It turned out later that the leak had come from McFarlane's counsel, Leonard Garment, who wanted his client's story to be the first put before the public. This was a good idea from McFarlane's point of view; by connecting Reagan more closely with the arms sales, McFarlane had instant credibility with the press. However, as we were to learn, McFarlane had changed his story several times. The public version he ultimately produced was at odds with the statements he had made privately to Poindexter and North in e-mail messages early in November 1986, when the NSC cover-up was under way.

On that same day, we received word from Senator Durenberger, through Bernie McMahon, that the committee had not found anything significant in its investigation, and would wrap up its work with a report to the effect that there was much less to the Iran-Contra matter than met the eye. There was only one small detail. The committee needed the testimony of Poindexter and North to complete the report, and they had refused to testify on Fifth Amendment grounds. According to McMahon, all the President had to do was pardon Poindexter and North—freeing them to give their testimony—and the committee could finish its work.

I invited McMahon down to the White House for a chat, and told him—speaking for myself and not the White House—that I thought the pardon idea was a non-starter. Unfortunately, I said, the best motives in the then current environment frequently produced the worst interpretations. A presidential pardon would certainly lead to speculation that this was part of a deal in which the President would pardon Poindexter and North and they in turn would clear him of wrongdoing. The charge that Gerald Ford had pardoned Richard Nixon as part of a deal for Nixon's resignation was much in my mind. Our best strategy for dealing with Poindexter and North was to hold them at arms' length, and not allow the perception to develop that we had or would have any contacts with them or their counsel.

Instead, I suggested, why didn't the committee grant use or testimonial immunity to Poindexter and North, which would have the same effect as a pardon but would be a much more common step in cases where congressional committees need testimony from witnesses who are concerned about possibly opening themselves to prosecution. This form of immunity prevents a prosecutor from using against a witness anything the witness says during his testimony before a congressional committee, but still permits prosecution of the witness on the basis of facts the prosecutor can develop independently. I told McMahon that I was reasonably sure the President would endorse use immunity if the committee voted it. McMahon, however, didn't like this idea. He said the committee would be reluctant to interfere with the Independent Counsel's investigation. We were at a frustrating impasse. If McMahon was correct, there was a Senate committee report that could improve the President's position substantially—and might be detailed enough to enable the President to rely on it in making statements to the American people and the press—but it would not be completed and published unless the committee could get the testimony of Poindexter and North. That of course was something we were powerless to deliver.

During the course of the Iran-Contra scandal, as in every major political crisis, a number of ideas were put forth by noncombatants and would-be advisers that can best be described as "goofy." In most cases, a little thought would have revealed even to their proponents that these ideas were unworkable. But at this point in the Iran-Contra crisis, the Sunday talk shows were suffused with just such silliness. Two ideas in particular seemed to gain currency: the President should appoint a special counsel who would investigate the facts and report directly to him, and the President should call North and Poindexter and ask them to tell him the whole story.

For one thing, it was not clear why a special counsel would have access to more information than the Tower Board, or would be able to assemble it any more quickly, or be treated as any more objective and credible. In addition, there was no reason at all to expect that North and Poindexter—who were relying on their Fifth Amendment privilege against self-incrimination—would say anything to a special counsel or to the President himself. Any such statement could vitiate the privilege, no matter to whom it was made. Finally, and perhaps most important, both ideas had the dangerous aspect that they would place the President in the middle of a controversy over the facts. What had he been told? Did that accord with his recollection? Did he disclose everything relevant from what he was told? These were only a few of the questions that would have led the President into an inescapable bog of ambiguity; worse than that, by making him the repository of the "facts" supposedly divulged by Poindexter and North, it would have made the President a much sought-after witness for all the investigations that were currently afoot.

But these ideas kept popping up, probably as the result of frustration among Republicans. And occasionally, they attracted interest in unlikely places. A good example occurred the following week. Regan asked me to join him for a meeting in a house on Jackson Place, across Pennsylvania Avenue from the White House, that is used by visiting former presidents. As we drove over there, Regan told me that we were going to meet with former Senator Howard Baker—ironically, the person who would ultimately replace Regan—about an idea the President himself had suggested. Describing it as either "the best or worst idea I have ever heard," Regan said the President had asked him to check out with various wise men whether the President should go up to the Hill and testify personally before the Senate Intelligence Committee. Regan had asked Baker to meet him at this place in order to discuss the President's suggestion.

I had no doubt about whether this was the best or worst idea; to me, it was clearly the worst—a scenario for disaster. The President seemed to have no sense of the dangerous waters in which he was now swimming. There were people on the Hill and elsewhere who would have liked nothing better than to terminate his presidency by showing that he was covering up wrongdoing or lying to Congress, or at least truncate his effectiveness as president by calling his credibility into question before the country. Our whole strategy was developed because we knew few of the facts about what had actually happened in the arms sales, and knew nothing at all about the diversion of funds. The President's news conference

on November 19—before we could gather reliable and authoritative information about what had occurred—should have been a good lesson.
Now he might be put under oath and asked to make definitive statements
about things he and the rest of us still knew little or nothing about.

To my surprise, Baker was ambivalent. He worried that the President might be asked questions that he couldn't answer, but on the other
hand said that if the President thought it would be to his political benefit he should do it. "The President," said Baker, "has the best political
instincts I've ever seen." Baker was a great phrasemaker. As a member of
the original Senate Watergate Committee, he had come up with the
summary question, "What did the President know and when did he
know it?" After the signing of the original Reagan tax cut, Baker had
called it a "riverboat gamble." I wondered how someone who thought a
tax cut was a riverboat gamble would describe the President's laying his
office on the line.

After Baker left, I told Regan my views. Regan listened but was non-
committal. Perhaps in his shoes I would have been, too. Regan was dealing directly with the President. His inclination, as I'd seen many times,
was to treat the President's ideas and suggestions with the utmost respect
and deference. In any event, despite my strong negative opinion, Regan
invited me to a lunch he had set up in the same place with Bob Dole,
then the Senate Republican leader, and Baker.

Dole was a good deal more negative on the idea of the President testifying than Baker had been, and that was good. But on the other hand
Dole had picked up the notion that the President should ask North and
Poindexter to tell him the whole story. Baker, who had become more
negative on the testimony proposal, suggested that the President should
appeal to North and Poindexter as military men. "If they'd take a hill on
the President's orders and risk their lives," said Baker, "why wouldn't
they do this in the national interest?" There was no resolution at this
meeting, but Regan had gotten fairly strong signals that Baker and Dole
were negative on the idea of the President testifying. I think he recognized, however, that the proposal for the President to call on North and
Poindexter, either to tell him what happened or to testify before Con-

gress, was almost certainly a non-starter. There was no reason for them to abandon their constitutional rights in this case, and there might be a backlash if the President asked them to do it.

But the ideas kept coming, and because I was the White House staff person most heavily involved in the Iran-Contra matter, I had to keep batting them down. The next day, James Baker, Regan's predecessor as chief of staff, dropped by my office with his idea: the President should ask all his advisers to sign affidavits that they never told him about the diversion of funds to the Contras. The President himself would then sign such an affidavit. I couldn't for the life of me understand what this was supposed to accomplish. If anyone had told the President, it would have been North or Poindexter, and neither of them was going to sign an affidavit. Moreover, putting the President under oath on this question was very dangerous. What if a document should turn up that showed the President was informed? This would not necessarily mean he had approved the diversion, but it would put him in a position of having been untruthful under oath. I noted to Baker that the President's denials of knowledge represented an implicit danger. As in Watergate, there is denial after denial, until a document or other definitive evidence is discovered that shows his denials to have been untruthful. At that point, the public believes they have been taken along for a ride, and the President loses all credibility. It is better, I said, for the President to keep silent than to try over and over again to demonstrate—ineffectively— that he did not know about the diversion of funds.

Baker's other idea was that the President should say he made a mistake in shipping arms to Iran. I told him we had tried that, and that the President would not say he'd made a mistake. Baker, of all people, must have understood what that meant. After four years as White House chief of staff, Baker surely had seen the President's views harden into convictions. In this case, Ronald Reagan had concluded that he had adopted the right policy toward Iran, had not traded arms for hostages, and would not say he'd made a mistake. This was the obverse of the conviction coin that served him so well in other cases. Now it would prolong the Iran-Contra controversy.

Although the notion of having the President solicit sworn statements from his staff and cabinet persisted for a few days, it eventually died away. None of the ideas that were offered to us—except a statement by the President that he had made a mistake—really made any sense in terms of our problem or our strategy. Our problem was that we did not have a clear idea of what actually happened, and could not find out without the assistance of Poindexter and North. Our strategy, as a result, was to cooperate with all inquiries and allow these investigations to bear the responsibility for reporting the facts. Any attempt we made to formulate a statement of facts was bound to be contradicted either by facts previously unknown to us or by the material that the media chose to select and report as facts. From the standpoint of the public, these were the same thing, although in reality they were very different. With respect to virtually every disclosure made by the White House, the media version could be relied upon to emphasize those elements that contradicted the position the President was taking. As a result, we hoped to make our case through other sources—sources that could make some claim to objectivity. The White House would give them access to as much information as possible.

Under these circumstances, we were hopeful that a good result would come out of the inquiry of the Senate Intelligence Committee, an investigation begun in November 1986 and now approaching its conclusion. As the committee's work proceeded we began to receive increasing indications that the committee had not found any serious problems with what the President had done. This was very encouraging and suggested that our rapid and full disclosure strategy might bear fruit. A favorable report from the committee, suggesting perhaps that the President's policy was in fact to open a communications channel to Iran—not to trade arms for hostages—and that such a policy was a credible one under the circumstances, might have gone a long way toward defusing the controversy. The fact that the Republicans had only a slim majority on the committee—a majority that would be lost in January 1987 when the new Congress convened—also encouraged us. It was possible that if the committee ultimately issued a report, some of the Democrats would sign it. We had been unable to break the impasse over how to get testimony from Poindexter and North, but it seemed as though the committee was now willing to proceed without this information.

Finally, on December 14, I was told by Rhett Dawson, the Tower Board chief of staff, that Bernie McMahon of the committee staff had briefed the Tower Board on the committee's conclusions, and was willing to discuss this material with me. I set up a meeting with McMahon the following morning, and received a report that was rather favorable from the standpoint of the President. The committee, according to McMahon, had concluded—although its conclusions had to be tentative without the testimony of North and Poindexter—that the White House had been the victim of a kind of scam. The arms sales program was sold to McFarlane by a combination of arms dealers and Israelis. The arms dealers wanted to sell advanced arms to Iran that were available only from the United States or Israel, and Israel was interested in supplying arms to Iran in exchange for Iranian Jews. McFarlane—looking for a Kissinger-like score on the international scene—was essentially taken in by the idea that this was an opportunity to achieve a strategic opening to Iran. However, Oliver North—who was assigned to carry out the program—was interested only in getting the hostages back, not in the broader purposes on which the policy was approved by the President. North did little reporting to McFarlane and perhaps even to Poindexter, neither of whom followed his activities very closely, or reported much of what little they knew to the President.

This interpretation accounted for a number of things—particularly the discrepancy between North's statements about the President's interest in the hostages and the President's insistence that he had approved a policy with a different and more strategic purpose. It also explained McFarlane's initial enthusiasm for the plan, how the President's plan became a trade of arms for hostages, and the President's lack of knowledge of the details. Nevertheless, this scenario had some pitfalls. Obviously, the President would be charged with some degree of dereliction and naïveté, in allowing a program of this significance to proceed without careful oversight, and in allowing himself to be scammed by the Israelis and a bunch of international arms dealers. Although other conclusions might have been preferable, given the President's current situation and the American people's waning respect for his truthfulness in this matter, it seemed to me that it would be better for him to be considered a fool than a liar. The picture of North that emerged from McMahon's report was also helpful to the President's case, since his image as a marine lieutenant colonel was otherwise that of a man who simply followed orders, rather than being the rogue operator he was in fact.

Shortly after I received McMahon's report, we heard from the Hill that the Senate Intelligence Committee would call Regan to testify the following day. Regan, who had initially objected when I suggested weeks before that we should not claim executive privilege if he was called to testify, was now eager to go before the committee. Accordingly, at 3:00 P.M., a group of us—including Ball, Thomas, my deputy Jay Stephens, Dawson, and I—convened in Regan's office to go over his testimony. We were in the midst of dealing with the opening statement when the President called. He said that he had a statement he wanted to issue, calling for the committee to grant use immunity to North and Poindexter in order to get their testimony. Regan argued with him a bit about putting the statement out now, but finally suggested that the President send it down to his office, where we would put it in shape to be released. Regan, who had to leave the office for a doctor's appointment, asked me to accompany him to the car. He told me he had heard virtually the same idea for a statement from Nancy Reagan that morning, and was certain that one of the lawyers the Reagans had been consulting had written it for them. In any event, this was the only time during the Iran-Contra matter that the President suggested any particular step be taken in his behalf.

At first I was concerned that the Attorney General would oppose the request to grant use immunity to North and Poindexter. The Justice Department usually objects to congressional grants of use immunity because these frequently create obstacles to prosecution. To my surprise, however, when I called Attorney General Meese he supported the idea and made a few suggestions about what he thought should be in it. He much preferred this approach, he said, to the idea of a personal appeal from the

President to North and Poindexter to testify, which he considered an unfair effort to pressure them to give up their constitutional rights.

When I read the President's proposed statement, I had some concerns about whether he fully understood its potential consequences—particularly the interpretation it might receive in the press—and went to see him. After greeting me, the President sat down at his desk and offered me a seat in the side chair to his right. As usual, he fixed me with a very steady gaze while I was talking with him. I said that I favored the idea of the committee granting use immunity, but was concerned about the initial request coming from him. The Democrats on the committee, I said, would likely turn down his request, saying that they did not want to interfere with prosecutions of North and Poindexter, and the press might suggest that the President was attempting to curry favor with the two people whose testimony could do him harm. Use immunity could help them avoid punishment—and ultimately did when, much later, a court overturned the convictions of North and Poindexter because they could have been based on immunized testimony. I noted, however, that the Attorney General had no objection.

Reagan showed a firm grasp of how use immunity worked, and told me that, despite my concerns, it still seemed to him that "it might work" and he "would like to try it." He said this in such a soft-spoken and non-assertive way that it almost seemed he would not have been offended if I'd told him I just wouldn't do it.

I left the Oval Office and returned to my office where I revised the President's draft to make it legally correct and to add in some of Ed Meese's ideas. I wondered, after reading the President's draft, whether in fact a lawyer had prepared it. It seemed rather to be the handiwork of a moderately sophisticated nonlawyer, and I would not have been surprised to learn that the President had drafted it himself. When Regan returned, I went back down to his office, briefed him on what the President and I had said, and distributed the redraft. At this point, the President called me, and I took the call outside Regan's office. The President asked whether the statement could be released the next morning. I said this was possible, but I was a little concerned about creating a flap prior to and during Regan's testimony. The President hesitated a moment and said that if this was the case we should release it at noon the next day, following Regan's testimony.

Regan's recollections of the Iran arms sales matter were very sketchy. He had no notes to refer to. Jay Stephens and I, who were briefing him, decided beforehand that we would not attempt to refresh his recollection with anything we had already learned from looking at documents that had been furnished to congressional investigators. Our view was that the best course was to allow him to tell the story he recalled, without any attempt to correct or enhance what he remembered. There were several reasons for this. The information we had seen was all in some sense contradictory and suspect. Each of the participants involved in carrying out the President's policy had his own perspective and in some cases his own agenda. It was difficult to know who was telling the truth. In addition, Regan's unadorned recollections were bound to be the best record of what the President was actually told, since he sat in on almost every national security briefing in which McFarlane or Poindexter had described the arms transactions to the President. Regan's memory, in my experience, was excellent—far better than the President's—and to the extent that he didn't remember details it was likely to be because those details had not been provided to the President himself. Thus, the testimony that Regan gave to the Senate Intelligence Committee was his unadulterated recollection of what the President was told in Regan's hearing, and likely to be the best record of the extent to which the President was briefed by McFarlane and Poindexter.

Perhaps, in preparing a client for testimony, some lawyers would not take this non-intrusive position. The client might be shown documents that refresh his recollection or enable him to be prepared for contradictory evidence. But this was not an ordinary deposition, or even ordinary testimony. We believed that there was some historical significance to what Regan was going to say, and that the historical record should be preserved intact. Neither Regan nor, we believed, the President needed any special defense. The facts, to the extent they were finally determined, might prove to be embarrassing to the President, but not fatal to his presidency. The important point was to let the chips fall where they may—to be sure the historical record was as accurate as possible. Stephens and I prepared Regan by asking him the kinds of questions he was likely to get from the committee and its counsel. The effect of this kind of preparation is to get the witness to recall as much as possible, to resolve conflicts in his own recollections, and to establish in his mind a chronologically arranged succession of important events. We did not, by and large, comment on his answers, except where one recollection seemed inconsistent with another.

One fact about which Regan had a distinct recollection was that the President did not approve the first Israeli arms shipment in advance— that he was told about it afterward by McFarlane and said something to the effect of "Well, what's done is done." Presumably, in describing this recollection, Regan knew that he was contradicting what McFarlane had said in his earlier testimony to the same committee. That testimony had been leaked to the press by McFarlane's lawyer, published by the *New York Times* on December 7, and generally accepted in the press as the definitive account.

By contradicting McFarlane's account, Regan must have known that he was taking on a lot. His only reason for doing this had to be that he believed it to be true. When the discrepancy in the testimonies was discovered, the press treated the difference between Regan's and McFarlane's recollections as a hugely significant issue, but from a legal point of view it meant nothing. Whether the President approved the arms shipment in advance, or condoned it afterward, was completely irrelevant to any important question in the Iran investigations. In both cases, the President had approved the sales, and in both cases the legal analysis was the same. It is a measure of the press's relentless focus on conflict— even trivial conflict—that no one ever bothered to evaluate whether this inconsequential detail had any significance.

Regan's testimony was a great success. His demeanor was open, honest, and candid. He freely admitted mistakes he made and occasionally an inability to remember. I was somewhat surprised to see that he was able to recall events in greater detail before the committee than he had been able to do when Jay Stephens and I questioned him, but there were no contradictions between what he had said to us the day before and what he testified to under oath. He made the point firmly that he was not the manager of the NSC staff, no matter what impression had been given by press accounts. His account of the President's demeanor when he learned of a plan to divert Iran arms sales funds to the Contras, and Poindexter's responses when Regan confronted him on November 25, were persuasive in their detail. After the hearing, Senator Durenberger, the chairman of the committee, said he now believed the President had not known about the diversion, much less approved it.

The President's statement on use immunity was released about the time that Regan's testimony ended. Fortunately, I was able to catch both Durenberger and McMahon and take them aside to explain what the President intended to do. It would not have been fair for them to be confronted with the President's statement without any prior notice. As we talked, it was clear that neither of them had a clear understanding of what use immunity was intended to achieve. It was not, as they seemed to think, a gift to the witness; it was a way of compelling the witness to testify to matters as to which he might otherwise—without immunity—have a privilege to keep silent. To be sure, use immunity complicated a prosecutor's task, but it was a good way to reconcile the interests of Congress and the judicial system. They agreed that the President's request justified the committee looking at the issue of immunity again.

Although Regan's testimony was widely praised on the Hill, the President's proposal for use immunity was not. When I got back to the White House, I was asked to brief reporters for the major newspapers and networks on both issues. Most of the questions were on the President's statement. Why had we waited until now to issue it? Wasn't it too late to do any good? Didn't we know that the request would be turned down? The implication was that the President was grandstanding, and knew that Congress would never agree. In fact, the committee did turn down the President's request, with not a murmur of protest in the press. The White House would have been severely criticized for any action that limited the amount of information the public received, but the Senate committee could do this with impunity.

By the following day, Regan's testimony that the President had not approved the August shipment in advance had reached Leonard Garment, McFarlane's lawyer. He called me to ask whether this was true, and I confirmed that it was. He seemed worried, and argued that McFarlane had no motive to authorize the Israelis to proceed without the President's specific approval. I said that this was, nevertheless, Regan's recollection. He pointed out that the Israelis would never have shipped the weapons unless they had assurances of replenishment, and I responded that Regan had testified only to the question of whether the President had approved in advance, not whether or when he had authorized replenishment of Israeli stocks. There was no point in arguing about this with Garment, but of course the Israelis would have shipped the arms if they believed that McFarlane had gotten the President's approval, even if he had not. In fact, if they thought the shipment of arms to Iran was in their interests—and there had been some suggestion to this effect in the Senate Intelligence Committee's unpublished draft conclusions—the Israelis might have shipped the arms on the basis of a wink and a nod.

We were still hopeful that the Senate Intelligence Committee's report would support the President's position on a few key points. This possibility became somewhat more realistic when Regan received a phone call from Senator Durenberger while Jay Stephens and I were preparing him for his next testimony—this time before the House Intelligence Committee. Durenberger said that he and Senator Patrick Leahy, the ranking member on the Senate Intelligence Committee, would like to come down to the White House and brief the President on the contents of the committee's report. Senator Leahy's presence, I thought, would be particularly valuable, if McMahon's description of the committee's conclusions was accurate, since it would indicate that at least some among the Democratic minority were on board.

I called McMahon and we agreed that the meeting should be confidential. He said that was the way Leahy and Durenberger wanted it. He said that the Democratic members of the committee had agreed that a public report would be made at the end of the committee's work, and that it would take about ten days to two weeks to prepare the report.

What the President would receive was a preliminary briefing. I said I'd recommend a meeting to the President and Regan. The meeting was scheduled for 2 P.M. the following day, a Friday, in the Library, a small room on the first floor of the residence part of the White House. The President was to leave for Camp David at 3 P.M.

When Durenberger and McMahon arrived, Leahy was not with them. This was not a good sign. Durenberger then spent a good deal of time explaining the political situation in the committee. This left little time for the actual briefing, which was done by McMahon. His report was not significantly different from what he had originally told me, but reduced by about two thirds. When the President and Regan left, it still seemed possible that the committee's report would be favorable.

However, after the President's departure, Senator Durenberger indicated for the first time that he was having difficulty getting the Democrats on the committee to agree to the interpretation of events just outlined by McMahon. This was very bad news, since at least a modicum of bipartisanship was necessary to give the report—and the interpretation of events we had been led to believe it would advance—any value. Previously, the only problem I had been told about was declassification of the report. Once that was solved, we believed, it could be released to the public. If the Democrats on the committee now did not agree with the report, it might not be released at all. Not only would this eliminate its value as a source of information, an unreleased report could actually do harm, since we could anticipate leaks by the Democrats of the portions that undermined the President's position. We could hope that the Republicans on the committee would be willing to leak favorable material, but that hardly ever worked. The media were just not interested in publishing material that supported the President's position. The best outcome under these circumstances would be for some senator to give the full report to a newspaper that would publish extended excerpts, but this seemed unlikely.

Nevertheless, by early January 1987, a committee of officials from the national security agencies had reviewed the report and declassified it for publication. Later, that declassification review would be described by Senate Democrats and some editorialists as a laundering. Still hoping for the best, I prepared a memorandum for the President in anticipation of the possibility that the committee would release the report. The memorandum summarized the report's conclusions and alerted the President to the kinds of press questions it would elicit. I asked him to think about the answers to these questions in advance of a meeting we had scheduled with him for January 3. However, calls from Will Ball and Bernie McMahon on January 2 indicated that whether the report would actually be released was becoming a closely contested issue within the committee. Not surprisingly, the Democrats, who were making political hay because of the President's discomfiture, were not enthusiastic about releasing a report that might give credence to the President's claims about his intentions. This was especially true in light of the fact that they were soon to take control of the Senate and would thus have a forum for continued investigation of what the President had done. A report at this point might limit their options. I was somewhat hopeful that press pressure for release of the report would influence the committee's decision, but there had been very little editorial comment on that subject during the preceding weeks and hence very little pressure on the Democrats to do anything but oppose release.

The meeting with the President on January 3 was my first opportunity to question him directly about his recollections concerning the Iran-Contra matter. It was a Saturday afternoon, and Regan, Jay Stephens, and I walked over to the White House residence and went up the elevator to the private floor where the Reagans lived. The President ushered us into a sitting room on the west end of the residence, and the meeting began. The sitting room faces west, and is dominated by a large fan-shaped window. A couch was situated under the window, a coffee table in front of the couch, and chairs on the two narrow ends of the coffee table. On the walls were paintings by American artists, borrowed from the National Gallery.

I briefed the President on the substance of the Senate committee report, and noted that it contained a number of elements that would be critical of him. Nevertheless, I said, it was better to have the facts out sooner rather than later, and the President agreed. I pointed out that the report would raise a number of questions about what he knew and what he did, and that the purpose of the meeting was to explore these questions. Regan asked me to give the President my assessment of whether the Senate committee report would actually be released, and I said that, although this question had become highly controversial within the committee, I was optimistic that media pressure would force the Democrats to let the report go. I was to learn otherwise.

I first asked the President whether he recalled approving the Israeli shipment of TOW missiles to Iran in August 1985. He said he had no recollection of this. He remembered something about a shipment of missiles that was to go from Portugal to Iran if the hostages were released, but would land in Israel if they were not. I said this sounded like the HAWK shipment in November 1985, and the President commented that this was all he could remember. He said that it would be helpful to him to have a chronology of events associated with the arms sales, because they all ran together in his mind. I told him that I would prepare one for him.

Regan then asked whether the President remembered a meeting in the White House residence with Shultz, Weinberger, Casey, and Regan, shortly after he returned to the White House after his colon cancer operation in July 1985. The President said that he could not remember this meeting, but did remember McFarlane coming to see him when he was in the hospital, and telling him that the Iranians wanted to open negotiations. He said he thought this was a fine idea. Regan then asked whether the President remembered saying that he did not want to ship weapons when we didn't know who we were dealing with, and the President again said he had no recollection of this.

At this point, it occurred to me that if the President didn't remember the actual events or the surrounding discussions perhaps he remembered his reactions to what he had been told. So I asked him whether he recalled being surprised when he was told the Israelis had shipped arms to the Iranians. To this he said yes, that he remembered being surprised to hear this. Regan then noted that this accorded with Regan's own recollection, and must mean that the President could not have approved the shipment in advance—otherwise he would not have been surprised. The President agreed.

We then moved on to the HAWK missile shipment in November 1985. The President said he had no recollection of approving the shipment but did recall that the shipment originated in Portugal, where "the Israelis had a warehouse," and that it was to go to Iran only if the hostages were released. Regan asked whether the President remembered the subject coming up at the time of the summit meeting in Geneva. He described the room—Regan's room—where McFarlane had briefed the President. This did not jog the President's memory. He knew part of the story associated with the HAWKs, but could not remember when it had been given to him.

I then asked him whether he could recall anyone telling him that if the Israelis shipped U.S. arms to the Iranians this had to be reported to Congress, and that he had decided not to report it. I had hoped this rather vivid description of the legal issue might refresh his recollection about his approval of arms sales in general, but it did not. Instead, he said—with reference to my comment about reporting—that he had been told that when there was danger to people's lives he did not have to report to Congress until the operation was over. This was a reasonably good description of how the National Security Act's requirement for reporting to Congress might be liberally interpreted. The Act generally required reports to Congress after the president had made a finding, but in special cases the report could be made "in a timely manner" after the operation was over. If the President reasonably believed that lives were at stake, he might be able to argue that the reporting obligation did not commence until after the hostages were all released or some other desired outcome involving the so-called moderates in Iran had come to pass.

I then moved to a series of questions about why the program was restarted in January 1986, after McFarlane had returned from a meeting in London and recommended that it be terminated. He seemed to have a recollection of having sent McFarlane on the mission to London because of uncertainty about whom we were dealing with. I said that both Shultz and Weinberger had thought the initiative was dead after McFarlane's report, but somehow and for some reason it was revived. The President said he recalled a "new Israeli" in the picture, whom he identified as Kimche—although it was probably a different official named Amiram Nir—who had said there was an opportunity to establish better ties with Iran through a new group in Iran.

I asked what kind of action was contemplated by the January 1986 finding, and he said that he thought the hostages would be released in exchange for a certain amount of arms, but that this was only a gesture of good faith on both sides—that the discussions were really for the purpose of opening up a channel of communication with a group that was opposed to Ayatollah Khomeini and wanted our support. When I asked whether he was aware of the trading going on—that North or others were offering weapons for hostages—he acknowledged that he had been told from time to time that weapons were being shipped and hostages would be coming out but he regarded that as part of the process of opening a channel of communication.

It seemed to me that this meeting was a good start. The President had only a weak recollection of what had happened in the arms sales matter, but perhaps the chronology I was asked to prepare would refresh his memory. Still, I faced the same question I faced with Regan's recollection; I did not want to put into the chronology information that I had learned as we had assembled documents for the various investigations that were now going forward. This information, even if it was accurate, might distort the President's recollection. When, later, I did not fully follow through on this policy, the results were what I had feared.

Meanwhile, our strategy was still focused on getting the Senate Intelligence Committee report issued, and I prepared a statement for Speakes to make at the outset of his press briefing on Monday, January 5. My hope was that the statement would stimulate press efforts—which had thus far been virtually non-existent, as far as we could tell— to get the report released, or at least to seek out a source who would leak the report. When I distributed my draft statement to Thomas and Ball after the daily operations meeting that day, Monday, they were opposed to issuing it. They pointed out that every time any one of us suggested to the reporters that they call for the release of this report, we were ridiculed for not ourselves releasing the North chronology. I said again, as I'd said to reporters seemingly dozens of times, the North chronology was—as far as I could tell—a tissue of lies. Nothing would be gained by releasing it except further confusion about what had actually happened, and further allegations of a White House cover-up. I also said I was afraid the Senate Committee report would never be issued unless there was pressure from the press, and I could see no other way of stimulating it. I noted my astonishment that while Senators Byrd and Dole had had a heated exchange on David Brinkley's Sunday morning talk show about whether the report should be released, not a word about the report or the disagreement had appeared in either the *Times* or the *Post* that morning.

Finally, we agreed that Speakes would not issue the statement, but would use it to answer a question, if any, about the report, and would release the statement only if he got no questions. As it turned out, there were no questions. I thought this must be a totally unprecedented situation. The press was complaining that they were not getting information about what actually happened in the Iran initiative. A Senate report had been prepared based on testimony from all the major players who would testify, and all the documents that could be assembled in the time allotted, and there was no enthusiasm in the press for seeing it. One could be forgiven for believing that the object here was not really to find out and report the facts, but to prolong the controversy. Thus, and predictably, when Speakes finally issued the statement calling for the release of the report he was met with a storm of questions about why we were calling for the release of this report when we had not released the North chronology.

The same day, the committee voted, 7–6, not to release the report. Senator William Cohen, Republican of Maine, voted with all the Democrats on the committee. Regan was hopping mad. "By not getting this report out," he said, "you and I have failed the President." I agreed, but I could not think of anything we could have done differently to get the report released.

A partisan fight erupted on the Senate floor between Republicans, who wanted the report released as the best available information at the present time, and Democrats, who called the report incomplete. Larry Speakes issued a statement after the vote and the Senate debate, reported by Bob Woodward in the *Washington Post* on January 7 this way: "In his statement after the committee vote last night, Speakes said, 'We are outraged and disappointed. We think the American people have the right to have this information and judge for themselves. The president will continue to do everything he can to see that all the facts come out as quickly as possible.' However, Speakes has repeatedly refused to release a chronology written by North before he left the White House."

The same day, however, the *Washington Post*'s lead editorial called for release of the Senate committee report, saying, "At the moment, the most important thing is to establish the credibility of congressional inquiry. This cannot be done if the Democrats act in a way to convey the idea that only information damaging to President Reagan will be allowed to flow freely into the public domain. Let's see the report."

And the *New York Times* carried a front-page article that day with the headline "North Falsified Information, White House Says." It picked up Speakes's comments about the inaccuracy of the North chronology and some of the details of the Senate report. A longer story the next day, styled as "News Analysis," contained a more detailed description, from Hill sources, of some of the report's conclusions. These pointed to the centrality of North in prosecuting the arms-for-hostages trade, and reviving it when it seemed to falter. He was quoted in the report as saying that if the arms trade fails, "the hostages will die." The *Times* said nothing editorially. None of this was a satisfactory substitute for a release of the report itself, but I was pleased that the report had gotten at least this much coverage.

Some of the articles illustrated the difficulty and frustration of dealing with the press. As I have noted, we had a number of reasons for wanting the committee's report to be made public—we thought it would establish a baseline of facts that would enable the President to cite a credible source when he stated a fact about the arms sales; it provided a credible explanation for how the initiative came to be and why it turned into what appeared to be a trade of arms for hostages; and it concurred that the President had been truthful when he said that he had approved the arms sales for a broader, strategic purpose. However, many of the articles about the report stated, as though it was a fact, that the White House wanted the report to be made public because it cleared the President of any involvement with the diversion of funds. This was not the reason. We did not imagine the President could ever be cleared of involvement in the diversion until Poindexter testified on the subject. There is no way to prove a negative, and we had no way of eliminating all likely channels to the President until Poindexter was willing to say that he had not told the President about the diversion.

However, when enough of the report was leaked that the press could see what it had to say about the diversion—that the committee had no evidence that the President was aware of it—they concluded that the White House staff was simply stupid for wanting the report to be disclosed, since it did not, in fact, clear the President of involvement with the diversion. Then there was commentary about the incompetence of the White House staff in pressing so hard for the disclosure of a report that did not even do what we purportedly wanted it to do.

But that was not the only fallout from the committee's report. I had been concerned that the failure to release the committee's report was only one of the setbacks we would encounter. The other would be leaks of portions of the report that were unfavorable to the President. That happened almost immediately. Late on January 8, I received a message from the press office that a portion of the report had been leaked to NBC, which was going with a story on it that evening. This was both good and bad news. If a network had a substantial amount of the report, it increased the chances that a newspaper—which would run large excerpts—would get the full report. The bad news was that network news was so truncated and summary that it was bound to report only those elements of the report that put the President in a bad light.

Sure enough, Chris Wallace reported that evening that the report showed the President had "signed a finding" in January 1986 to the effect that arms would be sold to Iran in exchange for hostages. This sounded like a tendentious interpretation of the finding, and I called

Wallace about it. He said he had a copy of the finding in the committee report, and I suggested that we meet so I could see what he had. I did not believe that the January finding said anything of the kind. Sure enough, when we met Wallace showed me a page of the report, but what he had was not a finding but a retyped version of the covering memo for the January finding. This was something I had not seen before; it was the memo that Poindexter had used to brief the President on the finding. I got a Xerox copy of the original, and read it.

My first reaction was that the memo as a whole tended to support the President's position that he had approved the arms sales as a way of opening a channel of communications with Iran. It contained a long explanation of the strategic considerations that favored an opening to moderates in Iran, and explained that the arms would both strengthen their position and provide a means to influence them. To the extent that the memo discussed the question of the hostages, it was in the context of establishing a precondition for further development of the relationship. I thought it unlikely that the memo and finding were simply a cover story for the trade of arms for hostages, since it makes no sense to create a cover story in a classified memo that was never intended to see the light of day anyway.

Because of the misleading NBC description, the press office asked me to brief the *Times, Post,* ABC, and CBS about the memo and the finding, and I did so by reading excerpts to them over the telephone. When this was done, the press office said I would then have to brief the entire press corps the following day, since we could not give a story this important to these selected outlets alone. With this, I realized that the whole memo and finding would have to be released, since I couldn't brief the entire press corps by reading them excerpts. Jay Stephens told me that both the memo and the finding had been declassified by the NSC staff when these materials were reviewed in connection with the declassification of the Senate Intelligence Committee report.

Accordingly, the following morning, after consulting with Regan, I authorized the distribution to the press of both the covering memo and the finding, and I spent about an hour and a half responding to questions. I had hoped that the memo would demonstrate to the press that the President understood his policy to be aimed at opening a channel to Iran, for which the hostage release was both a precondition and an added benefit of establishing the relationship. That is in fact what the memo said. But the press chose to focus on the few words in the memo that discussed the hostages and the relationship between the shipment of arms—the U.S. demonstration of good faith—and the release of the hostages—Iran's demonstration. The January 9 *Washington Post* headline, for example, was "Document Set Out Arms-for-Hostages Trade with Iran."

In all, the briefing—which was our last and most concerted effort to explain and support the President's position—was a failure. We simply could not overcome the press and public conclusion that the President had intended to trade arms for the U.S. hostages in Lebanon and had made up a cover story about opening a channel to Iran in order to put the best face on his real purposes.

A truncated version of the original Senate Intelligence Committee report was eventually released late in January 1987. The report had been substantially revised and reduced in size by the Democratic majority that now controlled the committee. The truncated version was in the form of a chronology and drew no conclusions. When this version was finally available, reporters raced through it looking for nuggets of sensational disclosure, which were published regardless of their truthfulness or the context in which they were disclosed.

A case in point was a statement in the report that North had told Meese that, when he tried to raise strategic issues with the President, the President only wanted to talk about the hostages. "With the President," North is quoted as saying to Meese, "it always came back to the hostages." What's wrong with this story is that North never had a chance to talk directly with the President. This was another of his fantasies. The press by this time had received information from the White House that North had never met alone with the President and was never more than a note taker in much larger meetings. Yet North's statement was circulated widely in the media and was reported in the *New York Times*.

Once again, North's fantasies provided wonderful fodder for the press, and did great damage to the President's credibility at this crucial

time. By prolonging the arms sales policy, diverting some of the funds
to the Contras, and participating in a cover-up of his own wrongdoing
after the arms sales were disclosed, North had caused the President significant harm.

In addition, in the original committee report, it was made clear
that it was North who was interested in using the arms sales to trade
for the hostages. The President might have worried about the hostages,
but the policy he had approved was not directed at trading arms to obtain their freedom. I called Gerald Boyd, the *New York Times* White
House correspondent, to complain about the *Times's* use of a quote
that he and they knew to be a complete canard. But this kind of effort
amounted to spitting in the ocean; all the press wanted out of the report was further evidence that the President had traded arms for
hostages, not an explanation of what actually happened.

This was unfortunate, and a disservice to the public, which was and
probably still is confused about what actually occurred and why the President appeared to have adopted such a senseless policy. The original Senate
committee report, if it had been made public, would have provided a realistic and credible explanation. For all their details, none of the subsequent
investigations—including the Tower Board, the Joint Congressional Committee that was later formed to investigate the Iran-Contra matter, and the
Independent Counsel—ever developed a comprehensive and understandable description of how and why the Iran arms sales policy came to be.
The Tower Board was charged with the task of gathering and reporting the
facts, and making management-style recommendations to the President
about how he should run the NSC. The board never tried to piece everything together by delving into the motivations of the players. The Joint
Congressional Committee focused, understandably, on the policy failure,
the deception and cover-up by North and Poindexter, and the failure to inform Congress. There was little effort expended in that report to understand why things happened as they did. The independent counsel, as a
prosecutor, focused solely on potential violations of law.

On the other hand, the 1986 Senate Intelligence Committee report
attempted to answer the question of why things developed as they did,

and for that reason produced what was potentially the most useful document of all. By looking at the issue this way, the committee made the whole process understandable, including why the President approved the initiative and why it degenerated into an arms-for-hostages swap. But the considerably altered and truncated version actually released to the public in late January 1987—after the Democrats had taken control of the Senate and the committee—simply pointed to a series of mistakes by the President and by his national security advisers. And a list of mistakes, while a suitable basis for criticism, did not help the President get the Iran-Contra crisis behind him. The Democrats understood this, which is why the original 1986 report—if it still exists at all—now molders in the committee's archives.

Thus, by the beginning of January 1987, the groundhog had seen his shadow; we were in for at least six more weeks of winter.

CHAPTER

9

IRAN-CONTRA: RECOVERY

He had a consistency about him, and he would stick
with things. Sometimes you'd wish that he wouldn't.
—George Shultz, on Ronald Reagan[1]

With the collapse of our hopes for release of the original Senate Intelligence Committee report, our focus turned to the Tower Board. The board had been given the assignment of investigating and reporting the facts about the Iran-Contra matter, and the President had urged them to act as quickly as possible. They took this charge seriously, promptly hiring a staff and setting to work assembling information.

The board started their investigation well, with an interview of Alton Keel, formerly Poindexter's deputy and then the acting national security adviser. Rhett Dawson, the board's chief of staff, invited me to sit in in case the board had any questions arising out of Keel's remarks. The board had invited Keel to describe the structure of the NSC, the nature of the relationship between the White House staff and the NSC staff, and the national security adviser's relationship to the President in the Reagan administration. Keel told them that the national security adviser reported directly to the President, and not through Regan. The NSC staff regarded Regan as the keeper of the President's schedule, but

not as a person in the chain of command up to the President. In response to questions from the board—which seemed to have absorbed
the press-created notion that Regan insisted on controlling everything—Keel cited several instances within his knowledge where
Poindexter met with the President without the meeting having been
scheduled by Regan and without Regan's presence, although he noted
that Regan was frequently invited along as a courtesy.

Presidential statements on foreign-policy or national-security matters involved a more co-equal relationship, Keel said, with the White
House staff having more to say about what the President said and how
he said it. But even here, he cited one instance in which Poindexter had
gone to the President directly after a speech had been through the White
House staff process and got a paragraph changed to the way he wanted
it, without consulting Regan. Keel made it very clear, I thought, that it
was the national security adviser, and not Donald Regan, who controlled
the furnishing of foreign and national security policy information to the
President, and was in charge of the President's foreign policy process. In
the end, the board seemed satisfied with what they had heard.

However, the pressures on the board to investigate and report
quickly took their toll. Tensions were rising between the board and the
agencies from which they were seeking information, and the board
seemed determined to get the White House into the middle of these
controversies. My first difficult encounter with the board's complaints
about the slow responses from the agencies they had contacted occurred
on December 10, only a week or so after the board had started its work.
I had been asked to come over to the board's offices to discuss an unspec-
ified problem. I arrived at the appointed hour and was shown to a conference room. Shortly thereafter, the board and its senior staff—Rhett
Dawson and Clark McFadden, the board's general counsel—walked in
and sat down across the table from me without a discernible greeting.
This was a substantial change from the atmosphere during the Keel
meeting. They were obviously very angry about something.

Apparently, the board had just received a letter from the Director of
the FBI, whose agency they had contacted for information. The Direc-

tor had suggested that they should not be looking into the Iran-Contra matter at all, and specifically denied them access to the FBI's files. I was not particularly surprised by this response, since bureaucracies, and especially law enforcement bureaucracies like the FBI, frequently react with hostility to broad requests for access to their files. What particularly alarmed me, however, was the board's attitude that this apparent lack of cooperation by the FBI signaled a lack of cooperation by the President. They seemed to think that the FBI's reaction was directed by the White House, and thus that the President was not going to cooperate with their investigation. Since we were operating in an environment in which the press was looking for any indication that the President was not cooperating with the board or any other investigating body, the board's dissatisfaction with the FBI's response, or the responses of other agencies, had to be dealt with quickly. If it should result in anonymous source stories that the White House or the President was not cooperating with the board, that would be very damaging indeed.

I told the board that the mere fact that the President appointed the board would not automatically mean that the FBI understood what the President wanted them to do. Obviously, in this case, the Director of the FBI did not understand that the President had appointed the board to look into the Iran-Contra affair and report to him, and that meant that the board was entitled to have the FBI's cooperation. I said I would contact the FBI, and every other agency where they encountered difficulties, and would make sure the heads of those agencies understood the priority the President placed on their cooperation. Shortly after I returned to the White House, Jay Stephens contacted the FBI and explained the situation; thereafter, the board received enough cooperation from the FBI so that we never heard any more from the board on the subject. But this experience convinced me that the board would need constant attention in the future.

Fortunately, late in December the President appointed a new figure who would take on the difficult job of dealing not only with the board but with all the other investigating bodies and power holders in Washington who had an interest in the Iran-Contra affair. The new arrival was David Abshire, who resigned his post as U.S. delegate to NATO to take on this role. In the words of the White House announcement, he was to coordinate "responses to Congressional and other requests for information in a timely manner." As many had been recommending for the preceding month, Regan and the President had agreed to bring in a respected and independent person to take on the task of managing the White House response in the Iran-Contra matter.

Abshire's appointment was announced on December 26, and by the end of the first week in January he and his staff were in place. Among others, Abshire had brought with him Charles Brower, a respected international lawyer, as his deputy. Although I did not know Abshire before his appointment, I soon found that he and I, and our staffs, could work smoothly together. There was certainly more than enough for all of us to do, and Abshire's affable personality, his perceived independence from Regan, and his seniority and reputation in Washington enabled him to serve as an honest broker between the groups demanding information and the slow-moving sources of supply in the White House, the national security agencies, and the NSC staff. Abshire could not necessarily make things move faster, but when he said—accurately—that the administration was doing all it could to expedite the furnishing of the necessary information, he was far more likely to be believed than the rest of us. Much of his work involved running interference for the Tower Board with the various agencies from which it sought information, to assure that it could complete its work as quickly as possible.

Many of us on the White House staff also held out hope that Abshire would eventually come to the view that it was in the President's best interests to admit that he had made a mistake—not in initially establishing the arms sales policy, but in not properly supervising how it was carried out. Richard Wirthlin's poll numbers showed that the American people did not believe the President when he said he had not traded arms for hostages, and every time the President issued a denial, his credibility with the public declined. If we were ever to get the President out before the public—where he would be asked about the Iran-Contra matter—we had to persuade him that there had in fact been a trade of arms for hostages, even though this had not been his policy. Understanding this, he might then be willing to say he'd made a mistake by not properly supervising those who were charged with carrying out the policy he actually approved.

The apparent unanimity of the staff on this question was reminiscent of the efforts of the White House staff, in 1981–82, to change the President's position on his economic policy. In that case, too, the President resisted all pressure. Here, however, there was an important difference. In 1981–82, the press was full of stories quoting anonymous White House sources about the President's stubbornness and weak grasp of basic economics. In 1987, with a different staff, there were virtually no press accounts that the President was being urged by his staff to admit that he made a mistake. Indeed, all outward indications—including Regan's on the record support of the President's position in a *Washington Post* interview—suggested that the White House staff was urging the President to stand his ground.

By mid-January, the Tower Board had been in operation for more than a month and had not yet interviewed the President. This was understandable; they wanted to have as much information as possible before asking the President to describe what he recalled. However, the press was becoming curious about why the board was hanging back, and were probably calling the board asking for an explanation. I suspect the Tower Board's staff left the impression that the White House was resisting a meeting. That would get the focus off them, and place it where the press likes to have it: on the White House. Over the weekend of January 18 and 19, the press story line was that the White House was sidestepping the Tower Board's efforts to set up a date for an interview of the President. At the same time, the board recognized that they would need an extension of their reporting deadline in order to complete their report. The two stories were then combined into a story that the board had to seek an extension of its deadline because the White House was delaying a meeting with the President. I was not involved in the negotiation of the date for the President's interview—Dennis Thomas was handling this with Rhett Dawson—but I knew that we did not want any delay.

Our objective and our every incentive were to get as complete a report as we could at the earliest possible time, and we knew that without an interview of the President, the board could not complete its report.

Indeed, the White House staff was increasingly frustrated by their inability to get the President out before the public, or at least in the news for something other than the Iran-Contra affair. For the six years prior to the advent of the Iran-Contra matter, the President and his agenda had always dominated the news. Since the arms-sales scandal broke, however, the President and the White House were working off the media's agenda—responding to the endless flow of stories and speculation about what happened. This in itself was probably responsible for a substantial portion of the decline in the President's approval ratings.

But there was little the White House staff could do about the situation. Since the President didn't have a definitive version of the Iran-Contra facts, and couldn't answer the most basic questions about what had happened and when, he couldn't be scheduled into events where he might be confronted by the press. The strategy had been to wait for one of the investigations to be completed and then to have the President rely on the facts thus disclosed in formulating his account. The initial Senate Intelligence Committee report would have been ideal for this purpose, but we couldn't get access to it. Now we were impatiently awaiting the Tower Board's report.

A meeting with the Tower Board did not raise the same difficulties as a meeting with the press. The Tower Board would want to know only what the President recalled about the origins of his policy and the approvals he gave for arms shipments. Presumably, they already had more facts than the President would ever have about the details of the operation. The press, however, could be expected to ask questions intended to have political impact—about whether the President complied with the law, or made a mistake, or failed properly to supervise North and Poindexter. The Tower Board might draw these conclusions in its report, but the press would ask the President to draw them himself.

But as usual, press stories moved the matter of a meeting between the board and the President higher up on everyone's to-do list—this is what it means to work off the media's agenda—and accelerated efforts on the part of both parties to settle on a date for the President's interview. On January 20, Regan told me that he and the President had cleared the following Monday, January 26, for the interview, and asked me to call Rhett Dawson to finalize arrangements. I did so, and the White House announced that afternoon when and where the President would be interviewed by the Tower Board. Now our efforts were devoted to preparing the President for the interview.

One of the issues that was sure to come up in the Tower Board meeting was whether the President had approved in advance the first shipment of TOW missiles in August 1985. McFarlane had testified to the Senate Intelligence Committee on December 1, 1986, that the President had approved the sale in advance, while Regan had testified that he recalled the President being told after the shipment had already occurred. The President had told me on January 3 that he did not recall when he had authorized the shipment, but recalled being surprised when he first learned of it. I had been preparing a chronology that I hoped would jog the President's memory, but I couldn't identify any meeting or phone call between McFarlane and the President—after the meeting in the hospital on July 18 and before the shipment of arms by Israel on August 20, 1985—in which the President might have authorized the Israelis to go ahead. Neither the White House phone logs nor the President's daily schedule disclosed a phone call or meeting during this period at which the approval might have been granted.

Although it seemed highly unlikely that the Israelis would have jeopardized their relationship with the United States by shipping U.S. arms to Iran without our approval, it was also unlikely that McFarlane would have authorized the Israelis to ship U.S. arms to Iran without authorization from the President. If he had done so, however, one can hardly imagine that he would now be saying that he didn't have the President's authority in advance. Authorizing the Israelis to ship arms to Iran would have been one of the worst bureaucratic and diplomatic blunders in history if it had been done without the President's approval. So McFarlane clearly had a strong incentive to remember that he had gotten authority from the President. But during the period when the Iran-Contra matter was being investigated, McFarlane was never able to identify a date when that had occurred.*

Moreover, my review of the documents associated with this matter indicated that McFarlane had told Poindexter and North quite the opposite when they were trying to assemble the facts for their own chronology shortly after news of the arms sales broke. In his first note to Poindexter (sent through an internal secure e-mail system maintained by the White House to which McFarlane had been given access), on November 7, 1986—just after disclosure of the arms sales—McFarlane wrote:

> It might be useful to review just what the truth is.
>
> You will recall that when the Israelis first approached us in June '85, I presented the idea of engaging in a dialogue with the Iranians—no mention at all of any arms exchange at all—and he [the President] approved it.
>
> We then heard nothing until August when the Israelis introduced the requirement for TOWs. I told Kimche [the Israeli intermediary at the time] no.
>
> They went ahead on their own but then asked that we replace the TOWs and after checking with the President, we agreed. Weir [one of the U.S. hostages] was released as a consequence of their action.[2]

I thought it was extremely significant that this note was private, for Poindexter's eyes only, and dated November 7—the day after the arms sales had begun to attract significant media attention. Moreover, to begin a private, presumably classified note, on a secure system, addressed

---

* As noted in Chapter 7, footnote 2, p.170, McFarlane—in a book published in 1994—identified an Oval Office meeting with the President on August 3, 1985, as the point at which he received approval to authorize arms sales by the Israelis. To my knowledge, this is the first time McFarlane was able to specify a date, and it came long after the various investigations had ended and long after it was possible to check White House records of his meetings with the President.

to a colleague who is the President's national security adviser, with the words, "It might be useful to review just what the truth is," strongly suggests that what follows actually *was*—even in Washington—at least somewhat close to the truth.[3] In addition, on November 18, 1986, McFarlane had written extensive portions of a chronology that was then in preparation in the NSC under the supervision of Poindexter and North. McFarlane's contribution reduced the President's involvement with the initiation of the arms sales by stating that the Israelis shipped the arms without the President's approval.[4]

These elements led me to believe that the President had not approved the shipment of arms in advance as McFarlane had testified, but only after the fact. I hasten to add that this has only historical significance and made no real difference as a legal matter. In both cases, without a finding or a subsequent report to Congress, it would have been difficult to square the President's actions with the requirements of the relevant statutes. If anything, McFarlane's later account—that the President approved in advance of the Israeli shipment—was slightly better for the President's legal case than Regan's recollection that the President learned of the shipment after the fact. This is because it might have been possible to argue that the President had made an "oral finding"—and in this sense complied with the literal requirements of the National Security Act—before he approved the Israeli shipment in advance. (An "oral finding" would be a peculiar thing. Presumably, the President would have to speak. I wondered whether he could make a "mental finding" and not speak at all.) It was harder to imagine that the President made an oral finding if he simply condoned those shipments after they occurred. But in the scheme of things, these legal niceties were not as important as the President telling the truth as he recalled it—since the real stakes involved were the President's credibility and avoiding any implication that he had participated in a cover-up.

The Tower Board made efforts to reconcile McFarlane's various accounts, juxtaposing his computer messages to Poindexter with his later testimony and explanations to the Board. McFarlane explained his initial position—outlined in the November 7 and November 18 memos to Poindexter—by saying that he was simply following up on and embellishing what he understood from press contacts was the White House position. When he was asked by the board whose position within the White House, McFarlane identified Regan.[5] It is conceivable (but unlikely) that Regan, who recalled the President being surprised by the first Israeli shipment, was telling the press on background that the President had not approved in advance, but why McFarlane would characterize this to Poindexter as "the truth"—when he knew it wasn't—remains unexplained. On November 21, however, McFarlane talked to Ed Meese, who told him—on the basis of the oral finding theory—that the President's legal position would be better if he had approved the Israeli shipment in advance.[6] Thereafter, on December 1, 1986, McFarlane gave his first public testimony on the subject, saying that this is just what the President had done.

This sequence of events leads to the intriguing possibility that Regan's recollection that the President had been surprised by the Israeli shipment—transmitted to McFarlane through calls from press contacts—influenced McFarlane's first account of November 7, which he embellished on November 18. However, this left open the difficulty of explaining why the Israelis would go ahead without U.S. approval, and the implication that McFarlane might have given that approval without the President's explicit authorization. When McFarlane learned from Meese that the President's legal position was better if he had approved in advance, it all fell into place: advance approval by the President was the best position for him to take, and that led to McFarlane's December 1 testimony.

At the same time, the evidence suggests that Regan's position—that the President did not approve in advance—was based on his recollection that the President was surprised to learn of the first Israeli shipment. Much of the press speculation that Regan was eager to get his view accepted because he was afraid of being charged with perjury is ridiculous. Regan had no motive for lying under oath; in fact, since McFarlane testified first, Regan could have simply agreed with him and avoided the controversy altogether. Regan certainly could not have been motivated by a desire to minimize the President's role in the arms sales, since he knew perfectly well that the President himself was saying to anyone who would listen that the arms sales were part of his policy of opening a channel to Iran. Finally, Regan knew from discussions with me that it made no significant legal difference under either the AECA or the National Security Act whether the President approved of the arms sales in advance, or simply agreed to replenish the Israeli stocks after the fact. Regan's only motive for testifying as he did, therefore, was probably that this was the truth as he recalled it, and he thought—as I did—that the historical record should be clear.

All of this speculation has the familiar government explanation—snafu—written all over it. The most likely explanation in my view is that with the large number of people involved in talking to one another about this initiative—Israelis, Americans, and Iranians, government officials, consultants, and arms merchants—the Israelis got the impression that the President either had or would approve their initial shipment of arms to Iran. The impression may have been given by a wink or a nod, or by a back-channel communication from someone who had talked to McFarlane and was told that the President was enthusiastic about the idea. It is likely that the Israelis had their own reasons for wanting to open a channel to Iran—that's why they had approached the United States with the idea in the first place—and thus their own incentive to proceed. This, together with the hints from Washington about the President's willingness to go ahead, led to their shipping the arms in the belief that their stocks would be replenished, but without any explicit approval. This would explain Regan's recollection that the President was surprised on first hearing of the arms transfers.

Of course, once the President agreed to replenish the Israeli stocks, the die was cast. The United States was now fully engaged. Since no one had explicitly authorized the Israelis to go ahead, no sustained thought had been given at this point to how all of this could be fit within the requirements of the law. It was also going to be very difficult to explain how the Israelis had gotten the impression that the shipment of arms was approved. From the vantage point of those involved in the matter at the time, an embarrassing congressional investigation was likely. All this led to the need for the extreme secrecy that attended the arms-sales initiative, and that in turn foreclosed the possibility of reporting to Congress. The action was turned over to Oliver North, and the rest is history. Someday, historians may be able to untangle all these threads, but based on the record known thus far, this seems to me to be the most likely explanation for the confusion about whether the President approved in advance, the extraordinary secrecy with which this initiative was pursued, and the cover-up by the NSC that ensued when the arms sales were ultimately disclosed.

As the date for the President's Tower Board interview approached, I met with Rhett Dawson to arrange the ground rules. We discussed the possibility of a transcript, both a classified and an unclassified report, and whether the meeting would be held in the Oval Office or the Cabinet Room. I told Dawson that we didn't want a classified report—it would only lead to press demands for the release of the classified section, and suggestions that the real skinny was in the material we were withholding. As to a transcript and the location of the session, I said I wanted to discuss these matters with Regan.

Although I initially favored a transcript, Regan thought it would be nothing but trouble. It would have to be released to the select committees of the House and Senate that had now been formed to investigate the Iran-Contra affair, and probably leaked to the press, and the President's words would be picked apart. The discrepancies, if any, between his account and the accounts of others would be highlighted in the press and his political opponents would suggest he was dissembling, at the very least. After thinking about it awhile, I agreed. Regan also thought the meeting should be in the Oval Office, where the President would be more comfortable. I communicated these items to Dawson, and the Tower Board agreed to these ground rules.

It was Wednesday, January 21, and I spent the rest of the day preparing briefing materials for the President. These included a chronology I had prepared from the materials we had seen and McFarlane's public statement to the Senate Foreign Relations Committee the preceding week, which the President had apparently seen on television.

The chronology was an effort to stimulate the President's memory. It did not contain anything that was not reported to or known to the President from published reports. As with Regan's testimony, I did not want to distort the President's recollection by putting into the chronology items that he could not have known. The chronology had a list of Iran-Contra events and dates (insofar as we knew them at this point) down the left-hand column and in the right-hand column a list of other events that were occurring at the same time. I hoped that putting the Iran-Contra events into the context of other events the President might remember would stimulate his recollections.

By the next day the President had read the briefing materials, and Abshire and I were scheduled to meet with him. Before that, however, I wanted to talk with the Vice President about whatever recollections he might have had which might fill out our knowledge. I met with the Vice President at 1 P.M. in his West Wing office. It was a relatively brief meeting. He recalled virtually nothing that added to our knowledge at that point.

At 2:00 in the afternoon, the Vice President, Abshire, Regan, and I met with the President. He had reviewed the briefing materials and made notes on them. The President said these notes were from his diary, which he had consulted the night before. Until that moment, I hadn't known the President had a diary, and a discussion ensued about whether it was a good idea for the President to reveal this to the Tower Board. The Vice President wondered whether this made sense. Wouldn't the board ask to see the diary? I said I didn't think so—the President was not under suspicion and the diary entries seemed to support his limited recollections. I can't imagine why I said this. Maybe I was thinking of the diary as something very personal that would not contain significant information about what the President was doing as president. As any fool would know, everyone who was investigating the Iran arms sales and the diversion of funds to the Contras would want to see the President's diary, or at least those portions that were relevant, once it became known that such a diary existed. In any event, no one made any further comments about the diary and we continued with the briefing.

The President's diary entries—as he had transcribed them to the chronology I prepared—contained very little useful information. As in the meeting in the White House residence in early January 1986, he could recall the hospital visit by McFarlane, but almost nothing else. He had some recollection of a briefing around the Geneva summit in November, but nothing very explicit. Interestingly, the diary was detailed enough to recall topics discussed in brief telephone conversations, but few details about the Iran initiative. Since the President had only checked his diary through September 1985, I suggested that he go through it all the way to November 1986, to see if he had any useful information noted down.

The same group met with the President again the next day, except that Brower attended instead of Abshire. This time, the President had gone completely through his diary by checking it against every date in the chronology, and had found some references to meetings in December 1985 and January 1986, and a reference to McFarlane's mission to Iran. The meeting made me very uneasy, however. The President seemed to have no independent recollection of what happened in the Iran initiative, although he was very clear that he had authorized the shipment of arms because he wanted to open a channel to Iran, and he wanted to see the hostages released because he wanted evidence that we were dealing with powerful people within Iran. It was not the President's conviction concerning his broader policy that was at issue, however; it was whether he had allowed or encouraged this initial idea to become a trade of arms for hostages. At another level—the level at which the press and the President's opponents were operating—it was whether the whole question of a strategic opening to Iran was simply a cover story for an arms-for-hostages swap.

It was difficult to believe that the President didn't know—or want to know—more about the arms sales than his answers implied. The press coverage of every detail and facet of this affair had been obsessive since the story broke in early November 1986. Anyone who read the newspapers or watched television would certainly have acquired a basic knowledge, and more than a limited curiosity about how all this came to pass. In the case of Ronald Reagan particularly, this was a crisis that many of his advisers thought threatened his presidency, so he had more than a little incentive to become as informed as possible about what had happened and why. Yet it seemed as though he had not been curious enough to consult his own diary until a few days before he met with the Tower Board, and he never asked any of us questions about what we had found in doing our own limited investigations. This lack of curiosity is an abiding mystery about Ronald Reagan, on which my thoughts were expressed earlier. The best explanation, in my view, was that he didn't believe that the whole Iran-Contra episode was as significant as the rest of us—who were caught up in it day to day—had come to believe. In this, once again, Ronald Reagan was right.

The President's interview with the Tower Board, on January 26, 1987, lasted about an hour and a quarter, and had some troubling elements. Attending were the three members of the board, plus Rhett Dawson, Clark McFadden, Charles Brower, and myself. Tower did all the questioning. He was respectful and sympathetic; in some cases, he seemed to be leading the President. The President was still unable to string everything together, or to answer questions about details without reading from the notes he had written on his chronology. But there were big and unwelcome surprises in some of his answers.

First, despite the fact that at three prior briefings he had said he had no recollection of whether he had approved the first Israeli shipment in advance, when Tower questioned him this time the President said that, although he was "still digging," he thought he had approved in advance.

Second, when asked about the HAWK shipment in November 1985, he said that the Israelis had shipped the HAWKs without our permission and that the missiles were called back. This was also completely new; in all the previous meetings we'd had on this subject, the President had said he remembered nothing significant about the HAWK shipment, including the briefing by McFarlane at the time of the Geneva summit. Moreover, this account was unpleasantly familiar. It was basically the false story that Poindexter had originally told me in early November 1986, when I first met with him about the Iran arms sales. I couldn't figure out, however, how the President had heard it.

My principal concern about these statements was that they were inconsistent with one another, and thus completely muddled the record. If the President had approved the first shipment in advance, he would not have disapproved the HAWK shipment and called it back. Moreover, we knew as a fact that he was never asked formally to approve the HAWK shipment, but only informed by McFarlane in Geneva that the HAWK shipment was going forward. On the other hand, if he had not approved the first shipment in advance—if he'd been surprised and annoyed as Regan had suggested in his own testimony—it was absurd to believe that the Israelis would have done the same thing twice.

None of this would solve the mystery of what actually happened. The most consistent interpretation of the two events would be that the President had approved the first shipment in advance, and having done so McFarlane was reasonably sure that he did not have to get the President's formal approval for the second shipment. But there was a good deal of evidence—including McFarlane's November 7 and November 18 notes to Poindexter and Regan's normally good memory—that the President did not approve the first shipment in advance, but only replenishment after the fact. I was quite worried about this discrepancy. There was a danger that the President would be seen as having been untruthful to the Tower Board—an event that would lead to renewed attacks on his credibility and charges of cover-up. At that point, however, I couldn't figure out where the President's inconsistent recollections had come from.

As the meeting ended, we all started to leave the Oval Office through a side door that leads directly out into a West Wing hallway. I was the last one out, and as I was leaving the President called me back. I walked over to his desk. With a smile, he took out of the top left drawer a sheaf of papers that were stapled at the top left and were folded back at the staple the way they would be if someone were reading through them. He showed this document to me and said that he had just come across it in his desk. He was pleased to have found it, he said, because "it told the whole story." I on the other hand was horrified. It was the false North chronology. Somehow, a copy had gotten to the President. After all my efforts to keep him from being influenced by facts he would not otherwise have known, he was influenced at the worst possible time by the worst possible source of facts. At least this explained where he got the tale about the HAWKs being called back.

It did not explain, however, where he had gotten the idea that he had approved the first Israeli shipment in advance. The North chronology said the opposite—that the Israelis had shipped the weapons without our approval. Then it occurred to me that I had put in his briefing book a copy of McFarlane's public testimony on this and other questions, both of which I had marked with yellow highlighter for his convenience in finding the salient points. He might have read it the preceding night, and found it persuasive. I realized that it was a mistake to have included the McFarlane testimony in his briefing materials. I had been scrupulously trying to preserve his recollections without any outside influence, but had violated my own rule by including the McFarlane testimony and highlighting the significant portions. It may be that he had paid so little attention to the news reports about the Iran-Contra matter that he didn't have any way to assess McFarlane's testimony as one view among many.

In any event, after I got back to my office, I called Jim Kuhn, the President's assistant, and explained the situation to him. I asked him to get the false chronology from the President—who already knew he should not have used it as a source for his testimony—and bring it to me. Shortly thereafter, Kuhn delivered it to my office.

In the aftermath of the Tower Board interview, Brower and I gave a brief statement to the press office, describing nothing of what was said there. I spoke to Rhett Dawson and he promised that the Tower Board would say nothing. However, later in the afternoon, I received a call from Gerald Boyd of the *New York Times,* saying that a *Times* reporter had a story that the President had said he couldn't remember whether he'd approved the Israeli shipments in advance. Ironically, that story would have been correct *before* the meeting. I told Boyd I couldn't comment but didn't believe anyone in the meeting would have described what the President said. This left somewhat ambiguous whether I meant the President hadn't said this or that no one in the meeting would have talked to the press. Boyd apparently took the cautious approach and killed the story. The *Washington Post,* however, went with the story, and the next day Boyd called me, angry as a hornet. He may have assumed that I'd given the *Post* reporter a better response than I'd given him, and said none of the *Times* reporters covering the Tower Board would talk to him now. I told him he had done the right thing, but didn't elaborate.

This episode shows how difficult and complex these situations are for government officials. Where did my loyalty properly lie? Boyd had an incorrect story, which did not reflect well on the President. Should I have let him publish it? I didn't have any obligation to make the *Times* stories accurate, of course, but I did have an obligation to prevent the publication of stories that were both wrong and damaging to the President. In addition, there was some sense of obligation to Boyd. As shown by the fact that he eventually killed the story, Boyd, to his credit, always tried to achieve accuracy. If I had let the *Times* publish an inaccurate story after he had given me a chance to correct it, was that being fair to him? Finally, we had all agreed, Brower and I and the Tower Board, not to speak to the press, and that created its own set of duties.

By Wednesday, Brower and I had worked up a summary of the meeting for the President and we sent it to him for review. The President called me late in the afternoon and said it looked complete to him. I mentioned that I was having some trouble with two of his answers and would like to talk with him about them. He said he was "stripped down" at that point—having just taken a shower—but maybe I could find some time in his schedule the next day. I said I would do so. I suppose I could have left well enough alone, but I still thought the historical record should be clear. More important, the President had put an obvious inconsistency on the record, in addition to repeating a story about the November HAWK shipment known to be false. If the Tower Board report noted all of this, and there was no reason to suppose it would not, the President's truthfulness could be called into question.

Also, there was the problem of McFarlane's November 7 note, which the President had never been told about. The note, then in the possession of the Tower Board and the other investigators, said that the President had not approved the Israeli shipment in advance. If this came to be the accepted view by the investigators—and that seemed most plausible to me—the President would be left with having made yet another incorrect statement to the Tower Board. Since this statement could be construed as motivated by the oral-finding theory, the Tower Board or others might conclude that the President was seeking to advance his legal case by claiming now that he had approved the shipments in advance. Such a motive could give rise to an obstruction-of-justice charge.

Had the President approved the August TOW shipment in advance or had he not? Was the HAWK shipment in November authorized or not? As things stood after the Tower Board meeting, the record was confused and inconsistent, and I was worried again about the President's vulnerability to a charge of cover-up or obstructing justice, however unfounded. In these circumstances, I was able to arrange a meeting with the President the following afternoon, and at 3 P.M. Regan, Abshire, and I met with him. I asked him whether he actually remembered approving the shipment of TOWs in advance, or only a subsequent replenishment. This was a distinction that had not been resolved by Tower in his questioning of the President. The President seemed unable to recall. Then Regan said that he remembered McFarlane telling the President that the Israelis had sent the weapons without our approval, and the President had been surprised and displeased, saying something like "Well what's done is done." As he listened to this the President seemed to have a recollection of this event. He turned to me and said, "You know, he's right," referring to Regan. This was the second time that the President had seemed to have a recollection of being surprised when he was told by McFarlane that the Israelis had shipped arms to Iran. The first time was on January 3, when I asked him whether he remembered being surprised by McFarlane's report and he acknowledged that he did.

On the question of the HAWK missiles sale in November 1985, the President really had no recollection, even though Regan described for him the circumstances under which he was briefed by McFarlane in

Geneva. Nor could he remember where he got the idea that the missiles were sent without our approval and had for that reason been called back.

In most cases, no memory is better than a faulty memory; at least the President was not further confusing things—and damaging his credibility—by claiming to remember something that didn't happen, or a decision he made that he never in fact made. The problem now was to determine what to do about the record created at the first Tower Board meeting. Eventually, I decided that there had to be another meeting with the Tower Board—one at which the President would have an opportunity to set the record straight. For history and for his own protection, I still wanted his best recollections to go into the record, no matter what they were. There was no way he could get into serious difficulty if he told the truth—including the fact that he didn't remember. On the other hand, if the record was left as it was at the end of the first Tower Board meeting, the President might be in some jeopardy.

The existence of the President's diary was not a secret very long. The *Washington Post* ran a story on the diary or notes—they didn't know which—on Sunday, February 1. To our surprise, there was no press frenzy the following day, although a number of media outlets carried the story. We were aware that the *Post* story was coming, and had prepared a statement in which we said that the notes were the President's personal recollections, and their release would be an infringement of his privacy rights. When, on Monday, I was asked whether we would assert executive privilege concerning the notes, I sidestepped the question by saying that we were confident that at the end of the ongoing investigations there would be no outstanding questions that required the President's notes to be disclosed.

Regan had had a discussion with the President that morning about the notes. He told me that if necessary the President was willing to make relevant personal notes (the term we chose instead of diary entries) available, but not all of his personal papers. Regan asked us to prepare a statement for the press office to issue that summarized the President's position. Dennis Thomas favored a more forthcoming approach in which the President would say he was agreeable to making all his notes available under certain circumstances. I continued to resist the idea, but Thomas was right. If we adopted my formula that allowed the President or one of us to determine the relevance of the notes, we would give the impression that the President was resisting, and when we finally gave in—as we would inevitably be required to do—it would look like a defeat. Thomas's point was that we should recognize the inevitable from the beginning, especially since the President himself was not opposing disclosure. My opposition, I think, arose out of my concern that if this President had to give up his personal diary notes no presidents would ever keep notes again. But my position was simply theoretical; the real question was how to prevent the President from taking another defeat in the here and now. At the issues lunch that day, the President approved a statement that he would turn over the relevant notes. The next confrontation, I knew, would be over how to determine relevancy for disclosure.

Nancy Reagan called me in the late afternoon. She had just seen the statement on the personal notes and was not happy. She asked what kind of legal advice I had given, and I told her that as a legal matter I thought the notes should and could be protected, but as a political or public-relations matter almost all the President's advisers thought the relevant notes would eventually have to be disclosed. I said I agreed with this judgment. She said no one on the White House staff had any public-relations sense, and she didn't think either that the diaries should be made available or that anyone should be permitted to look through them. I said I agreed with her concern, and that we hoped to make arrangements so that only the President would look through his diaries and select the relevant notes, but I warned that there would be a fight over how to determine relevance.

That afternoon, I called Rhett Dawson and started the ball rolling toward another meeting between the President and the Tower Board. This had to be done carefully, so as not to appear that the President wanted a meeting to correct anything in his testimony—this would, of course, immediately appear in the press—or that the Tower Board had discovered something dramatic that required the President to be re-interviewed. I suggested that the President had not been able to talk about process at the first meeting, and that he had some thoughts on the subject. Dawson agreed that the board would also like to hear the President's views about the NSC policy process. I had in fact prepared a set of talking points for the President for the first Tower Board meeting that explained his management style and the process he had expected the NSC to follow. For some reason, the subject never came up, and the President never used them. A second meeting, in addition to its other potential benefits, would provide the President with an opportunity to talk with the board about a subject—his relationship to the NSC—that was an important part of their investigation and would be included in their report.

Dawson then raised the question of whether the board would be able to see the President's personal notes. I told him that the President would be agreeable to letting the board see these notes, if the board would give me a list of the dates they considered important. When Dawson came over later in the day he had a list of dates on which in the board's view relevant events occurred, and he wanted to see any excerpts of the President's notes for those days that were relevant to the board's investigation. I said the President would search his notes for those dates and furnish copies of the relevant notes to me. The Tower Board would then have access to them.

Dawson eventually called me back about another meeting between the Board and the President, and we scheduled the second interview for Wednesday, February 11. I'm sure that Dawson and the Tower Board members were not fooled by my suggestion that the President wanted to talk about process. They knew something was afoot, probably having to do with the President's statements concerning the TOWs and HAWKs.

Other investigators were also interested in the notes, and Abshire and I met with them one by one, beginning with Lawrence Walsh, the independent counsel. I told him we were prepared to make available excerpts the President would select from relevant dates that Walsh would specify, and said that I would make the same offer to Congress. Walsh obviously did not want a confrontation at this point, and was agreeable as a preliminary matter to see the same notes that Congress would get. However, he warned that relevancy would eventually be a question. The following day, February 4, Abshire and I met with Senators Daniel Inouye and Warren Rudman, the chairman and ranking member of the Senate Select Committee on the Iran-Contra matter that would eventually join with a House Select Committee to carry on a joint investigation. I made my proposal, but they wanted something else. They suggested that I read the President's diaries and make the relevancy decision. I said we would consider this if they could bring along the House committee. I explained that I did not want to ask the President twice to let me go through his notes.

A similar meeting with the heads of the House Select Committee on Intelligence—Lee Hamilton and Dick Cheney—also went well, but they took a different tack. Hamilton said that it would not be satisfactory for the personal notes to be reviewed only for specific dates. The President might have made notes on other days that were relevant. He thought all the notes for the period should be reviewed. Surprisingly, however, he did not request that a third party do the reviewing; it would be sufficient, he thought, if the President did the review himself. I said that we would be happy to consider this idea, too, but that I thought the Senate and House should agree on a common request.

When I returned from the Hill, I had a call from Rhett Dawson, who said that Tower was sending a letter asking the President as commander in chief of the armed forces to order North and Poindexter to testify to the Tower Board. I was annoyed by this. Not only was it a surprise from a quarter where we should have at least received some more advance notice, but it put the President back in the middle of a controversy I thought had ended weeks before. What's more, it seemed completely pointless, except as a grandstand play to embarrass the President. I was reasonably sure that no military commander—including the commander in chief—could order subordinates to give up their constitutional rights. When the letter came in, moments later, I sent it over to Larry Garrett, the general counsel of the Department of Defense, for review and advice.

By Friday, February 6, I had received a response from Garrett, and, as I'd thought, under the Code of Military Justice an order from a commander to a subordinate that would require the subordinate to give up his constitutional rights would not be a lawful order. I drafted a letter, advising the Tower Board that the order they requested would be unlawful. The letter did not say that the President would not issue the order, but left the implication that he would not because such an order would be unlawful. I imagined we would not have long to wait before the Tower Board leaked my response to the press. My letter was sent on Monday, February 8, and by that evening the press office had received the first inquiry from a reporter. NBC went with the story in its evening newscast on Tuesday. The press office was ready with a briefing for other reporters, and the story had only a one-day life.

By this time, I was focused on preparing the President for his second interview with the Tower Board. At 3 P.M., on Tuesday, February 10, Regan, Abshire, and I met with the President in the Oval Office to prepare him for his interview with the board the next day. Despite many staff efforts over the preceding two months—now joined by Abshire—the President would neither say he had made a mistake in his Iran policy nor admit that the policy he had approved had devolved into a program of trading arms for hostages. We thought this meeting offered one last chance to press the President on this issue. I had prepared and sent to the President the previous evening a tough memo, arguing that his policy of a strategic opening to Iran had in fact—according to the available evidence—degenerated into an arms-for-hostages swap.

Abshire had an agenda for the meeting that was based on my memo, beginning with talking points I had drafted about the functioning of the NSC staff. The discussion of the NSC process was to be the first order of business at the Tower Board meeting, and the ostensible reason for the meeting itself. As Abshire talked, the President seemed inattentive. It did not appear that he had read the memo or the talking points concerning the NSC. Again, I was astonished at his apparent lack of interest in a subject that had occupied public discussion for months, had kept him confined to the White House, caused a huge decline in his personal standing with the American people, and apparently engaged even his wife in an effort to manage the crisis.

After Abshire's discussion of the process issues, we turned to the portion of the memo that addressed the appearance of an arms-for-hostages trade. An attachment contained a list of the items that seemed to show that there had been a trade. Abshire made the same point, as did Regan. We all felt strongly at this point, as we had for almost the entire duration of the crisis, that the President could only extricate himself from this mess and restore his credibility by admitting what the American people had already concluded had happened—that even if he had not formally approved it, his policy toward Iran had become a trade of arms for hostages. The President didn't actually have to say that this was his policy—only that a policy he had initiated for other purposes had been perverted to this end—but in that case he'd have to admit that he'd made a mistake by not adequately supervising his subordinates. The President seemed somewhat more engaged as we proceeded with this approach, but kept saying that he could not have traded arms for hostages if he had not actually dealt with the captors.

It is important to keep in mind why the President was so stubborn on this point. He had always contended that it was not possible for a president to supervise all the activities of his subordinates. The right way to conduct the office—indeed, the way he had conducted it—was to choose competent subordinates, furnish general guidance as to policy, and give them the freedom to act and improvise as necessary. In his autobiography, Reagan would write: "I don't believe a chief executive should supervise every detail of what goes on in his organization. The chief executive should set broad policy and ground rules, tell people what he or she wants them to do, then let them do it; he should make himself (or herself) available, so that the members of his team can come to him if there is a problem."[7] In Reagan's mind, where the inviolability of principle held a high place, admitting he had made a mistake in failing adequately to supervise McFarlane, Poindexter, and North was to say that a management style he had followed as governor of California and as president of the United States was flawed. It wasn't consistent to say both that broad responsibility should be delegated to subordinates and that these subordinates should be closely supervised.

In the course of the discussion, the President also said that if the hostages had not been involved he still would have offered arms to Iran in the hope of improving relations for the future. I thought this was highly significant, and told him so. He had never said this before, and while it might not have played well with the American people, who continued to view Iran with great antipathy after the hostage incident in the late 1970s, I thought it likely that the public would respect his convictions even if they did not agree.

We then turned to the subject of the shipments of TOWs and HAWKs during 1985. At our last meeting, the President had seemed to recall that he was surprised when told by McFarlane that the Israelis had shipped arms to Iran. He also said that he really had no recollection whatsoever of the HAWK shipment. This could at least form the basis for a consistent story. The President had been surprised by the Israeli shipment, but condoned it. Perhaps in his condonation or in later conversations with McFarlane he had made statements that approved going forward with further arms shipments. This might have led McFarlane to believe that the President had given blanket approval to Israeli shipments of arms. This theory wasn't completely satisfactory—it did not explain why Israel sent another TOW shipment in September and the HAWK shipment in November without getting the President's specific approval in advance—but it was better than the muddle that was left after the first meeting with the Tower Board.

I said that if this was his best recollection, he ought to tell this to the Tower Board at the meeting, because at the last meeting he had left them with a somewhat confusing account. He said he would, but with so little conviction that as we left the Oval Office Abshire suggested to me that I should prepare an *aide-mémoire* for the President to refer to before the next day's meeting.

That evening I received a call from Rhett Dawson, who said that the Tower Board had recently come across some materials in North's files that he thought I should be aware of—that would be subjects of the next day's interview with the President. When they were brought over, the documents turned out to be transcripts of a North meeting with several Iranian government representatives in Frankfurt in early October 1986. The transcripts were truly shocking. First they indicated that North had turned over to Iranians, for virtually nothing, significant intelligence information concerning the position of Iraqi forces.* The board had checked the value of the information with the Defense Intelligence Agency and had been told that it was real and could have been extremely valuable to the Iranians if they had wanted to use it to attack Iraq.

Even more amazing was what the transcripts showed North telling his Iranian counterparts. It is important to realize, in evaluating the significance of North's statements, that as far as the Iranians knew he was a representative of the U.S. Government and perhaps even a direct emissary of the President. North spoke of personal meetings he had with the President—at Camp David, no less, walking in the woods!—at which the President was quoted about policies toward Iran and the Middle East region that directly contradicted what our policy actually was. He also quoted the President as praising Islam and the Islamic revolution in Iran. I was very concerned about these revelations. It had been my experience that relatively little that came into the hands of the Tower Board was not shortly thereafter made available to the press, and I could imagine—or maybe a better phrase would be that I could *not* imagine—what would happen if the content of these transcripts were known to the press. At that point, despite repeated White House efforts, very few members of the public had been informed by the media that the President had never met alone with North. As far as the public knew, North was a Reagan confidant, and here was North recorded as saying in the name of the President the most outrageous falsehoods and contradictions of U.S. policy. If these things had become public, there would be almost no way to redeem the President's credibility with the American people. I asked

---

* Ironically, in August 2002, there were press reports that the United States had furnished intelligence information to Iraq during the Iran-Iraq war, allegedly because of concern that Iran might win. If true, this would mean that both sides in that conflict were receiving U.S. support—Iran in the form of arms and intelligence about Iraqi forces, and Iraq in the form of intelligence about Iranian forces.

Dean McGrath, an assistant White House counsel, to check on whether this material had gone to the Hill, and he said that it had. Fortunately, for once, these items did not leak from the Hill or, if they did, we were fortunate that they did not catch the sustained attention of the press.

I met with Regan early the following morning and briefed him on the North transcripts. We realized that we would have to find time in the President's schedule that morning—before the meeting with the Tower Board—to brief him. Not only would the transcripts be the subject of the Tower Board interview, but they were powerful evidence for the President that his original policy had been completely subverted by those who were charged with carrying it out.

At the meeting with the President, attended by Regan, Abshire, and me, I briefed the President from my notes on what North had said to the Iranians in Frankfurt. The President was shocked. When he heard what North had said—that the President wanted Iran to win the war against Iraq, that the President had said that North was "thinking small" when he proposed to the President a list of arms for Iran, and that the President had gone off for a weekend to pray and come back with the quote from the Bible that had been given to the Iranians—Reagan said it was all "horseshit, pure fiction." The President said that North had never been to Camp David and he, the President, had never said those things. I had seldom seen him so animated and angry. He expressed great annoyance with North and said that he had hoped not to have to criticize North when he finally testified, but this was something else again. On the intelligence issue, he said that he had no recollection of ever being told that we had given intelligence information to the Iranians.

At this point in the meeting, I gave the President the *aide-mémoire* that Abshire had recommended the day before. It said that the President recalled being surprised when he first heard about the Israeli shipment of arms to Iran, and that he had no recollection about the HAWK shipment in November. It noted that he could not remember where he had heard the story about the HAWKs being called back. The President took the memo, looked at it, and put it aside.

At about noon, Dawson called again, this time to say that the Board would require another week to finish its report, and suggested that we announce the extension now, before the meeting with the President, so it did not look as though the extension was necessary because of anything the President had said. We really had no choice on granting the extension. The Tower Board was the only game in town that offered us the possibility of getting the President out of the White House and around the country again. Dennis Thomas had developed a press and public-relations plan that began immediately after the Tower Board report. Among other things, the President would review the report, adopt its conclusions, and make a speech to the nation relying on the facts that the board had found. Shortly thereafter, he would hold a press conference. All of this was to occur in February. The Tower Board's request for an extension threw the initiation of the plan back a week. Now the board wouldn't report until February 26, and there could be no press conference in February. It meant at least one more week in purgatory for the President and the rest of us.

The meeting with the Tower Board—attended by the board members and Dawson, McFadden, Abshire, Brower, and me—began with the President reading from the talking points on NSC process that we had prepared for him. He did this quite well under the circumstances, and at the end Tower and Scowcroft said that the ideas he had advanced were similar to those of other former presidents they had talked to.

Tower then opened the discussion with a general question about whether the President had any different recollections from those at the last meeting. The President did not respond to this question, but began to talk about what we had discussed with him that morning—the North statements in the Frankfurt meeting with the Iranians. He said the statements were completely fictional and wrong. Tower pursued these points for a while, in order to determine that the President did not agree with and had not authorized anything that North said.

Then Tower asked a more pointed question about the August 1985 shipment of TOWs. The President got up, went to his desk, picked up my memo, and began to read from it. Unfortunately, the memo was written in the second person—that is, it was addressed to the President and referred to him as "you." Two of the first sentences, for example, said, "You recalled being surprised when you learned of the August 1985 Israeli shipment of TOWs. If that is still your recollection, you might tell this to the Tower Board." The memo did not suggest that he say any more than this, since that was the full extent of his recollection. The President made a limited attempt to summarize it, to put it in the first person, but in reading it aloud he included some of the second-person references, making it sound as though he had been told to say these things. He did this without any conviction, and then compounded it by mumbling something about this being a dispute between Regan and McFarlane.

I was horrified. It was not only a terribly embarrassing moment, but at a time when there had been much press attention to the canard that Regan was somehow interested in making sure that his view of this issue—rather than McFarlane's—was accepted by the President, it could reasonably have been viewed by the Tower Board as an effort to influence the President in the direction of Regan's view. Abshire and Brower shared my concern.

Nothing happened on this story until Saturday, February 14. I was in the office and received a call from David Hoffman of the *Washington Post*. He said he had heard from excellent sources that the President had contradicted himself in the second meeting with the Tower Board on the question of whether he had approved the first Israeli shipment in advance. I said that I would not tell him anything about what the President had said to the Tower Board. Later in the day, at home, I got a call from Bob Timberg of the *Baltimore Sun,* who asked whether the President had "clarified his position." Again, I told Timberg that I couldn't say anything about what occurred in the Tower Board meeting. Finally, I received another call from a *Post* reporter, virtually demanding that I confirm the story that the President had changed his testimony. I thought this was interesting. Reporters seldom are so peremptory in seeking confirmations of stories, and I guessed that the *Post* could not find a good source to confirm what they knew was a great story. I thought they'd find one, and dreaded the headlines of the next day, but surprisingly there was no story in the Sunday edition. This indicated that the *Post* had not been able to find anyone to confirm the report, and I thought this spoke well for the people from the Tower Board who were in the meeting.

It was not until the following Thursday that the story broke, with reports in the *Post, Los Angeles Times, Wall Street Journal,* and *Baltimore Sun.* The *Post* story had a particularly stinging twist. It said that the President had changed his story after speaking with and being pressed to do so by Regan. I could not imagine where this story had come from. Very few in the White House knew that Regan had met with the President about this subject, and the members of the Tower Board could not have known what Regan might have said to the President. Most important, the story had no foundation. Those in the meeting with the President on this subject knew that Regan had not in any sense "pressed" the President to accept Regan's own recollection. Whoever leaked this story, if anyone, probably intended to cast Regan in a highly unfavorable light, and indeed it had an immediate and powerful effect. Criticism of Regan and demands for his ouster reached a crescendo. But the story also damaged the President, making him seem much more malleable than he was in fact.

I realized that I had been largely responsible for this disaster. Regan never had any interest, as far as I could tell, in pressing his point of view on the President. It seems to have been, from the beginning, simply what he recalled, and he thought it was the truth. For that reason, he wanted the President to have the same recollection—but if the President did not, that raised no significant problems for Regan. In my concern for an accurate historical record, I had pressed the President too hard for a recollection. In trying to accommodate me, or to recall something that he thought he should have been able to recall, the President had reached too far. When someone suggested that he was surprised on hearing about the Israeli shipment of TOWs, he remembered being surprised, but when he read McFarlane's testimony, that also seemed correct. His finding the false North chronology in his desk—which may have caused him to adopt the false story about calling back the Israeli HAWKs in November 1985—

only added further complications. The truth was that he had no recollection of any of these events, and in retrospect I should have left things in this posture when I first heard him say, on January 3, 1987, that he remembered nothing other than McFarlane's visit to him in the hospital.

It is probably appropriate at this point to comment on the President's memory. Given the enormous controversy surrounding the Iran arms sales, observers might believe that this action was an important initiative for the President, and what happened and how it happened should have been clear in his mind. His inability to recall events, therefore, is thought by some to reflect a decline in his cognitive abilities at this point—perhaps even an early indication of the onset of his later Alzheimer's affliction. This view, to me, reflects a lack of perspective. There are dozens of enormously important things happening in and around the Oval Office every day. In some of these, the President was directly and continuously involved. His recollections of these events, shortly after they occurred, should be relatively sharp. Despite the significance they assumed later—in the midst of a press frenzy— the Iran arms sales were only a flicker in this constant conflagration. As far as the record shows, the President was told about the initiative while he was in the hospital in July 1985, met several times with his foreign policy advisers to hear their views, and then—after the initiative went forward—received periodic, and apparently rare, reports about arms shipments and hostages. It says much about the relative significance of the arms-sales initiative that McFarlane— seemingly as an aside—dropped a report about HAWKs being sent to Iran and the hostages being released into the middle of the President's briefing with his advisers when he was in Geneva for a summit meeting with General Secretary Gorbachev in November 1985. McFarlane had to report at that moment; the plane was on the way. Given the importance of the Geneva summit, and the concentration it required of the President, it would be surprising if he remembered anything of McFarlane's report.

In his autobiography, Reagan provided some sense of perspective on the question of what he was expected to remember: "On any given day, I was sent dozens of documents to read and saw an average of eighty people. I set the policy, but I turned over the day-to-day details to specialists. Amid all the things that went on, I frankly have had trouble remembering many specifics of the day-to-day events and meetings of that period, at least in the degree of detail that subsequent interest in the events has demanded."[8]

There is further, and I believe substantial, support for the view that Reagan was actually told very little about the Iran arms sales intitiative. Donald Regan attended virtually every meeting at which the President might have been briefed about the Iran arms sales—including the meeting in Geneva—and his recollection of what occurred and the sequence in which things occurred was also very unclear. There has never been any question about the quality of Regan's memory—at that time or since—and the fact that he also had trouble recalling how the arms sales unfolded is a clear demonstration of their relative insignificance and the limited amount of information provided to the President by his national security advisers after the initiative was approved.

The conflict in recollections between Regan and McFarlane is also instructive. Both of them were at the same meeting with the President when the President was advised of the first shipment of arms to Iran by Israel in August 1985, and they made diametrically opposite statements about what had occurred. Regan believed the President was surprised by what he heard; McFarlane insisted the President had already approved the shipment. My own view, for reasons discussed earlier in this chapter, is that the Israelis probably never got definitive approval from the President but enough good vibrations out of Washington to allow them to go ahead. The President was surprised at that first report, but afterward endorsed the Israelis' action in sufficiently broad terms to permit them to proceed with an additional shipment of TOWs in September and HAWKs in November 1985.

Although, as discussed above, there was no reason, from a legal perspective, for me to care whether the President accepted either Regan's or McFarlane's account, it was important that the President not seem to have been dissembling or involved in a cover-up. To the extent possible, his limited recollections of events should be consistent with one another. On February 20, the *Post* and *Times* each carried stories that McFarlane had admitted to the Tower Board that he had taken part in a cover-up—in McFarlane's case, a completely unnecessary effort to obscure the President's involvement in his own policy. There had also been a more sinister cover-up, carried on by North and Poindexter, that attempted to prevent public disclosure of the facts about what had occurred by manipulating the facts given to the President about the hostages and so-called moderates in Iran. The President had escaped the consequences of this second cover-up because the effort was truncated by the discovery of the diversion memo in late November and the subsequent dismissal of Poindexter and North. Now the Tower Board was looking into this episode, and I was sure the other investigators—including the independent counsel—would also do so. I wanted to be sure that the President was not in any sense implicated in either of the cover-up efforts.

My concern was that the President had once again left a muddled record with the Tower Board. He had in fact changed his testimony so that there was some consistency between his accounts concerning the sale of TOWs in August and the sale of HAWKs in November. However, he had done it in an unconvincing way that now had come to look as though he was simply responding to pressure from Regan. I thought we had to do something to extract the President from this position, since the Tower Board's report, by focusing on the President's inconsistencies and changes of view, could suggest that the President was intending to mislead them. This in turn might attract the attention of the independent counsel, who was known to be looking at the question of whether the President and his top advisers had participated in a cover-up of some kind.

For this reason, Abshire and I met with the President once more, on February 19, to see if we could get a definitive statement from him about what he recalled about the arms sales, or in the alternative to assure him that if he really had no recollection it would be perfectly appropriate to say so. In the course of the meeting, the President told us that he had no independent recollection of approving any of the arms sales, but having read McFarlane's testimony on the subject—which I had included in his preparation material for the first Tower Board meeting—he thought that made the most sense.

After this, Abshire and I went back to my office to consider what we should do. The Tower Board now had a contradictory record, and reason to believe that the President was being manipulated. The fact, however, was that the President simply didn't remember. I suggested to Abshire that he call Tower and ask Tower to call the President—to hear the President's statement that he really didn't recall anything about the arms shipments in August and November 1985. Abshire spoke with Tower, but after consulting with his colleagues, Tower said he wanted something from the President in writing.

Abshire and I then sent a memo to the President telling him of Abshire's conversation with Tower, and suggesting that the President might wish to clarify the situation by sending a letter to the Tower Board explaining that he simply had no recollection. The memo was sent to the White House residence about 7:15 P.M., through Jim Kuhn.

On the morning of February 20, Abshire and I had a painful meeting with Regan. Regan had been badly battered in the press at this point, including the very damaging—and false—*Post* story that he had changed the President's testimony. It is true that Regan had been in briefings of the President that Abshire and I conducted, but he had never in these meetings pressed the President with his view—only once offering in the President's presence that he recalled the President being surprised when he was first told that the Israelis had shipped TOW missiles to Iran. He also knew of the inconsistent McFarlane memos—one of which, on November 7, said that the Israelis had acted without our advance approval—and never in my presence mentioned this to the President. If Regan was trying to change the President's testimony, I didn't see it. Moreover, he had no motive to do so. It made no difference to Regan what the President remembered; he was never in jeopardy of prosecution for his recollections concerning the arms shipments, although he could have been if he had attempted to change the President's testimony.

Thus, I sympathized with Regan as we talked with him that morning. Not for the first time, he complained that no one was defending him. He expressed frustration that McFarlane's side of the story was out

because his lawyer—Leonard Garment—was freely leaking favorable
accounts of McFarlane's Tower Board testimony to the press. But every
time Regan said he wanted to tell his version, I told him he shouldn't
because it might bring him into conflict with the President's account.
He said he understood this, but what was his reward for being loyal to
the President? I had to admit that he was being badly hurt. I told him
that I had talked with all the networks the preceding day and told them
that Regan was not involved in changing the President's position, but
they all went ahead and reported that anyway. The fact is that they
wanted to hurt him, and they were going to do it no matter who spoke
on his behalf. Washington is a very mean town when some formerly
powerful person, already in disfavor, is down. It's like dogs or wolves
turning on a deposed leader of the pack to finish him off. The same
phenomenon was exhibited in the Deaver matter. After he left the
White House and began to build a successful public-relations business
in Washington, the possibility that he was violating the ethics laws set
off a wild press storm—far out of proportion to the facts involved or
the importance of the issue as news. I could never understand the vin-
dictiveness of the press in these cases; it must have some deep emotional
source, but it's a regular and regrettable phenomenon in Washington.

When I returned to my office, I had a call from one of the President's secretaries. She said the President had an envelope for me. When
I picked up the envelope, I found it contained a handwritten letter to
the Tower Board from the President. It generally followed the format
we had suggested—the President said he really had no recollection—
but it contained the line: "I let myself be influenced by others' recollections." I called Abshire and told him I had a letter from the President
addressed to the Tower Board. We agreed that the original should be
delivered, but it should be accompanied by a more formal typed version
that the President would sign. Abshire went down to the Oval Office to
have this done, and would try to see the President to determine whom
he meant by "others' recollections." Since "others'" was plural, I assumed that the President meant both Regan and McFarlane, but when
Abshire returned he said that the President meant only Regan. Abshire

then delivered the President's original draft on yellow paper and a more formal signed letter to the Tower Board.

Now things began to move very quickly. The news over the weekend was terrible. Much of it focused on Regan's conduct, and seemed to be coming out of the Tower Board. After hearing a CBS report that Regan had ordered a doctored chronology and lied to or misled the Tower Board, I called Rhett Dawson and asked him whether the Tower Board had any evidence that Regan participated in a cover-up or had misled the board. I told him I certainly had seen nothing of this kind. Dawson denied that the board had any evidence of this, and said that Regan's testimony had been holding up well. He said that if they had any evidence of Regan's participation in a cover-up they would give him a chance to respond. I called Regan and, to encourage him, told him about my conversation with Dawson; it must have been a terrible day. He seemed grateful and said even his own wife had begun to doubt him—since everyone else was saying he had done something wrong.

On Monday, February 23, Regan organized an Oval Office meeting of inside and outside advisers to discuss with the President how and when he should respond to the Tower Board report, which was expected later in the week. The group consisted of the Vice President; Paul Laxalt, a former Republican senator and a friend of the President; David Abshire; Jim Baker; Regan; Dennis Thomas; Dick Wirthlin; Tom Korologos, a Washington wise man; and me. Before discussion began, the President said he was leaning toward making a statement next week, which would be the first week in March. A number of people endorsed this idea, saying that the President should make a brief statement at the time the Tower Board report comes out, but wait a few days to make a comprehensive response.

Discussion then turned to the substance of this comprehensive response. Baker suggested that the President should say that he had made a "mistake of the heart"—that he wanted the hostages back and traded arms for them. Others endorsed this idea or minor variations of it. I thought this was remarkable; all of those in the room from outside the White House—all of whom were very sympathetic to the President's position, and had probably given him the benefit of the doubt on this question—had come to believe that the President had intended to trade arms for hostages. In other words, under the barrage of press reports, even those closest and most sympathetic to the President came to believe that this was actually his policy. As Baker framed it, it was "a mistake of the heart." This view was different from the approach Regan and the rest of us on the White House staff—without success—had been pressing on the President for about two months. We had accepted and believed that the President had never intended to trade arms for hostages and that his "mistake" was not in the policy he had adopted but in how it was implemented. Whatever their disagreements about what the President had actually done, however, all his staff and outside advisers seemed to agree that the President should say he had made a mistake of some kind and that, until he did so, his credibility problems with the American people would persist.

The President, once again, resisted the idea that he had traded arms for hostages. He immediately saw in Baker's formulation a real inconsistency with his own view. He insisted again that he had authorized the arms sales for the purpose of improving the U.S. relationship with Iran, and not to trade for the hostages. Responding to some of the other ideas, he seemed to admit that arms had been traded for hostages, but this arose out of the way the operation was handled and not as a result of his policy. This was a major advance in his thinking on this subject; prior to this, I had never heard him accept the idea that his policy had degenerated into an arms-for-hostages trade. Indeed, when he was asked whether he would do the same thing again, the President said yes, "but I would institute more controls." This was an important change of position and I was very pleased to hear it; he was coming close to saying that he had made a mistake in not following the implementation of his policy more carefully. It was this approach that would allow him to reconcile his deeply held view that he had approved the arms sales only to open a channel to Iran with the fact that there was strong evidence that arms were traded for hostages. He could then admit he had made a mistake in not following the implementation of his policy, without admitting—as he certainly would not—that his policy itself had been a mistake. I don't think most of the advisers from outside the White House recognized that this meeting had produced a significant shift in the President's position.

At the end of the meeting, Regan said he had an announcement to make. He said he and the President had talked that morning, and that after the President had responded to the Tower Board report, they would sit down and discuss Regan's future in the White House. It did not seem realistic that Regan would be able to stay much beyond the end of the week. The stories about the President's change of testimony, the near-unanimous demands from editorialists as well as Republicans in and out of Washington for Regan's head, caused me to believe that an indefinite arrangement, such as that he'd just announced, would not last. The previous day, a Sunday, the *Washington Post* had published one of its meaner editorials, entitled "Chaos at the Top," which went on about Regan as follows:

> Donald Regan, arguably the worst White House chief of staff ever. . . From the beginning he has been casual, even cavalier about the interests of the president he is alleged to represent, but absolutely dogged in trying to justify, defend and glorify himself. . . . He has long since forfeited any shred of dignity he had as he fought with the first lady and, more telling, sought to lay off blame on others for what happened. . . . Still, we do not blame Mr. Regan, as appalling and self-absorbed as his actions have been, for the plight of Mr. Reagan. We blame Mr. Reagan for continuing to leave things in the hands of Donald Regan.

There is almost nothing factual in this screed of name-calling and invective. I had been watching Regan from close up struggle through the Iran-Contra affair for four months, and still could not see anything he had done wrong. He was certainly not responsible for the policy itself, nor for the cover-up by North and Poindexter—which he had tried to prevent—nor for the President's refusal to admit that he had made a mistake. I concluded that he was guilty of not cultivating the Washington power structure—of which the *Post* and the rest of the media were certainly a part—and the penalty for that was having his name and reputation dragged through the mud. It's little wonder capable people frequently refuse to serve in government; the rewards are few and the penalties can be enormous.

At about the same time, Mike Deaver was indicted on five counts of perjury in connection with allegations that he had violated the ethics laws by contacting the White House, after he had resigned his position, about matters in which he was alleged to have had substantial involvement when he was the President's deputy chief of staff. It is significant that he was indicted for perjury and not for actual violations of the ethics laws. In other words, although there was not enough evidence to prosecute Deaver for any of the things that provoked the vast media feeding frenzy about him described earlier in this book, the independent counsel still found it necessary to charge him with something. Deaver was eventually acquitted on the perjury charges, but the excesses of his independent counsel—Whitney North Seymour—like the excesses of the *Washington Post,* and the media generally in the Iran-Contra matter, demonstrate that it is dangerous to put power in the hands of people who are reckless in its use against others.

Neither the President nor any member of the White House staff saw a copy of the Tower Board report until the morning it was made available to the press. Under the release plan ultimately adopted, the President would meet with the board to receive the report, then go over to a press conference at the auditorium in the Old Executive Office Building next to the White House, where he would introduce the board. The board would then summarize the report for the press, and answer questions.

Flipping quickly through the report, I came across the following statement about Regan: "More than almost any Chief of Staff of recent memory, he asserted personal control over the White House staff and sought to extend his control to the National Security Adviser. . . . he especially should have ensured that plans were made for the handling of any public disclosure of the initiative. He must bear primary responsibility for the chaos that descended upon the White House when such disclosure did occur."[10] I thought back to the board's interview with Alton Keel, in which he said that Regan had not attempted to control the NSC staff, and wondered where they got this stuff.

At 10 A.M. on February 26, the Tower Board met with the President. Also present were the Vice President, Regan, Frank Carlucci, the new national security adviser, Will Ball, Marlin Fitzwater, who had replaced Speakes as the President's deputy press secretary, Abshire, Brower and me. Tower opened the meeting by saying that the report was the unanimous view of all of the members. Then he stopped, as though he didn't expect to have to say more. Since we and the President had only seen the report an hour before, we were not really prepared—nor did we expect—to ask questions. We anticipated a briefing of the kind the board was going to give to the press later that morning. In the awkward silence that followed, the President finally asked where the money had gone—referring no doubt to the diversion of funds to the Contras. There was a 10- or 15-minute discussion of this issue, of which the conclusion was that nobody knew.

After this, having realized that the Board was not going to provide a briefing, I asked Tower to tell the President what the report said about trading arms for hostages. Tower said that although they thought the President may have had a different idea in mind, the program very quickly became a vehicle for an arms-for-hostages swap. The President immediately objected to this characterization, saying that he could not see how it could be a swap if no one in the U.S. Government was actually dealing with the captors, and anyway he had approved the policy for a different purpose. Tower told the President he had not been adequately informed by his subordinates. Scowcroft then broke in and said that when an airplane containing arms is waiting on the edge of a runway for word on whether hostages have been released, that is trading arms for hostages. The President didn't say anything, but moved his head and shoulders in such a way as to indicate that he had to concede the point. Tower said it was a good idea to try to achieve an opening to

Iran, but wrong to use arms for this purpose. There were no moderates in Iran, he said, just gradations of radicals. He also noted that the board's report said North had misrepresented both his access to the President and the President's policies.

The Vice President asked whether there would be new facts to deal with when North and Poindexter testified—a fairly clear reference to the diversion-of-funds issue—and Tower said he thought this was unlikely because of the extensive paper trail that both of them had left. Scowcroft said that he didn't think there was any "bombshell" out there.

The President asked what North and Poindexter were afraid of—why they didn't testify. Tower turned this question over to Clark Mc-Fadden, the board's counsel, who said he had not seen anything in what the board had found to indicate that they had criminal liability. McFadden was correct about this, if he was referring to the arms sales alone, but Independent Counsel Lawrence Walsh did find prosecutable violations in the diversion of funds. Ultimately, that prosecution was not brought for technical reasons, but North and Poindexter were indicted and convicted in separate trials for lying to Congress, obstructing Congress and conspiracy (Poindexter), and obstructing Congress, destroying documents, and accepting an illegal gratuity (North). After separate trials, both were convicted, but their convictions were overturned by the D.C. Circuit Court of Appeals, which found that the prosecutor's evidence had been tainted by knowledge of the testimony which North and Poindexter eventually gave under a grant of use immunity by the Joint Congressional Committees.

At this point, the meeting was almost over and no one had asked about a cover-up. Thinking about the *Newsweek* article only a few days before—charging that Regan had led a White House cover-up—I asked whether there had been a cover-up and, if so, who was responsible for it. Tower said the board did not use the term cover-up, but some of those on the NSC staff had "distorted the facts" in the aftermath. Tower then went on to say, somewhat gratuitously, that the chief of staff had to bear responsibility for the way the facts were disclosed. Regan, sitting next to me, asked Tower whether the board had asked him about his conduct when he testified. Tower did not have an answer, because the answer was no.

Carlucci then asked whether the board had recommended that the national security adviser report to the President through the chief of staff. I smiled to myself as I watched the board fall all over itself denying that any such thing would be appropriate. Carlucci, having set the trap, then sprang it. He asked how the board could have it both ways—how could the chief of staff have responsibility for what goes on in the White House when he doesn't have authority to direct the people who are taking action? The board was caught flat-footed. It had no answer. Tower just stared down at his copy of the report.

But notwithstanding all these weaknesses, the Tower Board had done the job it had been established to do: it had assembled the facts that would enable the President to cite a credible and objective source when he was asked about the Iran-Contra matter in the future. The report received extensive press coverage, with large excerpts reprinted in the *New York Times* and *Washington Post*, among other newspapers. All that remained was for the President to say that he had made a mistake in allowing his original strategic initiative to degenerate into an arms-for-hostages swap, and the Tower Board's report presented a powerful case that this is indeed what the President's initiative had become.

On March 4, the President finally made the speech that Regan and other members of the White House staff had been imploring him to make for the previous three months. He said he had made a mistake by failing to supervise the implementation of his policy toward Iran. The key sentences were "I take full responsibility for my actions and for those of my administration. As angry as I may be about activities undertaken without my knowledge, I am still accountable for these actions." The *New York Times* front-page headline was "Reagan Concedes 'Mistake' in Arms-for-Hostages Policy; Takes Blame, Vows Changes." Much of the President's speech to the nation discussed the Tower Board, the facts that it had arrayed for him, and its criticisms. As we had hoped when the board was first established, its comprehensive report allowed the President to rely on something credible in stating facts that he did not know himself. Just as important, it provided the factual predicate for the President to say he had made a mistake, and this enabled him finally to put the Iran-Contra episode behind him and get out again among the American people.

EPILOGUE

The Iran-Contra crisis essentially ended with the President's speech to the nation on March 4, 1987. The investigations continued for years afterward, but the American people were satisfied with his explanation and were ready to move on. At the time, he looked to many observers like a lame-duck president. His credibility with the American people was badly damaged, the press contained increasingly overt expressions of doubt that he had the intellectual or political resources to carry on, and he was well into the last two years of his presidency, when his ability to influence events would likely have been at their lowest.

Yet Ronald Reagan came back. In his last years in the White House he succeeded again, this time in achieving the last of the great goals he had set for his presidency: he signed the first arms-reduction agreement ever negotiated with the Soviet Union, and began a process that would end the Cold War—and even the Soviet Union itself—after he had left office.

Again, one had to ask: How could he have done this? The answer goes back again to the central point of how he governed—not with craft or manipulation, or through the gradual accretion of political power in Washington as Richard Neustadt would have supposed, but through his ideas and convictions. He believed, and acted on his beliefs; he stayed the course. With his extraordinary sense of mission, and faith in the American people, he was an irresistible force to Mikhail Gorbachev and the other Soviet leaders who could not muster the same faith in their system or themselves.

Since his term in office, Ronald Reagan's esteem among the American people has only grown. At the end of his presidency, 54 percent approved of his job performance—a better figure than the 46 percent who felt the same way in March 1987, but both numbers were well below the average of 63 percent during the 11-month period prior to the advent of the Iran-Contra crisis. By February 2000, however, a Gallup poll showed Reagan ranked as the fourth greatest president by the American people, just after Roosevelt but well ahead of all his other modern predecessors or successors except Kennedy. Most recently, in a Gallup poll in April 2002, 73 percent of the respondents approved, retrospectively, of how Reagan "handled his job as president."

None of this would have mattered much to Ronald Reagan. He would have wondered not whether the American people thought he'd conducted the presidency well, but whether they still believed that they, and not their government, bore the principal responsibility for themselves, their families, and their communities.

When Howard Baker replaced Don Regan as White House chief of staff, he brought in his own counsel, a fine lawyer and friend named A. B. Culvahouse. I stayed on for about a month to help with the transition and to pass along whatever knowledge I had about the Iran-Contra matter, which would now become Culvahouse's responsibility, working with David Abshire.

When I finally left the White House, almost a year to the day after I'd arrived, I had the satisfaction of knowing that Ronald Reagan was on the way back.

NOTES

PREFACE

1. Ronald Reagan, *Ronald Reagan: An American Life* (New York: Pocket Books, 1990), p. 287.

CHAPTER 1

1. In his autobiography, *Ronald Reagan: An American Life* (New York: Pocket Books, 1990), p. 532, Reagan recounts his reaction to the public's incredulity: "Those first few months after the Iran-Contra affair hit the front pages were frustrating for me. For the first time in my life, people didn't believe me. I had told the truth, but they still didn't believe me. While I was unhappy, I never felt depressed about the situation. There wasn't a gloom or 'malaise' hanging over the Oval Office, as some writers have suggested. I just went on with my job."

2. Fred I. Greenstein, *The Presidential Difference: Leadership Style from FDR to Clinton* (New York: Free Press, 2000), p. 157.

3. Frances Fitzgerald, *Way Out There in the Blue* (New York: Simon and Schuster, 2000), p. 175.

4. Ibid., pp. 217–219.

5. Robert Shogan, *The Double-Edged Sword* (Boulder, CO: Westview Press, 1999), p. 156; *Report of the President's Special Review Board* (the Tower Board) (Washington, DC: Government Printing Office, 1987), p. iv–10.

6. A good summary of the changes that occurred during Reagan's eight years in office appears in Dinesh D'Souza, *Ronald Reagan: How an Ordinary Man Became an Extraordinary Leader* (New York: Touchstone, 1999), pp. 25–28.

7. Richard E. Neustadt, *Presidential Power and the Modern Presidents* (New York: Free Press, 1990).

8. Ibid., p. 185.

9. Ibid., p. 270.

10. Ibid., p. 269.

11. Ibid., p. 270.

12. Ibid.

13. Fitzgerald, *Way Out There in the Blue* (New York: Simon and Schuster, 2000).

14. Ibid., pp. 353–355.

15. Lou Cannon, *President Reagan: The Role of a Lifetime*. First Public Affairs edition (New York: Public Affairs, 2000).

16. Edmund Morris, *Dutch: A Memoir of Ronald Reagan* (New York: Random House, 1999), p. 514.

17. Comments of Barton Bernstein, Conference of the Organization of American Historians, on *Reagan in His Own Hand*, Washington, DC, April 14, 2002.

18. Reagan, *Ronald Reagan: An American Life, (New York: Pocket Books, 1990)* p. 124.

19. D'Souza, *Ronald Reagan: How an Ordinary Man Became an Extraordinary Leader, (New York: Touchtone, 1999)*, p. 28.

20. Kiron Skinner and Annelise and Martin Anderson, eds., *Reagan in His Own Hand* (New York: Free Press, 2001).

21. Michael Deaver, *A Different Drummer* (New York: HarperCollins, 2001).

22. William Lee Miller, *Lincoln's Virtues* (New York: Alfred A. Knopf, 2002), p. 382.

23. Ibid., p. 397.

24. The full quote, from the *General Theory of Employment, Interest and Money*, is: "The ideas of economists and political philosophers, both when they are right and when they are wrong, are more powerful than is commonly understood. Indeed, the world is ruled by little else. Practical men, who believe themselves to be quite exempt from any intellectual influences, are usually the slaves of some defunct economist."

25. Americans for the Reagan Agenda, *A Time for Choosing: The Speeches of Ronald Reagan, 1961–1982* (Chicago: Regnery Gateway, 1983), p. 39.

26. Steven F. Hayward, *The Age of Reagan* (Roseville, CA: Forum, Prima Publishing, 2001), p. 57.

27. Lou Cannon, *President Reagan: The Role of a Lifetime*, First Public Affairs edition (New York: Public Affairs, 2000), p. 82.

28. Max Weber, *Politics as a Vocation*, in Gerth and Mills, *From Max Weber* (New York: Oxford University Press, paperback edition, 1958), p. 79.

29. Peggy Noonan, *When Character Was King: A Story of Ronald Reagan* (New York: Viking, 2001), p. 317.

CHAPTER 2

1. Reagan, *Ronald Reagan: An American Life* (New York: Pocket Books, 1990), p. 161.

2. Richard E. Neustadt, *Presidential Power and the Modern Presidents* (New York: Free Press, 1990).

3. John Podhoretz, *Hell of a Ride: Backstage at the White House Follies 1989–1993* (New York: Simon and Schuster, 1993), p. 129.

4. Tevi Troy, *Intellectuals and the American Presidency: Philosophers, Jesters or Technicians?* (Lanham, MD, New York, London: Rowman and Littlefield Publishers, 2002).

5. Richard E. Neustadt, *Presidential Power and the Modern Presidents* (New York: Free Press, 1990).

6. Quoted in William Ker Muir Jr., *The Bully Pulpit: The Presidential Leadership of Ronald Reagan* (San Francisco: ICS Press, 1992), p. 41.

7. Ibid., p. 181.

8. Ibid., p. 78.

9. Ibid., p. 78.

10. Ronald Reagan, *Speaking My Mind* (New York: Simon and Schuster, 1989), p. 78.

11. Kiron Skinner and Annelise and Martin Anderson, eds., *Reagan in His Own Hand* (New York: Free Press, 2001).

12. Lou Cannon, *President Reagan: The Role of a Lifetime*, First Public Affairs edition (New York: Public Affairs, 2000), p. 292.

13. Frances Fitzgerald, *Way Out There in the Blue* (New York: Simon and Schuster, 2000), p. 175.

14. Ibid., p. 103.

15. Ibid., p. 103.

16. Lou Cannon, *President Reagan: The Role of a Lifetime*, First Public Affairs edition (New York: Public Affairs 2000), p. 254.

17. Milton and Rose Friedman, *Free to Choose* (New York: Avon Books, 1981), p. 62.

18. Ibid., p. xix.

19. Ronald Reagan, *Speaking My Mind*, (New York: Simon and Schuster, 1989), pp. 61–62.

20. Ibid., pp. 94–96.

21. Michael Deaver, *A Different Drummer: My Thirty Years with Ronald Reagan* (New York: HarperCollins, 2001), p. 166.

22. Kiron Skinner and Annelise and Martin Anderson, eds., *Reagan in His Own Hand* (New York: Free Press, 2001).

23. Ibid., p. 221.

24. Ibid., pp. 262–263.

25. Everett Carll Ladd and Karlyn Bowman, *What's Wrong: A Survey of American Satisfaction and Complaint* (Washington, DC: AEI Press, 1998), p. 113.

26. Ibid., p. 96.

27. Ibid., p. 87.

28. Ibid., p. 239.

29. Fred I. Greenstein, *The Presidential Difference: Leadership Style from FDR to Clinton* (New York: Free Press, 2000), p. 157.

30. David Herbert Donald, *Lincoln* (New York: Simon and Schuster, 1995).

31. Ronald Reagan, *Speaking My Mind*, (New York: Simon and Schuster, 1989), p. 62.

32. Quoted in William Ker Muir Jr., *The Bully Pulpit: The Presidential Leadership of Ronald Reagan* (San Francisco: ICS Press, 1992), p. 184.

33. Ronald Reagan, *Speaking My Mind*, (New York: Simon and Schuster, 1989), p. 64.

CHAPTER 3

1. David Stockman, *The Triumph of Politics* (New York: Harper and Row, 1986), pp. 340–351.

2. Reagan, *Speaking My Mind*, (New York: Simon and Schuster, 1989), p. 80.

3. Ibid., p. 351.

4. Reagan, *Ronald Reagan: An American Life*, (New York Pocket Books, 1990), p. 314.

5. David Stockman, *The Triumph of Politics* (New York: Harper and Row, 1986), p. 349.

6. Ibid., p. 315.

7. Ibid., p. 349.

8. Kiron Skinner and Annelise and Martin Anderson, eds., *Reagan in His Own Hand* (New York: Free Press, 2001), p. 264.

9. David Stockman, *The Triumph of Politics* (New York: Harper and Row, 1986), p. 351.

10. Reagan, *Ronald Reagan: An American Life*, (New York Pocket Books, 1990)p. 315.

11. Lawrence Lindsey, *The Growth Experiment* (New York: Basic Books, 1990), p. 4.

12. Kiron Skinner and Annelise and Martin Anderson, eds., *Reagan in His Own Hand* (New York: Free Press, 2001), p. 299.

13. Ronald Reagan, *Ronald Reagan: An American Life* (New York: Pocket Books, 1990), p. 283.

14. Lou Cannon, *President Reagan: The Role of a Lifetime.* First Public Affairs edition (New York: Public Affairs, 2000), p. 121.

15. Ronald Reagan, *Ronald Reagan: An American Life* (New York: Pocket Books, 1990), p. 311.

16. Kiron Skinner and Annelise and Martin Anderson, eds., *Reagan in His Own Hand* (New York: Free Press, 2001), p. 279.

17. Ronald Reagan, *Ronald Reagan: An American Life* (New York: Pocket Books, 1990), p. 287.

18. Ibid., p. 288.

19. Ibid., pp. 314–324.

20. Donald Regan, *For the Record* (New York: Harcourt, Brace Jovanovich, 1988), p. 184.

21. Ronald Reagan, *Ronald Reagan: An American Life* (New York: Pocket Books, 1990), pp. 314-315.

22. Ibid., p. 355.

23. Ibid., p. 357.

24. Peter T. Kilborn, "Treasury Official Assists 'Inefficient' Big Business," *New York Times,* November 28, 1986.

25. Kiron Skinner and Annelise and Martin Anderson, eds., *Reagan in His Own Hand* (New York: Free Press, 2001), p. 228.

26. Ronald Reagan, *Ronald Reagan: An American Life* (New York: Pocket Books, 1990), p. 294.

27. Lou Cannon, "The New Era: Reagan and Gorbachev," in Center for the Study of the Presidency, *Triumphs and Tragedies of the Modern Presidency, Seventy-Six Studies in Presidential Leadership* (Washington, DC: 2000), p. 209.

28. Steven F. Hayward, *The Age of Reason* (Roseville, CA: Forum, Prima Publishing, 2001), p. 692.

29. Ibid., p. 692.

30. Kiron Skinner and Annelise and Martin Anderson, eds., *Reagan in His Own Hand* (New York: Free Press, 2001), p. 86.

31. Ibid., p. 79.

32. David Gergen, *Eyewitness to Power: The Essence of Leadership: Nixon to Clinton* (New York: Simon and Schuster, 2000), p. 206.

33. Frances Fitzgerald, *Way Out There in the Blue* (New York: Simon and Schuster, 2000), pp. 347-369.

34. Text of speech, October 14, 1986.

35. Lou Cannon, "The New Era: Reagan and Gorbachev," in Center for the Study of the Presidency, *Triumphs and Tragedies of the Modern Presidency, Seventy-Six Studies in Presidential Leadership* (Washington, DC: 2000), pp. 210-211.

36. A good summary of the controversy about this issue appears in Fitzgerald, *Way Out There in the Blue,* (New York: Simon and Schuster, 2000), pp. 347–369.

37. Donald Regan, *For the Record* (New York: Harcourt, Brace Jovanovich, 1988), pp. 262-263.

38. Ibid.

39. Kiron Skinner and Annelise and Martin Anderson, eds., *Reagan in His Own Hand* (New York: Free Press, 2001), p. 222.

CHAPTER 4

1. Kiron Skinner and Annelise and Martin Anderson, eds., *Reagan in His Own Hand* (New York: Free Press, 2001), p. xi.

2. Ibid., pp. xi–xii.

3. Edmund Morris, *Dutch: A Memoir of Ronald Reagan* (New York: Random House, 1999), p. xii.

4. Lou Cannon, *President Reagan: The Role of a Lifetime* (First Public Affairs edition (New York: Public Affairs, 2000) p. 141.

5. Ibid., p. 145.

6. Donald Regan, *For the Record* (New York: Harcourt, Brace Jovanovich, 1988), p. 184.

7. Ibid., at 225.

8. Lou Cannon, *President Reagan: The Role of a Lifetime* (First Public Affairs edition (New York: Public Affairs, 2000) p. 141.

9. Ronald Reagan, *Ronald Reagan: An American Life* (New York: Pocket Books, 1990), p. 538.

CHAPTER 5

1. The entire support for the *Newsweek* cover-up allegation consisted solely of the following paragraph: "The destruction of documents allegedly took place three days after former national security adviser Robert McFarlane, North and four aides collaborated in the sanitizing of the Iran record. First they wrote an opening statement for Reagan to give about the scandal at a press conference the next day. Then, starting at 10:30 or 11, McFarlane set about amplifying the chronology drafted by the CIA. McFarlane's successor, John Poindexter, had ordered up the chronology, ostensibly to help the administration get its story straight. One NSC staffer says Poindexter told him later that he was acting on instructions from Donald Regan. Another man present that night confirms the story." So, Poindexter asked for a chronology to be prepared so the administration could "get its story straight," and perportedly says—to an unnamed staffer some time later—he was acting on instructions from Donald Regan. That was enough for *Newsweek* to accuse Regan of orchestrating a cover-up, a possible crime.

2. Larry Sabato, *Feeding Frenzy: Attack Journalism and American Politics* (Baltimore: Lanahan Publishers, 2000), p. 93.

3. Timothy E. Cook, *Governing with the News: The News Media as a Political Institution* (Chicago and London: University of Chicago Press, 1998), p. 133.

4. Larry Sabato, *Feeding Frenzy*, p. 34; see also Herbert R. Molner, *Feeding Frenzies and the Rainbow Coalition* (Chicago: Aspen Books, 2002), p. 25.

5. Larry Sabato, *Feeding Frenzy: Attack Journalism and American Politics* (Baltimore: Lanahan Publishers, 2000), p. 35.

6. William A. Hachten, *The Troubles of Journalism: A Critical Look at What's Right and Wrong with the Press,* second edition, (Mahwah, NJ and London: Lawrence Erlbaum Associates Publishers, 2001), pp. xxii–xxiii.

7. Ronald Reagan, *Ronald Reagan: An American Life* (New York: Pocket Books, 1990), p. 394.

8. Thomas Patterson, *Out of Order* (New York: Knopf, 1993) p. 19.

9. Stuart Diamond and Michael Tolchin, "Deaver Inquiries Are Reported Extended to Asia," *New York Times,* August 11, 1986.

10. Everett Carll Ladd and Karlyn Bowman, *What's Wrong: A Survey of American Satisfaction and Complaint* (Washington, DC: AEI Press, 1998), p. 82.

11. Ibid., p. 86.

12. Ibid., p. 124.

13. Martha Joynt Kumar, "The President as Message and Messenger: Personal Style and Presidential Communications," in Robert Y. Shapiro, Martha Joynt Kumar, and Lawrence R. Jacobs, eds., *Presidential Power* (New York: Columbia University Press, 2000), p. 411.

14. Fred L. Israel, *Ronald Reagan's Weekly Radio Addresses: The President Speaks to America, Volume I: The First Term* (Wilmington, DE: Scholarly Resources, 1987), pp. 90–91.

15. Ibid., pp. 102–103.

16. Kumar, "The President as Message and Messenger," p. 416.

17. Donald Regan, *For the Record* (New York: Harcourt, Brace Jovanovich, 1988), pp. 255–256.

18. Donald Regan, *For the Record* (New York: Harcourt, Brace Jovanovich, 1988), p. 255.

19. Ronald Reagan, *Ronald Reagan: An American Life* (New York: Pocket Books, 1990), p. 393.

CHAPTER 6

1. The same is true, incidentally, in legal matters. People sometimes express puzzlement about why the president needs a White House counsel. The attorney general and the Justice Department, after all, should be able adequately to serve as the president's legal advisers. Indeed, the attorney general is the principal law officer of the land and should logically be the president's adviser on legal matters. However, the attorney general heads the Justice Department, which has institutional interests all its own, and the attorney general can be caught between supporting the institutional position of his agency and advising the president about what is best for the president. Because of this conflict, modern presidents have had their own counsel—known as the Counsel to the President—and the White House counsel staff has grown larger as the Justice Department has become more deeply involved in the administration of programs such as the Immigration and Naturalization Service, in defending the government in court, and in criminal prosecution. In the future, I believe it is likely that the White House Counsel staff will eclipse the Justice Department as the principal legal advisory group for the Executive Branch as well as the president, and the Justice Department will be limited to representing the government in court and administering programs. Indeed, the extraordinary range of authority apparently exercised by the White House counsel in the George W. Bush administration may be a harbinger of this development.

2. Sabato, Larry, *Feeding Frenzy: Attack Journalism and American Politics* (Baltimore: Lanahan Publishers, 2000), p. 71.

3. Lou Cannon, *President Reagan: The Role of a Lifetime.* First Public Affairs edition (New York: Public Affairs, 2000), pp. 506-520.

4. Ibid., pp. 610 and 691. In this case, absurdly, Regan's statement in a press interview that he was like the shovel brigade at the circus parade, cleaning up after the elephants, was taken to suggest that Regan thought the President was the elephant. This, of course, was not the case. The collapse of the talks at Reykjavik, which was precipitated by the President's refusal to back down on the Strategic Defense Initiative, could have been a

political disaster if the media's first reaction—to blame the collapse of the talks on the President—had been allowed to stand. The public relations barrage Regan organized following the Reykjavik meeting reversed this perception before it settled among the American people. The press were the elephants Regan was talking about, not the President.

5. Sabato, Larry, *Feeding Frenzy: Attack Journalism and American Politics* (Baltimore: Lanahan Publishers, 2000), pp. 48-53.

6. A particularly malicious story was that the aides who came over to the White House from Treasury with Regan were toadies and yes-men—a caricature popularized by the conservatives among the Reagan speechwriters, who began to refer to them as "the Mice." This idea was picked up by the media as another way of criticizing Regan. Again, this charge was false, but the White House press—knowing little and caring less about the fairness of the charge—retailed it to the public. Even Lou Cannon, a reporter for the *Washington Post,* who otherwise tried to be balanced in his assessments of the President, adopted this idea. In his biography of Reagan, Cannon identifies these aides by name and subsequently refers to them as the Mice. He spends pages criticizing Regan and the Mice for their alleged incompetence and at one point writes that Regan had "drummed into" the people he brought over from Treasury "that loyalty to him was the principal virtue, and they never transferred this loyalty to Reagan after they went to the White House." Cannon, *President Reagan: The Role of a Lifetime,* p. 501. Cannon cited no evidence for this statement, which—since it presumes to describe what four people were thinking—is absurd on its face. What Cannon fails to note is that the best evidence of where the loyalty of these men truly lay was in the fact that they never attempted to defend Regan by diminishing the President, despite many opportunities to do so. By repeating the canard that they owed their loyalty to Regan rather than the president, Cannon compromised the quality of his reporting.

7. Regan's note taking gave rise to an amusing story during the 1986 campaign. The President had gone to South Dakota to support the candidacy of James Abdnor, one of the Republican senators unexpectedly elected in the strong 1980 Reagan victory. After speaking to a group of farmers, the President and Regan took two of them to the airport in the presidential limousine to discuss the issues on the farmers' minds. Asked afterward whether they thought the President had listened to what they were saying, one of them responded, "Sure do. He even had another fella in there with him takin' notes."

8. Lou Cannon, *President Reagan: The Role of a Lifetime.* First Public Affairs edition (New York: Public Affairs, 2000).

pp. 488–503.

9. Ibid., p. 640. Cannon quotes Regan after the Iran-Contra affair caused his departure from the White House: "It took this crisis for me to realize, 'Oh, Jesus, I don't have a friend in town here. . . . Why don't I have a friend?'"

10. Havemann Judith and Lou Cannon, "Regan Prevailed in Rejection of Big Pay Hikes," *Washington Post,* January 15, 1987.

CHAPTER 7

1. In this and succeeding chapters, I disclose and discuss a great deal of information that might normally be covered either by executive privilege or attorney-client privilege—a form of executive privilege that applies to government lawyers. As a government attorney, representing the President in a matter directly connected to his government duties, I would ordinarily be covered by both executive privilege and attorney-client privilege. However, I believe I am permitted to make these disclosures for several reasons:

Ronald Reagan waived executive privilege, and hence attorney-client privilege, as to all matters relating to the Iran-Contra affair; several members of the White House staff, including the national security staff, testified both publicly and in private to investigators as to their discussions with the President about the Iran arms sales and related matters; the Attorney General testified before committees of Congress as to his discussions with the President, again without the President asserting any form of privilege; the White House and the Executive Branch, at least while I was White House counsel, disclosed to investigating committees of Congress, to the Tower Board, and to the independent counsel, all documents in their possession that were requested by and relevant to these inquiries; and the President himself answered questions as to his thoughts, recollections, and conduct in connection with these matters. As a result of the President's waiver and the subsequent disclosures, I do not believe that I am bound by either executive or attorney-client privilege in connection with my actions or discussions with the President or other officials in the Iran-Contra matter.

2. The *Washington Post* article—quoting a Lebanese newspaper—was a dispatch from Lebanon, and said only that McFarlane was in Tehran to discuss "a cessation of support to terrorist groups in exchange for purchases of spare parts needed for Iran's U.S.–made war equipment." However, both the *Wall Street Journal* and the *New York Times* that morning carried articles about U.S. efforts to free the hostages, although neither article mentioned arms sales.

3. Edmund Morris, *Dutch: A Memoir of Ronald Reagan* (New York: Random House, 1999), p. 605.

4. Michael Ledeen, *Perilous Statecraft* (New York: Charles Scribner's Sons, 1988).

5. Ihsan A. Hijazi, "Hostage's Release Is Linked to Shift in Iranian Policy/A More Pro-Western Element Is Ascendant in Teheran, Arab Diplomats Say," *New York Times,* November 4, 1986. It seems clear that this formulation is the genesis of the idea that there were "moderates" in Iran, even though Ledeen never uses the term in the article he published in the *Washington Post* on January 25, 1987, or in his book, *Perilous Statecraft.* Indeed, on page 139 of *Perilous Statecraft,* he writes, "We understood that these were not people who were interested in sabotaging the Shi'ite revolution; none of them could be accurately termed 'moderate' in the normal commonsense meaning of the term." Ledeen goes on to explain that this group was not opposed to the Khomeini regime as much as it was "Pro-Western" in its outlook. Given the rabid hatred of America preached up to then by Ayatollah Khomeini, however, "moderates" would be a fair description of a group within Iran who wanted to moderate the country's policies toward the United States. Somehow this idea became transmuted in someone's mind—possibly Oliver North's—into the notion that we were dealing with a group whose lives would be in danger if their identities were revealed. This turned out to be a useful fiction with which North and Poindexter could keep the lid on disclosures about the arms dealing.

6. Ledeen, *Perilous Statecraft,* pp. 118–119.

7. Examples of North's fabrications and fantasies abound. Late in its investigation of the Iran-Contra matter, the President's Special Review Board (known as the Tower Board, after its chair, former Senator John Tower) came upon tape recordings of a North meeting with Iranians in Germany. In the meeting, North described for the Iranians meetings with Reagan at Camp David that never occurred, and statements by Reagan that directly contradicted U.S. policy concerning Iran. When these statements were reported to Reagan, as described in Chapter 9, he was shocked. Another example appears in a White House memo of April 21, 1987, in which Peter Keisler of the White House counsel staff summarized statements given by another NSC official to representatives of the Senate and House

committees investigating the Iran-Contra matter. The memo records that North told this official, in early November 1986—just as the arms sales story was breaking—that the "real story" was "that we were 'scarfing up Iranians on the streets of Tehran.'" When asked what that meant, North said that "we were holding members of leading Iranian families in secure houses in Iran until the American hostages were released."

8. In the same April 21, 1987 Keisler memo, the former NSC officer is reported to have said that "in North's mind it was a 'straight one-for-one swap'" of arms for hostages, but he could not speak to how others, such as McFarlane, might have viewed the matter."

9. *Report of the Congressional Committees Investigating the Iran-Contra Affair* (Washington, DC: U.S. Government Printing Office, 1987), p. 295.

10. Ibid., p. 301.

11. Sofaer deposition, June 18, 1987, p. 39.

12. *Report of the Congressional Committees*, p. 301.

13. Donald Regan, *For the Record* (New York: Harcourt, Brace Jovanovich, 1988), p. 41-43:

I said, "John, what the hell happened? What went on here? What did you know about all this?"

The unflappability for which Poindexter was admired did not desert him now. He put down his knife and fork, dabbed at his mouth with his napkin, and repeated what he had told Ed Meese the afternoon before.

"I had a feeling that something bad was going on, but I didn't investigate it and I didn't do a thing about it," he said. "I really didn't want to know."

I asked him why not.

Poindexter did not grope for an answer. "I felt sorry for the Contras," he said. "I was so damned mad at Tip O'Neill for the way he was dragging the Contras around that I didn't want to know what, if anything, was going on. I should have, but I didn't."

14. The Tower Board's description of a few of North's deceptions, and the liberties he took in describing U.S. policies to representatives of the Iranian government, appear in its Report (*Report of the President's Special Review Board*, February 26, 1987), p. iii–18.

15. Facts on File, "Iran-Contra Arms Scandal: North Says Reagan Knew of Diversion; Other Developments," *World News Digest*, November 28, 1991.

16. *Report of the Congressional Committees*, p. 301.

17. At this point, many people around the President were seriously concerned about impeachment. See, for example, Lou Cannon's account of the worries of Ed Meese, Stu Spencer, Nancy Reagan, and Mike Deaver in Cannon, *President Reagan: The Role of a Lifetime*, pp. 626–627.

CHAPTER 8

1. If we'd had a little more time, and been somewhat more astute in our knowledge of Washington relationships, we might have made different choices. McFarlane had in the past worked for both Tower and Scowcroft, and was known to be close to both of them. Since he was a key player in the formulation and implementation of the Iran arms sales policy, I for one would have been reluctant to select Tower and Scowcroft to review his work. I had no reason to believe that they would not be objective, but I would have been concerned that the press would treat them as biased, and thus diminish the value of their report. As it turned out, the press did not see their connection to McFarlane as significant.

2. Ronald Reagan, *Ronald Reagan: An American Life* (New York: Pocket Books, 1990), p. 533.

3. Lou Cannon, *President Reagan: The Role of a Lifetime.* First Public Affairs edition (New York: Public Affairs, 2000), p. 640.

CHAPTER 9

1. Quoted in William C. Wohlforth, editor, *Witnesses to the End of the Cold War,* transcripts of a conference at Princeton University, 1993.

2. *Report of the President's Special Review Board* (Tower Board), February 26, 1987, p. D–4.

3. In addition, an article on December 6, 1986, in the *Washington Post* noted that McFarlane's testimony—that the President had approved the shipment in advance—contradicted a version of this sequence of events given to the *Post* the preceding month by a "person familiar with McFarlane's thinking." In this version, as recounted in the December 6 article, the President refused to consider sending arms to Iran when the idea was suggested by the Israelis, but after passing this message to the Israeli emissary, McFarlane was said to have "'had the strong expectation' that the Israelis would proceed with the arms transfer to Iran" without the President's approval.

4. *Report of the President's Special Review Board,* pp. D5–D7.

5. Ibid., p. D4.

6. Ibid., p. D10.

7. Ronald Reagan, *Ronald Reagan: An American Life* (New York: Pocket Books, 1990), p. 161.

8. Ronald Reagan, *Ronald Reagan: An American Life* (New York: Pocket Books, 1990), p. 516

9. *Report of the President's Special Review Board,* at iv–11.

INDEX

ABC, 232
Abdnor, James, 288n5
ABM treaty, 69
Abortion controversy, 154
Abshire, David, 164–165, 240, 249, 255, 258–262, 264–266, 270–273, 277, 282
AECA (Arms Export Control Act), 126, 172, 175, 176, 180, 185, 187–188, 190
AFL-CIO, 86
Air traffic controllers' strike, 52–55
Allied Chemical Corporation, 86
Alzheimer's disease
　disclosure of Reagan's, 84, 88–89
　question of effect on Reagan while president, 104–105, 268–269
American self-confidence, restoring, 6, 9, 34, 53–54, 55, 125–126
American values, traditional, 14
Anderson, Annelise, 12
Anderson, Martin, 12
Anonymous sources, 129–132, 144–146
Approval ratings, 45–46, 143, 168, 210
Arctic National Wildlife Refuge, 118
Arms control, Reagan on, 64
Arms Export Control Act (AECA), 127, 172, 175, 176, 245, 247
Arms race, with Soviets, 65
Arms sales to Iran, 2–3, 171–176
　alleged cover-up, 111
　diversion of funds to Contras, 208–210, 231

lack of congressional notification regarding, 178–179
question of presidential approval of, 171–172, 177–178, 211, 221, 266–267
Regan's recollections of, 220–222, 226–227
strategic reasons for, 169–170, 172, 176, 184, 231, 235, 250, 274
See also Iran-Contra
Ash, Roy, 25
Ash Council (President's Advisory Commission on Executive Organization), 25
Attorney-client privilege, 288n1
Attorney General, role of, 287n1
Authority, delegation of
　in Iran-Contra, xii, 21–23, 177–178, 258, 261–262
　as Reagan management style, xii, 10, 21–24, 27–29, 32

Baker, Howard, 104–105, 143, 163, 213–214, 282
Baker, James (Jim), 17, 94–95, 128, 131, 163, 215, 273–274
Balanced budget, 48
Ball, Will, 139, 153, 182, 204–206, 218, 225, 228, 277
Baltimore Sun, 127, 266, 267
Bay of Pigs, 8, 92, 155, 168–169, 189
Bernstein, Barton, 10
Biden, Joseph (Joe), 115

Bitburg (Germany) visit, 71–72, 92, 137, 158
Blackmun, Harry, 1
Bobbitt, Lorena, 115
Boren, David, 209
Bowman, Karlyn, 121
Boyd, Gerald, 131–132, 234, 253–254
Brady, James, 139
Brennan, William, 1, 2
Brinkley, David, 229
Brock, Bill, 76
Brower, Charles, 240, 250, 251, 253, 265, 266, 277
Buchanan, Pat, 77–78, 107, 139, 153, 182, 184, 200
Budget process reform, 173
Bully Pulpit, The (Muir), 29
Bureaucracies, Reagan's dislike for, 14, 63
Burger, Warren, 100, 149–150, 154
Burns, Arnold, 194
Bush, George H. W., 23–24, 46, 115, 249, 273, 277, 278
Bush, George W., 42, 69, 115, 160, 287n1
Business, role in Reagan administration, 62–63
Buttafucco, Joey, 115
Byrd, Robert, 229

Cabinet Council on Domestic Policy, 148
Cabinet Council on Economics, 25
Cabinet councils, 140–141
Cabinet government, 24–26, 78–79, 139–141
Cabinet members, influence of speeches on, 26, 29
Cabinets, stake in legislation, 142–143
Campaign contributions, 118–119
Cannon, Lou
    on calls for Regan's resignation, 207–208
    on INF treaty, 69
    Reagan biography, xi, 8
    on Reagan's disengagement, 15–16, 56
    on Reagan's relationship with Gorbachev, 64
    on Reagan's remoteness, 93
    on Reagan's speeches, 31
    on Reagan's view of nuclear disarmament, 32
    on staff loyalty to Regan, 287n3
Capitalism, 63–64
    depression as failure of, 33–34
Carlucci, Frank, 277, 279
Carter, James Earl (Jimmy), x, 11, 15, 16, 43, 115, 131
Casey, William (Bill), 131, 186–187, 193, 226
CBS, 117, 232, 273
Central Intelligence Agency (CIA), 86, 171, 178
Charismatic authority, 18–19, 94
Chavez, Linda, 97–98
Cheney, Dick, 95, 152, 259
Chew, David, 75, 83, 108, 139, 153, 182, 183, 196, 200, 206
Chief of staff position, 162–164
    Reagan's lack of concern over, 94–95
    See also Baker, James; Baker, Howard; Regan, Don
Classified information, leaked to press, 149
Clinton administration, scandal and media during, 115
Clinton, William Jefferson (Bill), x, 3, 11, 26, 42, 43
CNN, 143
Code of Military Justice, 260
Cohen, William, 229
Commission on CIA Activities in the United States, 86–89
Commission on the Bicentennial of the Constitution, 149
Communication, importance to Reagan, 113–114, 123–126
Competition
    deregulatory philosophy and, 28
    enhancing, 55, 58, 62–63
Condit, Gary, 115
Congressional notification, of arms sales, 172, 178–179, 227–228
Congressional pay raise, Regan and, 166
Connor, John T., 86
Conservative issues, Reagan and, 58, 77–78

Conservative Political Action
    Conference, 34
Contras
    diversion of arms sales proceeds to,
        195, 197, 198–201, 208–210,
        231, 234
    U.S. aid to, 95
Convictions, Reagan's commitment to,
    xi–xii, 3, 10, 18, 281–282
Cook, Timothy E., 114
Coolidge, Calvin, 7, 59
Cooper, Chuck, 184–185, 188, 190,
    193–195, 200–201
Corpocracy, 63
Corporate takeovers, 63–64
Correspondence
    disclosure of Alzheimer's disease, 84,
        88–89
    with ordinary Americans, 83–84
Council of Economic Advisors, 147
Council on Wage and Price Stability, 47
Counsel to the President, reason for,
    287n1
Cox, Chris, 151, 152
Culvahouse, A. B., 282
Cuomo, Mario, 134
Cynicism, role of press in increasing
    public, 122–123

Daily operations meeting, 137–139, 141,
    146–147, 167, 173, 193
Daniels, Mitch, 101, 139, 161, 174, 207
Darman, Richard, 63
Dawson, Rhett, 196
    access to Reagan's diary and, 258
    establishing ground rules for
        presidential interview, 248
    on Reagan's testimony, 273
    selecting review board, 197, 204
    as Tower Board chief of staff, 217,
        237, 238, 242, 243, 251, 253,
        257–259, 262, 265
Dawson, Tom, 130–131, 139
Deaver, Michael
    access for Edmund Morris and, ix, x
    Bitburg visit and, 71
    chief of staff appointment and, 94–95

as deputy chief of staff, 163
    ethics investigation of, 96–97, 115,
        119–121, 132, 147
    indictment of, 276
    on Reagan's interest in policy, 12
    on Reagan's shyness, 82
Debategate, 131
Deep Throat, 129
Defense Intelligence Agency, 263
Defense policy, 64–72, 125, 173
Deficits
    interest rates and, 48–49
    Reagan's acceptance of, 46, 48, 61
DeFrank, Tom, 111
Delegation of authority in Reagan
        White House. *See* Authority,
        delegation of
Depression, effect on American view of
        government role, 33–34
Deputy chiefs of staff, 163–164
Deregulation
    of banking, 27–29
    as political goal, 55, 125
    promotion of, 58
    as response to economic recession,
        46–47
Diamond, Stuart, 119
Diana, Princess of Wales, 115
Different Drummer, A (Deaver), 12
Dillon, C. Douglas, 86, 88
Disarmament, 32, 64
Disarmament agreement,
        with Soviet Union, 5, 9, 55,
        66–71, 143, 281
Disengagement, Reagan's reputed, 5–6,
        42, 55–56, 77–79
Dobrynin, Anatoly, 103
Dolan, Tony, 29, 30, 182
Dole, Robert (Bob), 102, 213–214, 229
Domenici, Pete, 47, 50
Domestic Council, 25, 141, 143
Domestic Policy Council (DPC), drug
        testing policy and, 73–74, 76, 77
Domestic policy, Reagan
        accomplishments in, 141–142
Donald, David, 41
Donovan, Ray, 92, 115

Drug testing policy, 72–77, 148
D'Souza, Dinesh, 11
Duberstein, Ken, 163
Durenberger, David, 206, 208, 211, 223–224
Dutch: A Memoir of Ronald Reagan (Morris), x–xi, 9

Economic growth, U.S. 6, 9, 14
Economics
    Reagan's writing on, 57
    as subject of radio addresses, 36
    supply-side, 45, 59
Eisenhower, Dwight D., 11, 43
Elites, role in media, 118
Energy and the environment, as subject of radio addresses, 36
Entrepreneurs, Reagan administration and, 62–63
Eureka College, 81, 101
Executive order
    on drug testing of government employees, 76–77
    on sales of arms to terrorist states, 175, 187–188
Executive privilege, 98, 148, 180–182, 206, 256, 288n1

Farewell Address (January 11, 1989), 21
Federal Aviation Administration, 52
Federal Bureau of Investigation (FBI), 147, 238–239
Federal Reserve, 48, 49
Feeding frenzies, media, 113, 115–116, 144, 168
Feeding Frenzy (Sabato), 113, 160
Ferraro, Geraldine, 116
Fisher, Amy, 115
Fitzgerald, Frances, 8, 31–32
Fitzwater, Marlin, 105, 277
Flowers, Gennifer, 115
Ford, Gerald R., 43, 86, 115, 160, 211
Foreign aid, 77
Foreign policy, 36, 64–72, 142
Fortune, 21, 22, 24
Free market system, Reagan on, 63–64
Free to Choose (Friedman & Friedman), 32
Free trade, 58, 61–63, 125

Friedman, Milton, 33–34, 39, 59
Friedman, Rose, 33–34, 39

Gallup Polls, 45, 122, 138, 143, 282
Garment, Leonard, 211, 223, 272
Garrett, Larry, 259
Geneva summit meeting, McFarlane briefing at, 194, 201, 250, 251, 252, 268
Gergen, David, 67, 94
Glass-Steagall Act, 28
Goals, presidential, 55–56
Goldwater, Barry, 14
Gonzales, Elian, 115
Gorbachev, Mikhail, 64, 66–69, 70, 143, 194, 268, 282
Governing with the News (Cook), 114
Government
    attitude of American public toward, 38–39, 121–122, 126
    placing limits on, 50
    press coverage of, 112–115
    Reagan philosophy of, xi, xii, 10, 14–17, 33, 35, 36, 39–40, 41–44, 56–58
Gramm-Leach-Bliley Act (1999), 28
Great Society, 42
Greenstein, Fred I., 39, 47, 85
Griswold, Erwin N., 86
Growth Experiment, The (Lindsey), 51

Hachten, William, 117
Hamilton, Lee, 259
Harding, Tonya, 115
Harding, Warren, 59
Hart, Gary, 115
HAWK (Homing-All the Way-Killer) missiles, sale of to Iran, 193–196, 201, 251–252, 254–255, 262, 264, 269, 270
    question of presidential approval of, 195, 226, 227, 251–252, 255
Hersh, Seymour, 86
Hill, Anita, 115
Hoffman, David, 130–131, 266
Holland, Dianna, 152
Hoover, Herbert, 59
Horner, Connie, 76

Hostages
    Reagan's concern for, 96, 234
    trading arms for release of, 167, 170,
        172, 228, 234, 274, 277
House Intelligence Committee, 193, 223
House Select Committee on the Iran-
    Contra matter, 259
Humor, Reagan's public, 100–103

Ideas
    centrality of to Reagan's presidency,
        23–24, 26–27, 44
    importance in myth of Ronald
        Reagan, 13–14
    Reagan interest in, 16–17
    Reagan's belief in power of, 33
Ideology, Reagan's, 13–14, 17–18, 33
IMF (International Monetary Fund),
    89–91
Inaugural Address (1981), 15, 34,
    41, 44
Independent counsel
    Deaver case, 276
    Iran-Contra, 209–210, 235, 270
Individualism, 14, 15, 34
INF (Intermediate Nuclear Force) treaty,
    69–70
Inflation, 49
Inflation psychology, 54
Inouye, Daniel, 259
Instant analysis, 114
Intellectual ability
    assessment of Reagan's, 5–6, 10,
        35–36, 84–91
    Reagan's reaction to perception of his,
        103–104
Intellectuals and the American Presidency
    (Troy), 26
Interest rates, deficits and, 48–49
Intermediate Nuclear Force (INF) treaty,
    69–70
International Monetary Fund (IMF)
    replenishment, 89–91
Intrater, Arnold, 152
Iran
    arms sale to. *See* Arms sales to Iran
    intelligence information given to,
        200, 263

    Reagan administration dealings with,
        175
Iran-Contra
    appointment of independent counsel,
        209–210
    appointment of review board,
        196–198. *See also* Tower Board
    arms sales to Iran. *See* Arms sales to
        Iran
    beginnings of, 167–168
    chronology from NSC, 195, 196,
        229–230, 244–245, 253
    chronology from White House, 249
    closure, 281
    cover-up by NSC staff, 111–112,
        176–181, 186, 187, 201, 211, 270,
        286n1
    diversion of funds to Contras, 195,
        197, 198–201, 208–210, 231, 234
    effect on Reagan's credibility,
        203–204
    effect on Reagan's effectiveness, 5
    explanations of, 182–184
    lack of congressional notification of
        arms sales, 172, 178–179,
        227–228
    legal issues, 180–181, 184–188,
        190–191, 193–194
    need for Reagan to admit mistake,
        92–93, 169, 189–190, 193,
        210–211, 215–216, 240–241,
        260, 273–275
    origins of, 169–171
    presidential findings on, 188, 195,
        232, 245, 246, 255
    press coverage of, 126–128, 168,
        229–230
    public opinion on Reagan's role in,
        240–241
    Reagan's admission of mistake,
        279–280
    Reagan's alleged approval of arms sales
        to Iran, 171–172, 177–178, 211,
        221, 266–267
    Reagan's management style and, xii,
        21–23, 177–178, 258, 261–262
    Reagan's reaction to, 2–5, 105, 203,
        283n1

Iran-Contra *continued*
 Reagan's recollections concerning,
  177–178, 225–228, 249–256,
  262, 264–265, 267–268,
  270–271
 Senate Intelligence Committee. *See*
  Senate Intelligence Committee
 significance of, 7–8
 strategic reasons for arms sale,
  141–142, 169–170, 172, 176,
  231, 235, 250, 274
 suggestion that President solicit
  affidavits from staff regarding
  affair, 215–216
 suggestion that Reagan testify before
  Senate Intelligence Committee,
  213–215
Iranian moderates, protection of, 180,
 289n5
Iraq, intelligence information regarding,
 200, 263
Israel, role in arms sale to Iran, 169–172,
 176, 188, 191–192, 217, 223,
 243–244, 247–248, 269
Issues lunches, 77–78, 95, 101–102, 104

Jacobsen, David, 167, 174
Jewell, Richard, 115
Johnson, Lyndon, x, 4, 8, 11, 40, 43
Joint Congressional Committee, 234–235
Jones, Paula, 115
Justice Department
 drug testing policy and, 73, 75, 148
 investigation of Michael Deaver, 96,
  97
 Iran-Contra affair and, 184–185,
  205, 206–207
 role of, 287n1
 Supreme Court nominees and, 151
 use immunity and, 219

Keel, Alton, 70, 168, 173, 182, 184,
 187, 189, 192, 237–238, 277
Keisler, Peter, 152, 289n5
Kemp, Jack, 115
Kennedy, John F., x, 8, 11, 13, 40–41,
 43, 91, 92, 155, 189, 282

Keynes, John Maynard, 14
Khomeini, Ayatollah, 170, 179, 228,
 289n5
Kim, Kihwan, 119, 120
Kimche, 228
Kingon, Al, 75, 103, 139
Kinnock, Neil, 115
Kirkland, Lane, 86
Kissinger, Henry, 31, 104
Koehler, Jack, 107–108
Kohl, Helmut, 71–72, 92, 158
Korologos, Tom, 273
Kruger, Bob, 152
Kuhn, Jim, 253, 271
Kumar, Martha Joynt, 123, 125, 129

Labor, Reagan relations with, 52–54
Ladd, Everett Carll, 121
Laffer, Arthur, 59
Law, importance of obedience to, 54
Laxalt, Paul, 273
Leahy, Patrick, 223–224
Leaks (information), 143–146
 avoiding, 149–154
 effect on consultation between White
  House and agencies/Congress,
  149–150
 effect on White House staff, 147–149
 from White House staff, 143–148,
  156–157
 See also Press
Lebanon, hostages in, 170, 180
Ledeen, Michael, 170, 289n5
Lee, Wen Ho, 115
Legislative strategy
 Reagan's role in, 58–59, 60
 White House staff and, 142–143
Lemnitzer, Lyman, 86
Levy, Chandra, 115
Lewinsky, Monica, 3, 115
Libya, bombing of, 149–150
Lincoln, Abraham, xi, 13–14, 41
Lindsey, Lawrence, 51
Little Red Hen parable, 36–38
Lobbying, Reagan's role in congressional,
 60
Los Angeles Times, 127, 157, 173, 267

Loyalty
Reagan's for staff, 96–97
staff for president, 78–79, 145

MAD (Mutually Assured Destruction),
66–67, 69
Management style, Reagan's, xii, 10,
21–24, 27–29, 32
Iran-Contra and, xii, 21–23,
177–178, 258, 261–262
Manchester Union Leader, 115
Marshall, Thurgood, 1, 2
Maseng, Mari, 139
McCain, John, 13
McFadden, Clark, 238, 251, 278
McFarlane, Robert (Bud)
delegation of arms sales, 22, 171,
204
executive privilege and testimony of,
206
Geneva briefing by, 194, 201, 250,
251, 252, 268
HAWK missile shipment and, 194
introduction of idea of arms sales to
Iran to Reagan, 169–170
Iran-Contra cover-up and, 178, 270,
286n1
November 7 note, 252, 254–255
relation with Tower and Scowcroft,
289n1
role in Iran-Contra, 22, 112,
217–218, 227
testimony before Senate Foreign
Relations Committee, 248
testimony before Senate Intelligence
Committee, 208, 211, 221, 243
testimony before Tower Board,
245–246, 290n3
testimony regarding presidential
approval of arms sales, 211,
243–246, 270
visit to Tehran, 167, 173, 179, 288n2
McGrath, Dean, 152, 264
McMahon, Bernie, 208, 211–212, 217,
223, 224, 225
McNamar, Tim, 165
Media. *See* Press

Meese, Edwin, 95, 163
on drug testing policy, 73–74, 75,
148
Iran-Contra investigation and, 3,
180, 194–197, 206–207,
209–210, 234
on legality of Iran-Contra, 176,
184–185, 190–191, 246
Scalia nomination and, 97–98, 151
on use immunity for North and
Poindexter, 218
Mellon, Andrew, 59
Meltzer, Allan, 59
Memory, state of Reagan's, 104–105,
268–269
Menendez brothers, 115
Meta-news, 116–117
"Mice, the," 287n3
Michel, Bob, 95
Miller, Jim, 138, 174
Miller, Roy, 106
Miller, William Lee, 13
Mitchell, Andrea, 192
Mondale, Walter, 101
Moral core, of Republicanism, 14
Morris, Edmund, ix–xi, 8–9, 12, 55, 93,
104
Muir, William Ker, Jr., 29
Muskie, Edmund, 115, 205
Mutually Assured Destruction (MAD),
66–67, 69

NAFTA (North American Free Trade
Agreement), 62
National debate, during Reagan
administration, 114–115
National Journal, 65
National Security Act, 173, 176, 180,
185, 188, 190, 227, 245, 247
National Security Council (NSC), 25
functioning of, 260–261
Iran-Contra cover-up by, 111–112,
176–181, 186, 187, 201, 211, 270,
286n1
structure of, 237–238
National Security Planning Group
(NSPG), 195, 196

NATO (North Atlantic Treaty
Organization), 64
NBC, 231–232, 260
Neustadt, Richard E., 6–8, 9, 10, 23, 26,
40, 53, 77, 123, 157, 281
New Deal, 40, 42, 43
News conference (November 19), 103,
189, 191–192
News initiative, 128–129, 242
Newsweek, 111–112, 115, 117, 132, 157,
278, 286n1
New York Times, 131–132
anonymous sources and, 144–145,
146, 149
CIA story, 86
Iran-Contra stories, 132, 157, 173,
208, 209, 211, 221, 230–231, 232,
233, 234, 255, 270, 279, 288n2
Iranian moderates story, 170
Mike Deaver story, 119–121
number of Iran-Contra stories, 127,
168, 186, 187
Oliver North story, 183
press frenzy and, 116
press standards and, 117, 134
Nir, Amiram, 228
Nixon, Richard, 11, 40, 43, 211
Noonan, Peggy, 19
North, Oliver, 2, 127
allegation that Reagan approved arms
for hostages, 233
attempted concealment of HAWK
missile shipment, 194
conviction of, 168
criminal charges against, 278
delegation of arms sale to, 22, 171,
204, 217–218, 231, 248
exaggerations of relation with Reagan,
182–183, 199–200, 289n7
false press about, 131
Iran-Contra chronology, 192,
229–230, 244–245, 252, 267–268
Iran-Contra cover-up and, 111–112,
178–180, 286n1
on Iranian moderates, 180, 289n5
pressure for resignation, 196
role in diversion of funds to Contras,
200–201

suggestion meet with Reagan to
disclose Iran-Contra story,
212–213
suggestion to grant use immunity to,
218–220, 222–223
suggestion to pardon, 211–212
transcripts of meetings in Germany,
262–264, 265
North American Free Trade Agreement
(NAFTA), 62
Nuclear disarmament, 32, 66–71. *See
also* Disarmament agreement

O'Connor, Sandra Day, 1
O'Meara, Vicki, 152
Office of Management and Budget
(OMB), 142, 147
Office of the Comptroller of the
Currency, 27
O'Neill, Tip, 198, 208–209
OPEC (Organization of Petroleum
Exporting Countries), 53
Oral finding theory, on arms sales to
Iran, 245, 246, 255
Oval Office, Reagan's respect for, 82
Overreporting, 115

Pack journalism, 119
Pardon, of Poindexter and North,
211–212
Passivity, Reagan's, 10–11
Patterson, Thomas, 118
Pentagon Papers, 118
Perilous Statecraft (Ledeen), 170, 289n5
Philadelphia Inquirer, 116
Philosophy of government, Reagan's, xi,
xii, 10, 14–17, 33, 35, 36, 39–40,
41–43, 57–58
Podhoretz, John, 23–24
Poindexter, John, 2, 22, 103, 112, 127,
139, 168
conviction of, 169
criminal charges against, 278
delegation of authority to, 204
direct access to president, 162,
237–238
executive privilege and testimony of,
206

Reykjavik events and, 70
Iran-Contra chronology, 244–245
Iran-Contra cover-up and, 171,
175–179, 180–181, 251, 286n1
knowledge of diversion of funds to
Contras, 197, 198–199
at news conference on Iran-Contra
(November 19), 189
opposition to Iran-Contra disclosure,
174, 182, 187, 191–192
pressure for resignation, 196, 197,
198–199
relations with press, 131
resignation of, 200, 201
suggestion meet with Reagan to
disclose Iran-Contra story,
212–213
suggestion to grant use immunity to,
218–220, 222–223
suggestion to pardon, 211–212
Policy development
cabinets and, 24–26, 139, 140–141
Executive Branch and, 24–27
Reagan's role in, x, 58–59, 64, 72–79
Policy issues, media coverage of,
114–115
Political coalition building, 40–41
Political operator, 40
Political risk, Reagan's willingness to
take, 18
Political skill, presidential success and,
40–41
Powell, Lewis, 1
Power
of cabinets, 139
of press, 133–134
of public, 125–126
use of, 4
of White House staff in Reagan
administration, 139
Presidency, Reagan's conception of, 2, 4
Presidential findings, on arms sales to
Iran, 188, 195, 232, 245, 246,
255
*Presidential Power and the Modern
Presidents* (Neustadt), 6–7, 40
Presidential reputation, 123
effect of leaks on, 157

Presidential success
Neustadt model of, 6–8, 9–10, 23
political skill and, 40–41
reasons for Reagan's, 4, 6–12, 42
President Reagan: The Role of a Lifetime
(Cannon), xi, 8
President's Advisory Commission on
Executive Organization (Ash
Council), 25
President's Special Review Board.
See Tower Board
Press, 111–135
anonymous sources and, 129–132,
144–146
coverage of Iran-Contra, 111–112,
117, 126–128, 157–158, 187,
229–230
decline in press standards, 117–119
decline in public confidence in,
122–123
feeding frenzies, 113, 115–116, 144,
168
government officials' cooperation
with, 130–131
lack of cooperation with, 154–158
maintaining presidential agenda in
face of, 123, 125–127, 128–129,
134-135
need for professional standards,
132–134
news initiative, 128–129, 242, 243
power of, 133–134
press coverage of government, 112–115
public opinion of public officials and,
121–122
public opinion of quality of
government and, 122
reaction to Senate Intelligence
Committee Iran-Contra report,
230–234
reliance on leaks, 143–146
Press conference (November 19), 103,
189, 191–192
Prioritization, political, 54–57
Productivity, 40, 64, 173
Professional standards, need for among
journalists, 133–135
Public employees, right to strike, 52–53

Public figure, concept of, 134
Public opinion
  on confidence in press, 122–123
  on integrity of public officials,
    121–122
  on quality of government, 122
  on Reagan as president, 282
  on Reagan role in Iran-Contra,
    240–241
  Reagan's approval ratings, 45–46,
    138, 143, 168, 193, 210
  on role of government, 38–39
Public policy essays, 35–36

Quayle, Dan, 115, 116, 160

Radio addresses, ix–x
  on defense and foreign policy, 65–66
  on drugs, 73
  as evidence of Reagan's intelligence,
    12, 35–38, 85–86
  ideology expressed in, 14–15, 17
  on public employees' right to strike,
    52–53
  Saturday morning, 123–126
  as source of policy ideas, 26, 30–31
  on tax policy and economics, 58–59
Ramsey, JonBenet, 115
Rancho del Cielo, 106
Raul, Alan, 151, 152
Reagan, Nancy, 11, 94, 97–100
  access for Edmund Morris and, ix, x
  anti-drug campaign, 73
  desire to keep husband's diary private,
    257
  on husband's reading habits, 35
  reaction to Iran-Contra, 203
  Regan resignation and, 92, 108
  role as husband's counsel, 105–108
  use immunity for North and
    Poindexter and, 218
Reagan, Ronald
  actions during air traffic controllers'
    strike, 52–55
  admission of mistake in Iran-Contra,
    279–280
  alleged knowledge of diversion of funds
    to Contras, 198–199, 209, 210

approval ratings, 138, 143, 168, 193,
    210
  attempt to restore American
    self-confidence, 53–54
  belief in goodness of people, xii, 11
  belief in power of ideas, 33–36
  bond with Nancy, 107–108
  charismatic authority of, 18–19
  commitment to convictions, xi–xii, 3,
    10, 17–18, 281–282
  on communication skills, 21
  correspondence with ordinary
    Americans, 83–84
  courtesy of, 96, 100
  on defense and foreign policy, 64–72
  definition of success, 4
  diary of, 256–257, 258–259
  disclosure of tax returns, 105–107
  disengagement with details, 5–6, 41,
    55–56, 77–79
  effect of Iran-Contra on effectiveness
    of, 5
  faith in American people, 14–15,
    57–58
  focus on speeches, 23–24, 29–32,
    42, 43
  focus on ideas, 10–14, 33–38, 40–43
  on free trade, 61–63
  goals of, 16, 55–56
  idealism of, 11
  influence on Bill Clinton, 42, 43
  intellectual ability of, 5–6, 10, 35–36,
    84–91
  interest in policy, 12
  legacy of, 38–39
  Little Red Hen parable, 36–38
  loyalty to aides, 96–97
  management style of, xii, 21–24,
    27–29, 177–178, 258, 261–262
  as member of Commission on CIA
    Activities in United States, 86–89
  memory of, 104–105, 268–269
  need to admit mistake in Iran-Contra
    and, 92–93, 169, 189–190, 193,
    210–211, 215–216, 240–241,
    260, 273–275
  modesty of, 82–84
  passivity of, 10–11

philosophy of government of, xi, xii,
10, 14–17, 33, 35, 36, 39–40,
41–44, 56–58
political legacy of, 42
as political myth, 12–14
political priorities of, 54–57
on presidency, 2, 4, 94
public opinion of performance as
president, 282
punctuality and, 82
reaction to assessment of intelligence,
103–104
reaction to Iran-Contra, 105, 203
recollections concerning Iran-Contra,
177–178, 225–228, 249–256,
262, 264–265, 267–268,
270–271
refusal to raise taxes, 46–49, 50–51,
54–55
relations with press, 112–114, 123,
126, 134
remoteness of, 93–96
role in securing tax cuts, 59–61
self-confidence of, 103
sense of humor, 100–103
shyness of, 81–82
significance of acting career on later
political success, 8–9
stubbornness of, 46–49, 50–51,
69–72, 91–93
success of presidency, 6–12
and Supreme Court, 1, 150–151
taking political risk, 18
thoughtfulness of, 97–100
view of self, 19
as visionary leader, 11–12
writing style of, 86–89
Reagan in His Own Hand, ix–xi, 12, 35,
36, 58, 65, 73, 85, 91
Reaganism, 12–13, 17–18, 33
Reaganomics, 45
Reagan Presidential Library, 36, 107
Recession (1981–1982), 9, 45–49
Regan, Ann, 160
Regan, Donald, 128, 130
alleged influence on Reagan's Iran-
Contra recollection, 267,
271–272, 273

alleged role in Iran-Contra, 111–112,
117, 286n1
on Bitburg visit, 71–72
briefing Reagan for Tower Board
interview, 249–250
as chief of staff, 17, 70, 74, 75, 76, 81,
82, 94, 98, 102, 129, 143, 144,
146, 153, 160–162, 165
as chief of staff during Iran-Contra,
92, 180, 182, 195, 196–198, 229,
243, 256–257, 260–261, 264, 274
criticism for performance as chief of
staff, 158
limits of authority as chief of staff,
161–162
loyalty of staff to, 287n3
loyalty to presidency, 163
loyalty to president, 153, 154–156,
157–158, 161
management style of, 159, 164,
165–166
pressing Reagan on Iran-Contra
"mistake," 155–156
on raising taxes, 285n2
on Reagan, 11
on Reagan's role in Iran-Contra, 127,
172
recollections regarding Iran-Contra,
220–222, 226–227, 246–247,
267, 269
relation with NSC staff, 237–238
relations with press, 154–158,
160–162, 275–276
resignation as chief of staff, 107–108,
207–208, 275–276
selecting members of Iran-Contra
review board, 204–205
soliciting policy initiatives, 137–138,
141
on suggestion that Reagan testify
before Senate Intelligence
Committee, 213–215
testimony before Senate
Intelligence Committee, 218,
220–222
Tower Board report and, 276–277
as Treasury secretary, 17, 28, 48–49,
60, 89–90, 159–160

Rehnquist, William, 1, 97–98, 100, 151, 152–153, 154
Reputation
 presidential, 123
 ability of press to destroy, 134
Reykjavik (Iceland), meeting with Gorbachev, 66–68, 69, 70, 287n3
Rice, Donna, 115
Rich, Marc, 115
Ripon Society, 87
Rockefeller, Nelson, 86, 87–88, 148
Rodman, Peter, 42–43
Roe v. Wade, 154
Rome, lesson of ancient, 39
Ronald Reagan: An American Life (Reagan), 57
Ronald Reagan: How an Ordinary Man Became an Extraordinary Leader (D'Souza), 11
Roosevelt, Franklin Delano, 9, 11, 13, 39, 42–43, 52, 282
Roosevelt, Theodore, ix, 55
Rudman, Warren, 259

Sabato, Larry, 113, 115, 116, 129, 144, 160
SALT II, 65
Saturday Night Live, 10
Scalia, Antonin, 1, 98, 100, 151, 153, 154
Scandal, hunt for by media, 115, 119–121
Scott-Finan, Nancy, 152
Scowcroft, Brent, 205, 265, 277–278, 289n1
SDI (Strategic Defense Initiative), 66–68, 69–70, 287n3
Sears, John, 32
Senate Foreign Relations Committee, 249
Senate Intelligence Committee
 Casey testimony, 193
 Iran-Contra investigation, 206
 Iran-Contra report, 223–226, 228–229, 230–235, 242
 McFarlane testimony, 208, 211, 243–244
 preliminary conclusions on Iran-Contra, 209, 216–218
 suggestion Reagan testify before, 213–215
Senate Select Committee on the Iran-Contra matter, 259
Seymour, Whitney North, 276
Shannon, Edgar F., 86
Shepherd, Mike, 152
Shultz, George, 77, 85, 91, 180, 194, 226, 228, 237
Simpson, O. J., 115
Skinner, Kiron, 12
Small Business Week, 124
Social issues, Reagan on, 77
Sofaer, Abe, 188, 193–194, 201
Soundbite, 113
Soviet Union
 arms race with, 65
 breakup of, 6
 disarmament agreement with, 5, 9, 55, 66–71, 143, 281
Speakes, Larry, 70, 103, 105, 139, 148, 153, 167, 173–175, 182, 193, 200, 228–230
Special counsel, appointment of in Iran-Contra, 212–213
Special Trust (McFarlane), 169, 172
"Speech, The," 14, 17, 30
Speeches
 ideology expressed in, 14–15, 17
 as instrument of governance, 29–34
 Reagan focus on, 42, 43
 as source of direction for staff, 23–24
 as source of policy ideas, 26, 29, 31
Spending cuts, tax increases and, 60–61
Sprinkel, Beryl, 139
Stahl, Leslie, 160
Stephens, Jay, 152, 218, 220–222, 223, 226, 233, 239
Stockman, David, 45, 46, 47, 48, 49, 50, 91, 156, 285n2
Strategic Defense Initiative (SDI), 65–68, 69–70, 287n3
Strategic missiles, 70–71
Strike, right of public employees to, 52–53
Subtext, 160
Success
 presidential, 6–12, 23, 40–41

Ronald Reagan and presidential, 4,
6–12, 42
work and, 38
Supply-side economic theory, 45, 59
Supreme Court lunch (November 25,
1986), 1–2, 4, 5, 201–202
Supreme Court nominations, 97–98,
100, 149–154
Svahn, Jack, 75, 139

Tabloids, mainstream media and, 115
Taxes
cuts in, 50, 55, 58, 59–61
pressure to raise during recession,
46–49, 50–51, 54–55
reform of tax system, 9, 61, 137, 143
radio addresses on, 58–59, 124–125
Tax Reform Act (1986), 61, 138
Tax returns, disclosure of Reagans',
105–107
Testimonial immunity, 212
Thatcher, Margaret, 58
Theodore Rex, 56
Thomas, Clarence, 115
Thomas, Dennis, 70, 75, 128, 139, 153,
156, 164, 182, 187, 189,
196–198, 200, 204–205,
210–211, 218, 228, 242,
256–257, 265, 273
Thomas, Evan, 111
Thompson, Paul, 188–188, 193–194, 201
Timberg, Bob, 266
Time magazine, 117, 157, 209
Tolchin, Martin, 119
Tort reform, 119
TOW missile shipment, 192, 193, 262,
266–267, 268, 270
question of presidential approval of,
171, 226, 243–245, 251, 255,
266–267
Tower Board, 234
access to Reagan diary, 256–257,
258–259
appointment of, 196–198, 204–207
beginning of investigation, 237–238
composition of, 289n1
consideration of McFarlane
testimony, 245–246

degree of difficulty in obtaining
information, 238–239
Don Regan and, 161
interview with Reagan, 241–242,
243, 248–249, 251–252
McFarlane testimony before, 170
North tape recordings and, 289n5
Reagan letter to, 272–273
Reagan's change of testimony before,
104
on Reagan's management style and
Iran-Contra, 21
report of, 93, 276–280
request for Reagan to order North
and Poindexter to testify, 259–260
second Reagan interview with,
257–258, 260–262, 265–266
Tower, John, 205, 265, 271, 277,
277–279, 289n1
Trade policy, Reagan's writing on, 57
Treasury Department, 27–29, 89
Triumph of Politics, The (Stockman), 45
Troubles of Journalism, The (Hachten),
117
Troy, Tevi, 26
Truman, Harry S, 43
25th Amendment, 105
Turner, Carlton, 74
Tuttle, Bob, 139

Under Fire: An American Story (North),
200
United Press International, 157
United States-Canada Free Trade
Agreement, 62
USA Today, stories on Iran-Contra, 157
Use immunity, granting to North and
Poindexter, 212, 218–220,
222–223

Vietnam War, 8, 118

Wallace, Chris, 231
Wallison, Ethan, 99
Wallison, Jeremy, 99–100
Wallison, Rebecca, 99–100
Wall Street Journal, 127, 157, 186, 267,
288n2

Walsh, Lawrence, 209, 258–259, 278
War on Poverty, 41
War Powers Resolution, 149–150
Warner, Margaret, 111
Washington Post, 130, 131, 161
  anonymous sources and, 144
  decline in press standards and, 117
  Don Regan stories,143, 156, 160,
    166, 275–276
  Iran-Contra stories, 157, 167–168,
    208–209, 230, 232–233,
    254–255, 256, 266–267, 270, 279
  McFarlane visit to Tehran story,
    288n2
  Michael Deaver story, 147
  number of Iran-Contra stories, 127,
    168, 186, 187
  press frenzy and, 116
Washington Times, 127
Watergate
  comparison of Iran-Contra to, 187,
    196, 199, 215
  decline in press standards and, 118,
    129–130
  decline of confidence in government
    and, 122
Way Out There in the Blue (Fitzgerald), 8,
  31
Weber, Max, 18–19

Weinberger, Caspar, 180, 226, 228
What's Wrong (Ladd & Bowman), 121
White, Byron, 1
White House, press coverage of, 112,
  114, 115
White House Correspondence Unit,
  83–84
White House counsel's office, 151–152
White House press corps, 130–132
White House staff
  conflict between loyalty to president
    and self-advancement, 144–145
  effect of leaks on, 147–149
  effect of leaks by, 148–154
  leaks from 145–148, 156–157
  loss of news initiative during Iran-
    Contra, 242, 243
  power of, 139
  pressures on, 143–144
Whitewater, 115
Will, George, 13
Wilson, Woodrow, 7, 35
Wirthlin, Richard, 186–187, 193, 240,
  273
Woodward, Bob, 230
Writing style, Reagan's, 86–89

Zerkle, Charlene, 152
Zero-zero option, 64